PRAISE FOR
NO

D0187938

Notorious Royal Marriages

"For those who tackled Hilary Mantel's *Wolf Hall*, and can't get enough of the scandal surrounding Henry VIII's wives, [*Notorious Royal Marriages* is] the perfect companion book."
—*The New Yorker*

"Carroll writes with verve and wit about the passionate—and occasionally perilous—events that occur when royals wed. . . . Carroll's fascinating account of nine centuries of royal marriages is an irresistible combination of *People* magazine and the History Channel."
—*Chicago Tribune* (5 stars)

"Sex! Intrigue! Scandal! Carroll's newest offering chronicles well-known matrimonial pairings among European royals during the last 900 years. With a breezy and lively narrative, she gives the dirt on a parade of often mismatched couples."
—*Historical Novels Review*

Royal Affairs

"Carroll . . . has a true talent for weaving fascinating narratives. Her entertaining writing style makes this one book you do not want to put down. Entertaining, impeccably researched, and extremely well written, it will appeal to all readers with an interest in British history."
—*Library Journal*

"There are lots [of] royal romps cataloged in this entertaining, enormously readable book."
—*Las Vegas Review-Journal*

"A sumptuous treat of romance, sex, jealousy, and scandal. Carroll gives you a historical work, but in an entertaining style."
—*Pittsburgh Examiner*

Also by Leslie Carroll

Notorious Royal Marriages

Royal Affairs

Royal
PAINS

A Rogues' Gallery of Brats, Brutes, and Bad Seeds

Leslie Carroll

 New American Library

New American Library

Published by New American Library, a division of Penguin Group (USA) Inc.,
375 Hudson Street, New York, New York 10014, USA
Penguin Group (Canada), 90 Eglinton Avenue East, Suite 700, Toronto,
Ontario M4P 2Y3, Canada (a division of Pearson Penguin Canada Inc.)
Penguin Books Ltd., 80 Strand, London WC2R 0RL, England
Penguin Ireland, 25 St. Stephen's Green, Dublin 2,
Ireland (a division of Penguin Books Ltd.)
Penguin Group (Australia), 250 Camberwell Road, Camberwell, Victoria 3124,
Australia (a division of Pearson Australia Group Pty. Ltd.)
Penguin Books India Pvt. Ltd., 11 Community Centre, Panchsheel Park,
New Delhi - 110 017, India
Penguin Group (NZ), 67 Apollo Drive, Rosedale, North Shore 0632,
New Zealand (a division of Pearson New Zealand Ltd.)
Penguin Books (South Africa) (Pty.) Ltd., 24 Sturdee Avenue,
Rosebank, Johannesburg 2196, South Africa

Penguin Books Ltd., Registered Offices:
80 Strand, London WC2R 0RL, England

First published by New American Library,
a division of Penguin Group (USA) Inc.

First Printing, March 2011
10 9 8 7 6 5 4 3 2 1

Copyright © Leslie Carroll, 2011
All rights reserved

 REGISTERED TRADEMARK—MARCA REGISTRADA

LIBRARY OF CONGRESS CATALOGING-IN-PUBLICATION DATA

Carroll, Leslie, 1959–
    Royal pains: a rogues' gallery of brats, brutes, and bad seeds/Leslie Carroll.
    p. cm.
    Includes bibliographical references.
    ISBN 978-0-451-23221-2
    1. Kings and rulers—Conduct of life—History. 2. Royal houses—History. I. Title.
    D107.C293 2011
    940.09'9—dc22   2010039898

Set in Sabon
Designed by Patrice Sheridan

Printed in the United States of America

Without limiting the rights under copyright reserved above, no part of this publication may be reproduced, stored in or introduced into a retrieval system, or transmit-
ted, in any form, or by any means (electronic, mechanical, photocopying, recording,
or otherwise), without the prior written permission of both the copyright owner and
the above publisher of this book.

PUBLISHER'S NOTE
While the author has made every effort to provide accurate telephone numbers and
Internet addresses at the time of publication, neither the publisher nor the author
assumes any responsibility for errors, or for changes that occur after publication.
Further, the publisher does not have any control over and does not assume any
responsibility for author or third-party Web sites or their content.

The scanning, uploading, and distribution of this book via the Internet or via any
other means without the permission of the publisher is illegal and punishable by law.
Please purchase only authorized electronic editions, and do not participate in or
encourage electronic piracy of copyrighted materials. Your support of the author's
rights is appreciated.

For "Hun,"

who has always marched to the beat

of his own drummer.

I love you, Daddy.

Contents

Foreword xv

KING JOHN

1166 or 1167–1216

Ruled England: 1199–1216

1

VLAD III OF WALLACHIA ("VLAD THE IMPALER")

1431–1476

Ruled Romania: 1448; 1456–1462; 1476

33

GEORGE, DUKE OF CLARENCE

1449–1478

AND

RICHARD, DUKE OF GLOUCESTER, LATER RICHARD III

1452–1485

Ruled England: 1483–1485

56

IVAN IV ("IVAN THE TERRIBLE")

1530–1584

Ruled Russia: 1533–1584

97

LETTICE KNOLLYS

1543–1634

135

ERZSÉBET (ELIZABETH) BÁTHORY

("THE BLOOD COUNTESS")

1560–1614

161

PRINCE HENRY, DUKE OF CUMBERLAND AND STRATHEARN

1745–1790

183

PAULINE BONAPARTE

1780–1825

217

ARCHDUKE RUDOLF,
CROWN PRINCE OF AUSTRIA, HUNGARY, AND BOHEMIA

1858–1889

256

PRINCE ALBERT VICTOR,
DUKE OF CLARENCE AND AVONDALE

1864–1892

300

PRINCESS MARGARET, COUNTESS OF SNOWDON

1930–2002

336

Acknowledgments 385

Selected Bibliography 387

Disobedience is my joy!

—Princess Margaret, sister of Queen Elizabeth II,
to film director Jean Cocteau

ROYAL PAINS

Foreword

According to an anonymous source addressing the subject of a major mid-eighteenth-century scandal, a royal's conduct was "a matter of national as well as private concern, such a dangerous influence do they derive from their titular and elevated station." In other words, the members of a royal family had a duty to both crown and country to behave themselves.

Dereliction of that duty is what this book is all about.

When I selected the subjects for this volume, I had no single overarching definition of "royal pain" other than classifying them according to the broad characterizations delineated in the subtitle. But as the chapters took shape, it became clear that each royal pain had his or her own standard for inclusion.

Contained within these pages are profiles of a number of brats, brutes, and bad seeds, whether they were the monarchs' brothers, sisters, cousins, or offspring (and sometimes the rulers themselves). They represent a panoply of vibrant characters whose rotten behavior scandalized the kingdom in their own day. Their actions earned them a lasting reputation in the pantheon of rotten royals, and shaped the course of history within their respective realms.

Some members of the cast, such as Ivan the Terrible, Vlad Dracula, and Richard III, merit inclusion because they rank near the top of a proverbial "A-List" of regal evildoers, responsible for the assassinations of members of their own families, or for the deaths of thousands of their own subjects. Other royal pains in this volume, like the Duke of Cumberland and Pauline Bonaparte, embarrassed their reigning relatives and, by extension, the crown and kingdom, with their numerous ill-advised and publicly conducted "sexcapades."

And whenever and wherever there was a free press, some of these royal pains made newspaper headlines, victims of their own celebrity. Whether openly or obliquely, their misbehavior ended up splattered across the front page.

Deprived of the opportunity to do anything substantive well into adulthood, the last three royals chronologically profiled here—Rudolph, Eddy, and Margaret—became lost souls. The exercise of their oversize sense of noblesse oblige led to ill-conceived associations and churlish behavior, exposing not only themselves but the entire royal family in an unflattering light.

The gothically gruesome pact that Crown Prince Rudolf of Austria made with his teenage lover Mary Vetsera very likely evolved into a murder-suicide that became the focus of an international cover-up. During his brief lifetime, the shy Prince Eddy was internationally believed to be not only lazy and stupid, but an active player in London's dicey homosexual subculture. Sexy and flamboyant Princess Margaret, caught smoking a cigarette in a nightclub, became a royal cause célèbre. And her star-crossed romance with a divorced courtier put the crown itself in the hot seat, accused in 72-point type of rampant hypocrisy.

Occasionally, the sovereigns themselves were bad news, real bastards—in the unofficial sense of the word—and brutes par excellence. They ruled their realms with iron fists—and saw no need to glove them in illusory velvet. They thought nothing of torturing their own subjects; even the most loyal adherents might find themselves at the wrong end of a sharp object if their sovereign perceived that they had crossed him.

In this volume, jealousies, lusts, and betrayals are played out on the world stage, pitting relations against one another for the highest possible stakes; it's sibling rivalry and combative cousins on metaphorical steroids. You may never look at your own family the same way again.

KING JOHN

1166 OR 1167–1216
RULED ENGLAND: 1199–1216

SCHOOLCHILDREN LEARNING ABOUT THE MIDDLE AGES may have heard phrases like "wicked Prince John" and "evil King John" to describe this English royal. And much of what we think we know about John stems from his characterization as an archvillain in the various Robin Hood legends.

But fictional depictions aside, John did indeed plot against his father, Henry II of England, as well as his elder brother Richard, whom he betrayed on numerous occasions. As king, Richard awarded John considerable preferment, but it was never enough; he always wanted more. After John legitimately ascended the throne, his insistence on wedding a barely pubescent girl promised in marriage to one of his most powerful vassals set in motion a conflict that would redraw the map of Europe. Years later, he upped the enmity ante by sexually harassing his barons' wives and daughters.

John was a usurper, a hedonist, and a hypocrite. And as far as his barons (and even his mother) were concerned, very much a royal pain.

He was the youngest of the seven surviving children born to Henry II and Eleanor of Aquitaine. And in due time John would become the apple of Henry's eye and the bane of Eleanor's. She was forty-four years old when she gave birth to John (forty-five, if he was born in 1167). Meanwhile the proud papa, eleven years younger than his queen, was carrying on a torrid affair with a sixteen-year-old Welsh blonde named Rosamund.

John was born into a family of willful, competive, passionate, and brilliant political strategists; it was no surprise, then, that his childhood was the scene of more than one pitched battle royal. "From the Devil they came and to the Devil they will return," declared the venerated Abbé Bernard of Clairvaux, speaking of the hot-tempered Angevin kings of England. Their French dynastic name derived from the first Angevin, John's father, Henry II, who had been the Count of Anjou. Popular medieval legend held that the family was descended from Satan's daughter Melusine, and those of their contemporaries who had been on the receiving end of Angevin wrath gave it credence.

The royal line of Henry II was also known as the Plantagenets (because of the sprig of yellow broom or *planta genista* that the men jauntily wore in their caps). Henry's relationship with his four sons, two of whom would die during his lifetime, was fraught with mistrust and hostility. When they were mere boys, John's older brothers—young Henry, Geoffrey, and Richard—were ceded the counties of Normandy, Anjou, and Aquitaine (in name only, not in governance). John, the baby of the family, was long denied any continental territories, earning him the nickname "Lackland." In 1173 Henry's three oldest sons took up arms against him, encouraged by their mother to revolt because the king intended to take back some of their holdings and bestow them upon John instead. Henry planned to name John as his heir, in part because at only six or seven years old the prince was too young to have joined his brothers' rebellion.

However, John's tender years were no guarantee of his eventual loyalty or trustworthiness. During the reign of his father, and later that of his brother Richard, John switched allegiances almost as often as he bathed. (As an aside, royal records of his own reign show that he paid his ewerer for twenty-three baths over sixteen months.) John initially supported their father when Richard made a bid for the throne. But after he realized that he was backing the losing man, he became a turncoat, fighting alongside Richard against Henry II in 1189. Henry died that July with the shock of John's betrayal on his lips. Some medieval chroniclers were fond of claiming that it was John's treachery, not illness and battle fatigue, that killed the king.

John was not named Henry's heir. Richard had bested their father in battle and compelled the dying Henry to leave the kingdom to him. John did, however, inherit the famous Angevin temper. According to the twelfth-century chronicler Richard of Devizes, Prince John once broke out in such a rage against Richard's chancellor William Longchamp that "his whole person became so changed as to be hardly recognizable. Rage contorted his brow, his burning eyes glittered, bluish spots discolored the pink of his cheeks, and I know not what would have become of the chancellor if in that moment of frenzy he had fallen like an apple into his hands as they sawed the air."

Richard was crowned king of England on September 3, 1189. Just a few days earlier, on August 29, John had wed one of their cousins, Isabella of Gloucester, to whom he had been betrothed since 1176, when the pair were mere children. John's marriage to Isabella made him heir to his father-in-law, which entitled him to be styled the Earl of Gloucester and enabled John to collect the revenues from cousin Isabella's property, but that was the extent of his connubial perquisites. The couple never dwelled together as man and wife. In fact, the horrified Archbishop of Canterbury had protested the marriage on the grounds of consanguinity. The spouses, both descendants of Henry I, were too closely related, and a papal dispensation that would have permitted the couple to wed had never been issued. John then intervened with a papal legate to secure the document. Yet even though the couple thus became legally married on paper, Archbishop Baldwin had forbidden them to have conjugal relations, or even to cohabit.

To satisfy his sexual urges John had numerous affairs, but they didn't satisfy his lust for land—and for as much power as he could wield, although Richard's wedding gift to his younger brother had included Nottinghamshire and six other English counties (from which John would derive extensive revenues), as well as a county in Normandy that entitled John to be titled Count of Mortain. After Richard's coronation, although John was also styled Prince John of England, he would use his French title throughout his brother's reign.

None of the Plantagenets trusted one another as far as they could spit. Any alliances were matters of expediency and were sundered as often as they were cemented. Richard was fully aware of his brother's jealousy, as well as John's penchant for treachery. Nonetheless, the new king was extremely generous to his sibling and perhaps there was a method to his madness, but medieval historians didn't see it.

The contemporary chronicler William of Newburgh was of the opinion that Richard was far too bountiful and lenient with John, believing that such largesse would only swell the Count of Mortain's head and lead him into the temptation to acquire more by any means.

Richard had scarcely become king before he prepared to go on crusade in the Holy Land. Wary that his younger brother might incite the barons to rebellion, or even to usurp the throne, he ordered John to stay out of England for a period of three years—by which time he expected to have returned from the crusade. Although John had never been Eleanor's favorite son, her maternal instincts got the better of her political ones. She urged Richard to release John from his oath to remain on the Continent. The consequences of Richard's acquiescence to their mother's request were disastrous—for John did nothing whatsoever to curb his duplicity.

Not only was Prince John prepared to commit treason by allying himself with England's greatest enemy, but his treachery was about to take the form of bigamy.

In 1191, the king of France, Philip Augustus II, offered John all of King Richard's continental lands if John would marry his sister Alys. When she was a little girl, Alys was officially betrothed to Richard and was sent to live at the English court among her future in-laws; but when she reached her midteens she became the mistress of King Henry, instead of his son's bride. Richard refused to honor the marital treaty with France because Alys was damaged goods. He eventually wed Berengaria of Navarre in a match arranged by his mother and then proceeded to ignore his queen for the better part of their marriage. Initially unaware of why his sister had been jilted by Richard, then disgusted by the discovery that she had soiled her honor and that of France by warming Henry's bed, Philip had a sour taste in his mouth from the whole ordeal, and he was eager to find a way to stick it to Richard.

John seriously considered Philip's offer of Alys's hand in marriage. However, Philip was in no position to redistribute the territories in France that formed part of Richard's kingdom. And John was already married to Isabella of Gloucester, regardless of the fact that they had never consummated their union. Nevertheless, John was about to make a secret dash for the Continent to parley with Philip when his mother discovered his plans. Eleanor rushed from Aquitaine to England to prevent John's departure, threatening him with the forfeiture of all his lands if he insisted on pursuing an unholy alliance with Philip of France.

John obeyed his mother only to the extent that he remained in England. By then, he wanted more than his brother's continental lands. He wanted the entire kingdom. And because John had been born on English soil (Richard was born in Aquitaine), he thought he deserved to wear the crown. Besides, he was *there*—and ready to rule!

John began laying the groundwork for claiming the crown while Richard was still in Cyprus. A master of spin-doctoring centuries before it became standard operating procedure in every political campaign, he traveled throughout the realm spreading rumors that Richard had named him as his successor, adding in dramatically dire tones that the king would never return from the Holy Land. John even intimated that Richard was already dead—although no one believed him. The following year, John extracted oaths of loyalty from various barons, and appropriated funds from the exchequer for his own use.

In December 1192, on his way home from the Holy Land, Richard was taken prisoner by Duke Leopold V of Austria. A few weeks later, he was handed over to Leopold's cousin, Holy Roman Emperor Heinrich VI, who kept Richard captive, demanding an exorbitant ransom from England. But rather than do his level best to effect his brother's swift and safe release, John endeavored to waylay into his own coffers the ransom money their mother fought so hard to obtain, soaking their subjects until they had no more to contribute. When countless silver marks somehow disappeared, instead of questioning her treacherous younger son about the missing money, Eleanor insisted on increasing the taxes on an already financially strapped populace until the ransom was raised.

By the spring of 1194, when Richard returned to his kingdom, it was evident that John's assumption of authority had been entirely unauthorized and the barons had been duped into supporting him. Although Richard may have slept with one eye open from then on, he forgave his twenty-seven-year-old brother. "Think no more of it, John; you are only a child who has had evil counsellors," Richard told the contrite and humbled prince. "Now, what can I give you for dinner?"

On April 6, 1199, Richard died in Eleanor's arms. He had been shot in the shoulder by an archer standing on the parapet of Châlus Castle near Limoges, a fortress Richard was preparing to invade. The wound turned gangrenous and Richard died from the infection. Eleanor now had no choice but to support John as Richard's successor, regardless of his previous efforts to usurp his elder brother's throne and pillage the kingdom for his own greedy ends. John was a royal pain, but he was still her son.

King John inherited a disastrous economy. Richard had constantly bled his subjects dry in order to finance his numerous wars. In addition, years of baronial resentment over the Angevin monarchs' taxation and arrogance were finally coming to a head, but John was compelled to raise taxes yet again to cover domestic expenditures. He also chose to purchase peace with his continental vassals for the sum of twenty thousand marks; it was a vast amount of money, but cheaper than going to war against them. The move further angered England's barons. For preferring the price of peace in this most martial of eras, John earned the nickname "Softsword."

It was an age of constantly shifting loyalties and frequent betrayals. Allies one month might be mortal enemies the next. The Angevin empire covered England, Ireland, and parts of France; however, it was exceptionally difficult for an English king to govern his continental lands from across the Channel. He had to rely on administrative stewards, or seneschals, to ensure that taxes were collected and the counties running smoothly, while staving off potential rebellions from neighboring nobles or the encroaching Capetians, the royal house of France, who were always seeking to add to their holdings.

The Angevins and the Capetians sought the same lands. It was as if France were a chessboard or a quilt, and each dynasty wanted to be sure it controlled enough connecting squares. Three adjacent counties in particular—Lusignan, La Marche, and Angoumois—were of vital importance to everyone, because whoever controlled those lands held the balance of power in the region. One of those three territories held a particularly attractive set of assets.

Isabella of Angoulême was the heiress of a region within

Aquitaine also known as Angoumois, a wealthy and desirable county near the west coast of modern-day France. Her father was the powerful Count Aymer (sometimes written as Adomar) Taillefer of Angoulême, and her mother's family was descended from and related to a number of kings, including the monarchs of France and Hungary.

In order to create an unbroken swath of continental territory that would be considered part of England's dominion, John needed to find a way to control the centrally located county of Angoumois. On the tic-tac-toe board of France he had already placed a metaphorical X in the northern box of Normandy and in the southern one of Aquitaine. The dowager queen Eleanor had made over her inheritance of Aquitaine to John after Richard's death in 1199, but that was no assurance that her barons would be loyal to him as their new duke.

And John needed as many continental allies as possible. During the first nine months of his reign, he made an effort to checkmate the encroaching king of France, Philip Augustus, by purchasing the loyalty of a couple of powerful vassals, including the formidable Lusignan family, ceding them large portions of Aquitaine in exchange for their support.

By the summer of 1200, John had been king of England, as well as duke of Normandy and Aquitaine, for little more than a year. Although his crown was the ultimate accessory, he nevertheless dressed to impress, being quite the clotheshorse, with a stable of fine garments and jewels. According to measurements taken of his remains when his tomb was opened in 1797, John was about five feet, six and a half inches tall. Self-conscious about his inferior height (even for those days), he swaggered in order to keep pace with taller men. Still, he was considered fairly attractive, with bright eyes, dark hair, and a mocking sense of humor; and although he'd been clean shaven in his youth, as king he affected a trim mustache and beard. As John matured, his taste for good living got the better of his metabolism and he evidently grew paunchy.

In August of 1200, John visited Aquitaine, and from the accounts of contemporary chroniclers, became utterly smitten with young Isabella. Their meeting changed the course of Western history.

Isabella's physical appearance has never been described, although medieval chroniclers frequently referred to her lustful appetite, painting her as a sexually precocious Lolita. Twelve was considered the age of consent at the time, and it is generally accepted that Isabella was that age when she met John, though some historians believe she might have been as old as fifteen. Other scholars believe she may have been as young as eight or nine, which would have to put the lie to the story that has been repeated for centuries, namely that John was so taken with her beauty that he couldn't wait to bed her. Even in the year 1200 it would have been viewed as child molestation and would certainly have been added to the lengthy list of "evil King John's" transgressions. But if Isabella was indeed twelve years old in the summer of 1200, John (if born in 1166) was nevertheless considered middle-aged at thirty-three.

Whether it was lust or politics that drove him, John was ready to do whatever it took to marry Aymer's daughter, including securing an annulment of his unconsummated first marriage.

A scandal of international proportions was about to commence. First, John consulted six bishops—three in Normandy and three in Aquitaine—before putting aside Isabella of

Gloucester. At least their annulment proceeding was evidently amicable; long after they'd been divorced, John sent his ex-wife generous Christmas gifts. Isabella of Gloucester would eventually marry twice more. But John, always looking for an angle, found a way to make some money from it. He charged Geoffrey de Mandeville (Isabella's second husband) the exorbitant sum of twenty thousand marks for the right to wed her. In his quest to secure allies by any means possible, the fee was John's way of forcing his ex-wife's new husband to become indefinitely indebted to the crown, aware that Geoffrey's income and revenues couldn't begin to offset the expense. In fact, Geoffrey never even fully paid the first installment.

John disentangled himself from his first Isabella, but there was a major hitch in his plans to wed the heiress of Angoulême. According to the chronicler Roger of Howden, before little Isabella had reached the age of nubility, and "on the advice and at the wish of King Richard," she had been betrothed to someone else. Count Aymer had already promised her to Hugh le Brun, lord of Lusignan and a loyal vassal of John's—one he could ill afford to anger. The le Bruns of Lusignan were powerful and important barons in the lower region of Poitou, and an illustrious crusading family, having accompanied King Richard to the Holy Land.

Hugh de Lusignan IX was also a powerful rival of Count Aymer of Angoulême. Adopting the strategy of keeping his friends close but his enemies closer, initially Aymer had thought it made perfect sense to forge an alliance by wedding his little Isabella to Hugh. Their marriage would unite two warring formidable families—making them allies, and making King John nervous.

Count Aymer of Angoulême and the le Bruns of Lusignan

were rivals for a wealthy, sprawling territory just to the east of Angoulême known as La Marche. And before John learned of Isabella's marriage plans, he had been backing Hugh de Lusignan's claim to it. But John quickly recognized that if Hugh were wed to Isabella, *he* would then control all three key counties—Lusignan, Angoulême, and La Marche—tipping the balance of power in the area, and making Hugh a rival John would have to reckon with. It was therefore vital for him to prevent Hugh's marriage to Isabella of Angoulême. Although right up until that month, John had been seriously considering a union with the princess of Portugal, after he saw Count Aymer's daughter, those plans went out the window. He recognized that if he were to espouse Isabella himself, it would prevent the creation of a powerful dynastic alliance between the houses of Angoulême and Lusignan.

Little did John realize that the fallout from this hasty marriage would cost him half his kingdom.

Many chroniclers, especially those writing during the High Gothic era, believed that John's sudden interest in Isabella was primarily sexual. Other historians, perhaps with the benefit of seeing the bigger picture, believed the match was politically motivated, intended to check the Lusignan barons' land grab. The truth probably lies somewhere in between.

According to the custom of the times, in arranged marriages between powerful families the young bride-to-be was sent to live in the household of her prospective groom until she came of age and could be a true wife in every way. In John's defense, Isabella's betrothal to Hugh may not have been regarded as fully ironclad because, in the words of Bishop Philip of Durham, she "had not yet reached her nubile years. Hugh had not wished to marry her *in facie ecclesiae*. So her father snatched her from the custody of Hugh le Brun, and she was immediately married to John by the archbishop of Bordeaux."

According to the chroniclers, John fell in lust with Isabella on sight. "He believed she possessed everything he could desire," wrote one of them. Naturally that cryptic sentence could just as easily apply to the county of Angoumois as to her physical attributes.

Evidently, John had made it worth Count Aymer's while to back a different bridegroom. Agreeing to support King John against the Lusignans—the very family he would have otherwise made his in-laws—Aymer signed two treaties with John: one private and the other public. In exchange for his preadolescent daughter, Aymer received John's support for his claim to La Marche. Consequently, as a direct result of John's marriage to Isabella, both the Angoumois and La Marche were brought under Angevin control.

Aymer removed Isabella from the home of Hugh de Lusignan on August 23, 1200. Although there had been a thirteen-year gap between John's betrothal to his first wife and their wedding ceremony, by this point he was no longer a pimply adolescent, but an impatient middle-aged monarch (politically, sexually, or both) and had zero interest in a lengthy engagement. So on August 24, King John of England married the young—very young—Isabella of Angoulême. A few days later he presented his child bride to his ailing mother, Eleanor, who was living at Fontevrault Abbey. Apparently, Eleanor liked what she saw in the girl.

But something must not have been entirely kosher with his second marriage ceremony, because John went out of his way to obtain the consent of several bishops to his union with Isabella of Angoulême. This clue has caused historians to surmise that she might indeed have been well under the age of consent at the time the king "stole" her from his vassal Hugh de Lusignan, and gives further credence to the Bishop of Durham's remark that she "had not yet reached her nubile" years. Isabella was said to have looked so young when she arrived in England that many who saw her were skeptical that she had even reached the advertised twelve years of age.

Isabella was crowned queen of England on October 8, 1200, by Hubert Walter, Archbishop of Canterbury. About thirty pounds were spent on her royal robes, an exorbitant sum at the time, considering that the annual income of a knight was only about a hundred and fifty pounds. Yet, barring the expense of her coronation, Isabella was treated by her husband with precious little pomp, while John continued to spend lavishly on his own accoutrements. He loved good music, fine food, and expensive clothes, and his court was a lovely one, filled—to excess, some chroniclers claim—with music and gaiety. So was something sinister at work or was the rotten condition of England's economy to blame for the fact that Isabella had been permitted the tiniest of retinues when she came to England, and had no income of her own?

During his brother Richard's imprisonment in Germany, John had already demonstrated his rapaciousness, as well as his capacity for appropriating funds that were not his to collect. It must have been a difficult habit to break, because he essentially began stealing from his own wife.

After Isabella gave birth to their first son, John began to pocket the "queen's gold" (the name for the tax of one gold mark for every hundred marks of silver paid by the Jews for the privilege of living and working peaceably in England). Queen's gold was traditionally used by the consort to fund her personal expenditures or for philanthropic bequests. So, where his young wife was concerned, was John still unjustly lining his pockets with others' largesse, or was he just an inconsiderate husband? It's possible that once Isabella did her royal duty by begetting an heir, her spouse no longer felt he had to be generous to her.

Unfortunately, Isabella's feelings on the issue (if they were recorded at all) have been lost to history. But there were others whose discontent with John's lack of noblesse oblige was most certainly noted.

The Lusignans bided their time after John wed Isabella, expecting him to offer them some recompense for snatching away Hugh's intended bride. But when John ignored them instead, the enraged and embarrassed Lusignan family threw its support behind the prematurely bald and perennially paranoid King Philip of France.

And with that John's continental headaches had only just begun. Over the next several years, he became embroiled in various skirmishes on French soil, all of which could be traced to his marriage.

For starters, in 1202, John received desperate messages from Count Aymer of Angoulême and from Eleanor of Aquitaine, who remained a force to be reckoned with although she was then residing in Fontevrault Abbey. They urged John to sail to France immediately to smooth things over with the Lusignans, who were doing a lot of saber rattling in Poitou.

But John had trouble marshaling any backing from his English barons. They were reluctant to finance his continental ventures (much less to accompany him abroad). This should have come as no surprise, as John had already informed them of his plans to limit baronial authority in their own counties. Ruling through intimidation rather than respect, John threatened to confiscate the castles of those who refused to support him in France.

Although at this stage in the game John and Philip of France were on the outs, John, as duke of several French territories, was still Philip's vassal. Upon John's arrival in France the monarchs "played nice" in an effort to suss out each other's plans. Uncertain of John's martial strength, and no doubt hoping to glean some information as to the size of John's forces, Philip advised the Lusignans to tread softly while he lavishly entertained John and Isabella.

The le Bruns of Lusignan had formally appealed to Philip against John, accusing him of unjustly attacking and despoiling them, taking over Hugh's county of La Marche, harassing Hugh's brother Ralph, and encouraging his officials to "do all the harm they could" to hassle them. John retaliated by charging the Lusignans with treason, challenging them to fight a judicial duel with champions—a contest involving knights, not lawyers—where might would make right.

John promised to uphold his part of the agreement by turning over three castles in surety to the contest's arbitrator, King Philip of France. But when he failed to appear for the combat, Philip attacked Normandy and bestowed John's holdings there on the English sovereign's teenage nephew, Arthur of Brittany. Because Arthur had been raised in the French court, many believed him to be far more inclined to support Philip than to back his own uncle John.

Between 1202 and 1204, John's mercenaries faced off against forces supported by Philip of France. But once a spoiled brat, always a spoiled brat; by bullying important vassals and thumbing his nose at his own continental overlord, the king of France, John began losing battles and hemorrhaging lands. Although John was in his mid-thirties by this time, and only two years younger than Philip, he still behaved like a feckless baby who petulantly took whatever he wanted (his brother's ransom money, his vassal's fiancée) and then blamed everyone else when things blew up in his face.

He did assert himself, as a man and as a king, when Eleanor of Aquitaine became caught in the civil cross fire. After John received the news that his eighty-year-old mother was being held hostage in the castle at Mirebeau by the Lusignans and her own grandson, Arthur of Brittany, John marched his army eighty miles in two days to reach her with all due speed. On the night of July 31, 1202, his soldiers stormed the castle and rescued Eleanor. Arthur, still a teenager, was among the rebels captured and paraded in manacles across the country. John's cruelty to his captives was noted in *L'Histoire de Guillaume le Maréchal*: "He kept his prisoners so vilely and in such evil distress that it seemed shameful and ugly to all those who were with him and saw his cruelty."

John's treatment of his nephew Arthur of Brittany was the most ruthless of all; but the king's conduct was not entirely without reason. Not only had Arthur allied himself with the French king and rebelled against John in Normandy, but the boy had also held his aging granny hostage. After the battle at Mirebeau, Arthur was taken prisoner by John and was never heard from again. Stories abounded that he was tortured and eventually murdered (in April 1203), possibly by John himself, adding to the king's reputation as an "evil" man. According to the chronicles written at Margam Abbey in Glamorgan, Scotland, "After King John had captured Arthur and kept him alive in prison for some time, at length, in the castle of Rouen, after dinner on the Thursday before Easter, when he was drunk and possessed by the devil . . . he slew him with his own hand and tying a heavy stone to the body cast it into the Seine. It was discovered by a fisherman in his net, and being dragged to the bank and recognized, was taken for secret burial, in fear of the tyrant, to the priory of Bec called Notre Dame de Près."

Yet some historians believe that the information detailed in the Margam annals may be fanciful; their supposition lies in the documented evidence that John treated Arthur's sister Eleanor very well during the remainder of his reign. Although she was more or less under permanent house arrest as a captive of the crown, John routinely presented her with costly gifts of furs, textiles, clothes, and saddles, in addition to an annual allowance from the royal exchequer.

The supreme court of France condemned John for Arthur's murder, even though no corpse was ever submitted as evidence. And it made a convenient excuse for France to invade England; therefore, the revolt of John's French barons can be seen as a direct consequence of his alleged murder of his nephew.

The victory at Mirebeau had been the pinnacle of John's continental success. In August of 1202, he had returned to Normandy triumphant, having eliminated the Lusignan threat. By autumn the rebel strongholds were in his hands and he and Isabella celebrated Christmas in Caen, according to a contemporary chronicler, "dining sumptuously and lying in bed till dinner-time."

The royal marriage had begun with the scandal perpetuated by John's petulant "theft" of Isabella from her intended bridegroom. And tongues never did stop wagging about them, nor pens cease their scratching. Many of the enduring historical accounts of John and Isabella's marriage began with the writing of Roger of Wendover, a monk at St. Albans during the early thirteenth century. Although Roger larded his chronicles with improbable embellishments, historians have dined out on that fatty biographical feast for generations, repeating and regurgitating the even more implausible flourishes supplied by Matthew Paris, Wendover's successor at St. Albans.

Paris was also wildly imaginative, and pro-baronial, and it is his depiction of Isabella of Angoulême as "an incestuous, evil, adulterous woman" that has survived the ages and cemented her (erroneously earned) reputation as a harpy. Paris's *Chronica Majora* reported the alleged firsthand findings of master Robert of London who in 1211 was King John's emissary to the emir of Morocco. Robert of London, evidently well out of his embassy, informed the emir that John was married to a harridan, "hateful to him, and who hates him, too. She has often been found guilty of incest, sorcery, and adultery, so that the king her husband, has ordered those of her lovers who have been apprehended to be strangled with a rope in her own bed."

Well, that's juicy stuff—quite the lurid picture of this royal marriage—but not one scintilla of proof has appeared over the ensuing centuries to bolster Paris's assertions. The same treatment of fancy as fact holds true for Paris's predecessor. Roger of Wendover (writing in 1225, some nine years after John's death) staunchly maintained that the reason King John lost Normandy within a year of his spectacular victory at Mirebeau was because he was overcome by "sorcery or witchcraft"—so infatuated with his wife, "finding all kinds of delights in his queen," that nothing else mattered to him but lying in her arms, indulging his passion for her in "incorrigible idleness," making love, not war. Roger asserted that John "was enjoying every kind of pleasure with his queen, in whose company he believed that he possessed all that he wanted."

But there has never been any proof of the charges that John preferred to loll about in lascivious luxury with Isabella instead of ruling his country. In fact, the pair were married for more than six years before Isabella became pregnant. If the numerous tales of unbridled lust are true, they don't take into account that Isabella bore her husband no children from 1200 to 1207. There was no mention of miscarriages, nor of ill health on the part of either party, although John did spend a considerable amount of time on the battlefields of France. So, if the medieval chroniclers, as well as one of John's more recent biographers, the twentieth-century historian Alan Lloyd, are to be believed—and the royal couple behaved like a pair of randy rabbits during their first few years of marriage, yet Isabella did not become pregnant for several years—where is the evidence of their libidinousness? They weren't exactly practicing birth control, and Isabella's one job as queen was to beget an heir to the throne.

She gave birth to their first child, the future Henry III, in 1207—another reason some scholars like to posit that she may have been prepubescent at the time of her marriage. Between 1207 and 1215, Isabella bore John five children— two sons, followed by three daughters. By 1207, when John was gray-haired and somewhat stout, but nonetheless filled with energy, Isabella was probably still in her teens.

Therefore, it is possible that John and Isabella's hyperactive sex life is merely mythological, handed down through the centuries as fact. And it's also doubtful that Isabella was to blame for encouraging John to make another fatal error in judgment that cost him England's continental lands. He was, after all, not a terribly brilliant military strategist. For example, he had released the Lusignans in exchange for their oaths of loyalty. Unsurprisingly, they broke their promises as soon as it was convenient to do so, and renewed their intriguing against him.

By June 1204, the entirety of Normandy was in Philip's possession. John had also lost Anjou, Maine, Touraine, and Brittany—and all within a single year, as one by one his vassals had capitulated to Philip, and his territories had fallen like a row of dominoes into the French king's hands. Only Poitou and Aquitaine remained in English possession. But in 1205, Poitou, too, fell to Philip's invading army. By then, John had scarcely a friend on the Continent.

It could be argued that few English kings were as unpopular as John. There's probably a superstitious reason as to why there has never been a King John II. John's distracting sexual passion for his wife, whether real or imagined, was only one reason he was soundly disliked and accounted a royal pain by his subjects. They had plenty to gripe about. Rather than appoint local nobles to administer his estates, he gave mercenary captains these prominent (and powerful) positions as seneschals, or stewards, of his Norman holdings. These mercenaries treated John's vassals as enemies, pocketing their tributes and tax payments.

Their corrupt behavior naturally engendered the enmity of John's barons, whose anger was compounded by the king's practice of surrounding himself with foreigners, landless knights, "bachelors" (young unknighted men), and bannerets (poor men he had raised up from nowhere and trusted to handle his affairs).

John managed to keep his thumb on the barons by squeezing exorbitant sums from them. There was a tax, levy, or fine on just about everything from marriages to inheritances to purchasing his goodwill, in case a noble fell out of royal favor for whatever reason. John levied two major tallages (a form of taxation) in 1203 and 1207; and in 1210 he instated a massive tallage against the Jews, the medieval monarchs' perennial cash cows. Brutal measures were implemented to ensure payment. After one Jew balked at having to forfeit the astronomical sum of ten thousand marks of silver (the amount levied upon each Jew in the kingdom), John commanded that a tooth be extracted for each day he continued to resist. After seven days, the man painfully relented. The 1210 tallage angered Christians as well. Many of them owed enormous sums to the Jewish moneylenders and were forced to repay their loans so that the Jews had the coin to hand over to the crown.

John was also fully capable of disliking men just because they were rich or powerful. And he made a practice of taking his own subjects as hostages. Sons of prominent barons were made security for their fathers' obedience; and the king made good on his threats. In July 1212, John hanged twenty-eight sons of Welsh chieftains who had broken their faith with him. And he impounded nobles' lands when they defaulted on loans from the crown, forcing the men and their families into penury and starvation.

It was no surprise, given his cruelty, that John feared assassination. The queen and their children were closely watched and John went everywhere with an armed bodyguard. His mania for secrecy rivaled that of America's two political Dicks, Nixon and Cheney; he demanded that members of his entourage spy on one another, and developed a system of secret verbal codes and signals. However, because John was too paranoid to write them down and stash them in a safe place, he occasionally forgot his own signs.

By the end of 1212, with enemies mounting on all sides, John recognized the necessity for a major ally. He had angered Pope Innocent years earlier by insisting on his own choice of archbishop, and in 1209 His Holiness excommunicated him. The papal interdict extended to all of John's subjects. They were deprived of the sacraments, unable to receive baptism, a church-sanctioned wedding, or burial in consecrated ground. It was Innocent's hope that the interdict would turn John's subjects against him. But the common man was not as concerned with the strictures of the Church as the pope had surmised. John did lose a number of his clerical ministers, who, fearing for the future of their souls, fled to the Continent or quit the king's service in protest of his apostasy. But he also had several lay counselors and administrators in his employ; and consequently, the business of governing the realm remained largely unchanged.

Finally, in 1213, John hit upon a plan to obtain military and financial aid from Rome so that he could defend England from the threat of French invasion. He shrewdly made himself a vassal of the pope by agreeing to go on crusade—at an unspecified date, of course, in order to indefinitely prolong having to make good on his promise.

It was a classic "you scratch my back, I'll scratch yours" strategy. Here's why the delay was a good move for the Vatican as well: If John were to depart immediately for the Holy Land, rather than postpone his crusade, King Philip of France might take advantage of his absence to invade England and claim the crown. The last thing Rome wanted was the creation of such a vast royal dominion, because it would challenge, if not diminish, papal power and authority.

The Barnwell annalist, a less biased medieval chronicler than his contemporaries, wrote of John's decision to ally himself with Rome: "The king provided wisely for himself and his people by this deed, although to many it seemed ignominious and a monstrous yoke of servitude. For matters were in such extremity . . . that there was no shorter way—perhaps no other way—of evading the impending danger. For from the moment he put himself under apostolic protection and made his kingdom part of St. Peter's patrimony, there was no prince in the Roman world who would dare attack him or invade his lands to the damage of the Apostolic see; since everyone stood in greater awe of Pope Innocent than of his predecessors for many years past."

But the pope did expect John to *eventually* make good on his promise, warning the king that if he reneged on his bargain, his excommunication, and that of every one of his subjects, would be reinstated. But the pontiff never bothered to scold or lecture John on his personal morals. And looming large was the issue of marital fidelity to the woman he had once been so besotted with that he was willing to risk his kingdom.

Depending on the source, John is said to have sired

between five and twelve royal bastards by various mistresses, one of whom was a noblewoman. He was largely reputed to have seduced several of his barons' wives and daughters (or at least tried to), an early form of sexual harassment that was soundly censured in his day, as well as by modern chroniclers of his reign. Recent historians suggest that all of the royal bastards were born before John's marriage to Isabella of Angoulême, and the illegitimate children were given the surname Fitzroy (which means "son of the king").

But even though John may not have impregnated women after his second marriage, there is no indication that he stopped hitting on them. Some of his lovers have been identified. There was the "widow Hawise," a woman named Suzanne, and another named Clementia. In 1212, the king sent a chaplet of roses, plucked from his justiciar's garden, to an unnamed mistress. John was also rumored to have lusted after the wife of one of his vassals, Eustace de Vesci, but the woman cleverly hired a professional prostitute to take her place in the bed. Eustace de Vesci was one of the nobles who took up arms against John in the baronial uprisings of 1212–1216, so it's possible that the king's libido had something to do with de Vesci's hostility.

A "maidservant of the king's friend" named Susan also received gifts from John. And the wife of John's chief forester, Hugh Neville, had to promise the king two hundred chickens in exchange for the privilege of sleeping with her own husband.

Now that the litany of John's licentious transgressions has been recited, it should be noted that much of what has been written about John's libido, particularly that his purported lust for women of his own class earned him the enmity of his barons, was composed several years after his death, offered as one of the key reasons the nobles rebelled against him in 1215. But these lurid stories deserve to be mentioned because they have been repeated through the centuries, helping to cement John's reputation as an evil man and an even worse king.

And they do help to explain some of the abuses of power that so angered a number of John's barons, leading to their demands for the codification of a king's responsibility to his vassals and vice versa. That document, considered by history to be John's crowning achievement, would become known as the Magna Carta. Centuries of schoolchildren have been taught that the Magna Carta was a lengthy charter of laws that John was forced to sign under duress at Runnymede on June 15, 1215, as a result of a mass uprising of rebellious knights and barons.

Not quite. For starters, John didn't actually sign the document; he affixed his great seal to it. More important, the barons had been angry with John for years over a number of issues, leading to several violent skirmishes between their armies and John's knights. Many of the rebels believed that John had committed *personal* wrongs against them and their families, including unlawful confiscation of their castles and other property. The barons had grown increasingly testy because they'd seen the government of the counties pass from hereditary lords to the king's sheriffs. Royal tribunals increasingly impinged on the authority and existence of the barons' own courts. And John had elevated to positions of authority in his government foreigners, mercenaries, and professional administrators, instead of promoting from within the ranks of the nobility.

In 1214, baronial discontent reached a boiling point, according to John's biographer W. L. Warren. The barons sought a restoration of the laws and rights established by King Edward I—except for one hitch. No one knew just what those laws and rights were. The nobles were lost in a haze of nostalgia for a less tyrannical reign.

On May 17, 1215, the rebels easily entered London. Friends opened the gates for them and they took the city with little resistance. These barons and their supporters then sent letters to every man who was still loyal to John, threatening them with violent reprisals if they did not switch their allegiance.

So on June 10 at Staines, John committed himself to an early draft of what would become the Magna Carta, affixing his seal to a document titled "The Articles of the Barons." The treatise was then submitted to the rebels and underwent a few revisions during the ensuing days.

The Magna Carta was the result of at least four slightly different documents, a negotiated settlement that was the work of many hands and influences. Essentially it reduced the king's role from autocrat to chief executive operating under the supervision of a baronial committee.

Many of the clauses in the Great Charter were written as a direct result of, or a response to, John's abuses of power—including taking English subjects as hostages for perceived disloyalty or nonpayment of debts to the crown; his engagement of foreigners or "aliens" in his armies as seneschals of his castles; and his burdensome taxation.

Although the Magna Carta began as a verdict on John's reign, some clauses in the charter, such as "The English Church shall be free" or "To no one will we sell, to no one will we deny or delay right or justice" have stood the test of time. The latter was a tremendous advance for the common man. No longer could a moneyed landowner buy his way out of a lawsuit or a judgment against him.

But the version of the Magna Carta that King John approved survived just a little longer than ten weeks, repudiated by extremists on both sides and declared invalid by Pope Innocent III, who agreed with John that kings ruled by divine right and had no business capitulating their power to recalcitrant nobles.

During the months following the signing of the Magna Carta, John prepared to withstand a French invasion led by Louis, the son of Philip of France. Louis sought to claim the English throne on the grounds that his wife, Blanche of Castile, was a granddaughter of Henry II. Some of John's most disenchanted barons had even chosen to accept Louis as their lord.

In the summer of 1216, Louis arrived on English shores and his army quickly took control of the southern counties. Meanwhile, Alexander of Scotland was marching down from the north. Numerous powerful lords, including John's own half brother, William of Salisbury, were among the defectors to Louis's camp.

King John, who had already lost his continental lands, was now in danger of losing England.

At the end of September, John was in Lynn arranging for supplies to be sent to his Norman strongholds; but evidently, he feasted too well during his sojourn there, and contracted dysentery. The medieval chronicler Roger of Wendover, who was fond of listing gluttony among John's catalog of sins, insisted that the king aggravated his condition by "surfeiting himself with peaches and new cider."

Still ailing and in great pain, John traveled through the chilly mists and fogs from Lynn to Wisbech on October 11, and the following day his caravan began the arduous journey over the numerous rivers that empty into the Wash. His destination was Swineshead Abbey in Lincolnshire. But John was about to encounter more bad luck. Roger of Wendover wrote that the king's baggage train met with an accident as the carts attempted to ford the Wellstream (now the River Nene; the Wellstream is the Nene estuary). Because the caravan was in too much haste to wait for the tides to recede, the packhorses and some of John's servants were mired in quicksand. According to the chroniclers, John's household effects and the equipment of his portable chapel, including its holy relics, were lost in the goop.

The disaster seemed to aggravate John's physical condition. Over the following week his health worsened. Although his body was racked with fever, he was nonetheless determined to press on and confront his enemies. When he reached the Bishop of Lincoln's castle in Newark on October 16, the abbot of Croxton was summoned to attend him.

John was too ill on October 18, 1216, to read his messengers' dispatches, which contained peace offerings from a number of rebels. But he was able to dictate a will before the abbot heard his confession and administered last rites. He died that night. In accordance with the tradition of burying a sovereign's internal organs in locations other than where the body is interred, King John's intestines were taken away by the abbot of Croxton. John's corpse was laid to rest according to his wishes in the Church of the Blessed Virgin and St. Wulfstan in Worcester. The last of the Angevin kings was gone for good.

His enemies celebrated his demise in a nasty little couplet:

With John's foul deeds all England is stinking
As does hell, to which he is now sinking.

John's innovations as king of England often suffer the same fate of his baggage caravan: They get lost in the muck. Rarely has a kind word been said of him over the centuries. The *Histoire des Ducs de Normandie et des Rois d'Angleterre*, composed in 1220 (just four years after John's death) by the subordinate to one of John's own generals during the civil war, described him as "A very bad man, cruel and lecherous." The thirteenth-century chronicler Matthew Paris, who succeeded the opinionated (and fanciful) Roger of Wendover as the historiographer at the parish of St. Albans, co-opted Roger's negatively embellished version of John's life, referring to the sovereign John as "nature's enemy." Gerald of Wales believed John to be "the most atrocious tyrant on record." According to the Barnwell annalist, "[H]e was generous and liberal to aliens [foreigners] but he plundered his own people; he ignored those who were rightfully his men and placed his trust in strangers; before his end his people deserted him, and at his end few mourned him." Even the nineteenth-century historical biographer Kate Norgate noted John's "superhuman wickedness."

He was cruel, he was paranoid, and he was petty. Certainly when the accounts are tallied they tend to render King John more villainous than virtuous. But on his sheet of credits should be included his reform of the English currency system, continued strides in the reformation of the country's judicial system, the formation of a navy, and an entire reconfiguration of governing. Because John could not rely on baronial support, he declared the whole kingdom of England a commune, and "all men, great or humble, should swear to uphold it." In doing so, he instituted a greater form of self-governance and called on the burghers to defend their own towns. Armies could then be raised independent of feudal lords, mustering a national levy when appropriate, to be coordinated by the king's own law officers, the chief constables of the various shires.

In 1209, when the price of grain soared due to poor crops, John ordered his sheriffs to provide cheap loaves for the impoverished. He also routinely fed great numbers of the poor, although the gesture may have been a superstitious penance for his perpetual disregard for Church doctrine, such as eating meat on fast days and going hunting and hawking on Sundays and other holy days.

During John's reign London Bridge was completed, with a chapel at its center. And on the west coast of England, he founded a port of trade and access to Ireland, which had been one of the territories made over to him in 1185, when his father, Henry II, was still king. Although John's reign over England lasted less than seventeen years, he was Lord of Ireland for just over three decades.

Henry, the nine-year-old son of John and Isabella of Angoulême, succeeded his father on the throne of England. He was crowned Henry III on October 28, 1216. John's death ended up bringing the rebel barons into the royal fold, because none of them had any quarrel with young Henry, and vastly preferred to see him wear the crown than Philip's son, the foreign Louis of France. Louis's forces were routed in August 1217, and on September 12, peace was restored to England.

Henry III ruled England for fifty-six years. Despite his parents' bad reputations, he was a good son and a noble king. In him, John—for all his vindictiveness, paranoia, and cruelty—had left England a very fine legacy indeed.

Vlad III of Wallachia

"Vlad the Impaler"
1431–1476
Ruled Romania: 1448; 1456–1462; 1476

*I*n 1897 London stage manager–turned-author Bram Stoker had an international bestseller on his hands with his novel about a vampiric Transylvanian count named Vlad Dracula. The inspiration for Stoker's doomed romantic anti-hero was a fifteenth-century Romanian prince. But the real Vlad was far more of a monster than any Victorian gothic novelist could have imagined. He also merits a niche in the pantheon of royal pains who had terrible, psychologically scarring childhoods. Nonetheless, while Vlad's boyhood may have shaped his adult behavior, it cannot excuse it.

Capricious, vicious, and malicious, Vlad Dracula—who would become known far and wide within his lifetime as "Vlad the Impaler"—was born in the citadel of Sighişoara, Transylvania, to an exiled member of the Wallachian nobility, known as Vlad II, and his wife, the Moldavian *Chiajna* (also spelled *Cneajna*) or princess, daughter of Alexander the Good.

Wallachia, a region roughly the size of New York State, is now the southern part of Romania, but in the Middle Ages it was a principality located to the immediate south of Transylvania, separated by the rugged Carpathian Mountains. Although the senior Vlad was a descendant of the house of Basarab, Wallachia's ruling family, the prince, or *voivode*, of Wallachia did not rule by hereditary sinecure. Instead, the *voivode* was elected by the (often corrupt) boyars, the region's landholding aristocracy. And if a prince was expecting too much of them, financially or militarily, they were quick to replace him. Might made right as well, and there were as many coups and usurpations of the throne as there were legitimate elections.

In 1431, the year of little Vlad's birth, dad Vlad had taken an oath to protect and defend the Holy Roman Empire against the encroaching Ottomans, becoming one of only twenty-four knights in Holy Roman Emperor Sigismund's Societas Draconis, or Order of the Dragon. This meant that the elder Vlad was permitted to spiff up his knightly wardrobe and accessories with the emblem of a dragon and was henceforth known to his people as Vlad Dracul—Vlad the Dragon, in Romanian. The status-conscious new knight was terrific about showing off all his cool new dragon gear, but he would prove less enthusiastic about keeping his oath to the emperor.

When he returned home to Wallachia he discovered that his half brother Alexander Aldea had usurped his throne. On the outs with his people, not to mention his own family, Vlad senior fled to Sighişoara, a walled medieval city, fortified by guard towers at its gates. It was there that his second son, baby Vlad, was born.

From his own father, little Vlad, called Vlad Drăculea or Dracula—"son of Vlad the Dragon"—would learn the hard way that vows were made to be broken.

Young Vlad lived in a world where three vast empires vied for dominion over the geography as well as the religion of its subjects. Most of western Europe was part of the

Holy Roman Empire, which practiced Roman Catholicism. Wallachia and Transylvania were located in the increasingly shrinking Byzantine Empire, a realm that incorporated elements of the exotic East and the Christian West, practicing a religion known as Eastern Orthodoxy. However, the Wallachians' appearance, at least in terms of dress, more closely resembled that of the Muslim Turks, whose Ottoman Empire sat to their east. The Ottomans were constantly trying to gobble up portions of the Byzantine Empire in the hopes of eventually conquering the Holy Roman Empire as well; their ultimate goal was to convert all of Europe to Islam. Wallachia lay directly in the Ottomans' path, so by default it was the line of first defense.

In 1436, when little Vlad was barely five years old, his father decided it was high time to reclaim his throne. The only problem with this grand idea was that he lacked the forces to do it. Although Holy Roman Emperor Sigismund offered his moral support, no *military* support was forthcoming. So Vlad Dracul formed a strategic alliance with princes Ilias and Stefan of neighboring Moldavia. The price for their support was that the elder Dracul should espouse their sister Eupraxia (and begin a new family with her). Obviously, that meant he'd have to ditch his current wife, the mother of little Vlad and his elder brother, Mircea, even though she had also been a Moldavian princess (albeit from a family that had fallen from power). Evidently Vlad didn't think this was such an onerous demand, although it made his children's mother the odd woman out. While there is little enough information about her, historians assume that she was sent packing—possibly back to her parents—and out of her young sons' lives forever.

With the aid of Moldavian troops, Vlad senior marched into Wallachia's capital city of Târgoviște. After grabbing the crown from his dying half brother, he relocated his family, which by now included little Vlad's baby half brother, Radu cel Frumos—"Radu the Handsome."

In Wallachia, Vlad junior received the typical education of a medieval princeling, tutored by an old boyar, a noble from the realm's ruling class. The boy learned literature and languages and the skills required to become a knight. That same year, 1436, although he would not turn five until November, Vlad Dracula was initiated into the Order of the Dragon. He would grow up to be the ruthless son of a ruthless father.

The elder Vlad had a fluid concept of loyalty. He routinely cut deals with his enemies and consistently betrayed his friends. After Holy Roman Emperor Sigismund died in 1437, Vlad violated his oath to defend the empire and instead signed a peace treaty with the Holy Roman Empire's archenemies, the Ottoman Turks. Their combined forces promptly invaded Transylvania.

But the new emperor had a champion, János Hunyadi, a Hungarian nicknamed "the white knight." Because of the era's shifting sands of international diplomacy, both the senior and junior Vlads would end up having a love-hate relationship with Hunyadi that lasted until the Hungarian's death in 1456.

In 1441 Hunyadi journeyed to Târgoviște to parley with the elder Vlad, inviting him to join a crusade against the Turks. Vlad hedged his bets, as he often would (a tactic his namesake would adopt as well), and opted to remain neutral, blithely looking the other way as the Ottoman army invaded Transylvania.

But Hunyadi successfully repelled their forces. For good measure he kicked Vlad senior off his throne and out of Wallachia. When Vlad fled to the Turks seeking asylum, they imprisoned him instead. He must have been surprised to learn that everyone else was as duplicitous as he was.

Having handily sacrificed his first wife to political expedience, Vlad didn't blink when one of the terms of his release in 1443 was the forfeit of his two youngest sons, Vlad and Radu, as hostages. The two boys found themselves imprisoned in a fortress seven hundred miles away while their double-crossing father was permitted to return home and reclaim his title as prince of Wallachia.

Imagine Dracula's reaction when at the age of twelve or thirteen he learned that his dad had used him as a bargaining chip. Although the Turks would provide young Vlad with an excellent education and treat him fairly well (when they weren't brutally whipping him for having a bad temper and an insubordinate attitude), he was extremely wounded by his father's callous and cavalier behavior toward his own sons, and would never trust the man again.

The youthful Vlad proved himself to be quite the astute student, alertly observing events around him. While he was a captive in Turkey he picked up some nifty tips on torture and mutilation and witnessed his first impalements. This method of execution commonly practiced by the Ottomans would eventually become the Wallachian prince's bloody and brutal signature.

In time, Vlad junior and Radu were moved to Adrianople, the capital of the Ottoman Empire, five hundred miles closer to Wallachia. There they were raised in the court of the sultan, Murad II. But the boys' life there was not all sunshine and roses. The fifteenth century was a violent

one across the globe and Murad made sure that if his enemies made the mistake of crossing him, they didn't get the
chance to do it again. Two Serbian princes he had captured were blinded with hot irons after they were caught
writing clandestine letters to their father. Vlad and Radu
got the message.

During his sons' captivity, Vlad II performed another
political flip-flop. Judging that it was the best course for
Wallachia, he allied himself with his former adversary, János
Hunyadi—an extremely risky move, given that he was
breaking his oath to the Turks, who still had custody of
his children. As part of Vlad's strategem to play both sides
at the same time, he personally remained neutral, but sent
his oldest son, Mircea, off to fight in Hunyadi's crusade
against the Muslims.

Rather than punish the elder Vlad for his duplicity, the
sultan recognized that the Wallachian boys were worth
more to their father alive than dead, so he compelled the
Wallachian prince to sign a peace treaty with the Turks in
order to secure his sons' release. Vlad seemed to have no
qualms about switching sides again; and in 1446, at the age
of sixteen, Vlad Dracula was released.

But he would never see his traitorous father again. In
addition to his foreign enemies, the elder Vlad had plenty
of detractors within Wallachia as well. Two generations
earlier, his family had splintered into two warring factions:
the Drăculesti and the Dănesti. Both sides were descendants of the ruler Basarab and each of them vied for pri-
macy in Wallachia.

At the end of December 1447, the teenage Vlad received
a visit from a boyar who had been a friend of his father's.
The nobleman brought the boy two gifts: the sword and

the medallion that Vlad senior had received when he became
a knight of the Order of the Dragon. Then came the bad
news. Vlad's father had been murdered in the marshes of
Bălteni by members of the rival Dănesti clan, at the instigation of his sometime friend and frequent adversary, the Hungarian "white knight," János Hunyadi. The violence didn't
stop there. The assassins had blinded young Vlad's older
brother, Mircea, with hot irons and then buried him alive.

Although his father's idea of parental devotion had been
to ship him off to his enemies, Vlad had been too thoroughly indoctrinated in the culture of revenge to ignore
the man's death, much less his brother's. His life now had
a purpose: to avenge their murders.

In September 1448, while Hunyadi was busy launch-
ing yet another crusade against the Turks, Vlad Dracula
seized his opportunity to grab the throne of Wallachia
without a fight. But his triumph was short-lived, and by
the end of the year, the barely seventeen-year-old Vlad
was both homeless and throneless. Only two months after
he had claimed the crown, an ally of Hunyadi's, Vladislav
II, drove the youth out of office and out of town, pushing
him all the way into Adrianople. Not so coincidentally,
Vladislav II was a member of the Dănesti branch of Vlad's
family—the same faction that had been responsible for the
murder of Dracula's father and brother.

The next few years were fraught with political assassinations and ever-shifting alliances. In 1451 Vlad found
himself on the run from Hunyadi's army for several months,
yet the following year, the Hungarian leader changed his
tune entirely, offering the twenty-year-old Vlad a job guard-
ing the southern border of the Holy Roman Empire from
the threat of Turkish invasion. Vlad was stationed in the

city of Sibiu, just fifty miles from his birthplace of Sighişoara. In exchange, Hunyadi pledged to help Vlad retake
the throne of Wallachia. Vlad spent the better part of the
next five years on the battlefield.

Bubonic plague was sweeping the region, and citizens
were fleeing in droves. On August 11, 1456, Hunyadi, too,
became a victim of the deadly disease. It was sweet revenge.
But Dracula was far from satisfied. Everyone who'd had any
connection to the deaths of his relatives would pay the price.
Vlad seized the opportunity to grab the throne. He marched
over the Transylvanian mountains with a modest force and
confronted Vladislav II on the battlefield. His adversary
retreated but was cut down on August 20 by Dracula's supporters. The Impaler himself might even have participated
in the killing of his nemesis.

Vlad entered Wallachia's capital city, Târgovişte, in August
1456. Taking up residence in the stone castle where he had
spent his boyhood, he declared himself prince.

As Prince of Wallachia, Vlad began to make peace treaties with his neighbors and even agreed to pay the Turkish sultan—now Mohammed II, the son of Murad II—an
annual tribute, permitting Mohammed's armies to march
through Wallachia on the way toward distant territorial
conquests. When his subjects learned of these apparent
concessions, they weren't sure whether Vlad was naive or
canny.

However, the new *voivode* was far less welcoming to the
boyars, Wallachia's aristocratic, landowning ruling class
who for centuries had been accustomed to sharing power
with whoever happened to be prince. They had long made
trouble for the *voivodes* by seeking to control the workings
of the government themselves.

On Easter Sunday, 1457, Vlad invited two hundred boyars and their families to an enormous feast. His guards surrounded the boyars as they were getting up from the table. Vlad scanned their faces in an effort to guess their ages, or asked them pointed questions about how many princes' reigns they had lived through. He was trying to determine who among them was old enough to have participated in the plot ten years earlier to oust his family from Wallachia, and who might have had a hand in the assassination of his father and brother.

Several dozen of the older boyars were immediately ushered outside and taken to a place beyond the city walls, where one by one they were impaled upon stakes. The ground became stained with blood. But Vlad wasn't finished. Instead of leaving the mangled corpses where they lay, he had their bodies artistically arranged in rows along the hillside as a warning to other would-be traitors. The site soon became known as the Forest of the Impaled.

What emerged as Vlad's favorite method of dispatching his enemies was a particularly slow and brutal form of torture and death. Vlad Dracula was by no means the only medieval ruler to favor impalement (the Turks used it to great effect as well), but he was certainly the only autocrat to raise it to an art form, and it was observed that he took particular enjoyment in it as well. The stake was oiled and honed to a point—but not too sharp, so as to cause maximum pain. Then it was inserted into the victim's anus and forced through his body until it came out his mouth. The "express" version of the torture involved impaling directly through the torso. Age was no guarantee of absolution; Vlad was known to have impaled infants through their mothers' chests. For additional amusement, on occasion he impaled people so they would hang upside down on the stakes. Death was far from instantaneous and it delighted Vlad to watch his anguished victims slowly expire.

Throughout his brutal reign he would employ other methods of torture as well. He was fond of mutilation, dismembering and disfiguring, and scalping—both the head-slicing form we would recognize as a former practice of some Native American tribes, and the eastern European version where slits are made in the victim's head and the skin is peeled back from the face. Vlad also enjoyed boiling his enemies alive, and leaving his victims to die of exposure or animal attacks.

Vlad hit upon a particularly ingenious method of dispatching the boyars and their families who had survived the Easter 1457 impaling unscathed. But he wanted to be sure they made themselves useful while they were dying. Sparing neither women nor children, he force-marched the nobles (who were still arrayed in their holiday finery) fifty miles up the Argeş River to the foot of a craggy mountain. At the mountain's summit stood the ruin of a stone castle. Vlad had decided to renovate this remote "eagle's nest" and make it his residence in times of political crisis. He put his captives to work rebuilding what would become the Poenari Fortress, also known as Castle Dracula. Those at the bottom of the mountain slaved over hot ovens making bricks. A human chain moved the building materials up the side of the cliff, as the last group of slaves did the castle's reconstruction work at the summit. Untold noble families died during this literally backbreaking work, their clothes shredded to tatters, their bodies starving and exhausted.

Vlad's overweening distaste for the aristocracy led to

his preferment and promotion of members of the laboring classes. He drew from the lower ranks of society to staff the three types of defense forces he created to police his principality: The *viteji* was the military unit that would lead the Wallachian army into foreign wars. The *sluji* were Vlad's national guard, also in charge of chasing criminals and flushing out his domestic political enemies. And the force that no one wanted to encounter was the *armasi*—Vlad's institutionalized execution force. The *armasi* were highly trained in various forms of weaponry, but the tool they wielded with the most zeal and frequency was the stake, the hallmark of Vlad's cruelty. For this the prince would eventually earn the nickname Vlad Tepes, or "Vlad the Impaler" in Romanian. He was an equal opportunity impaler as well. His victims came from all walks of Wallachian life, from corrupt noble to cheating merchant to petty thief. And he practiced other methods of execution with equal dexterity. One day Vlad decided to round up all the beggars he could locate—the lame, the halt, and the homeless—and invite them to a grand feast. He genially plied them with spirits and after the ragtag guests were good and drunk he set fire to the hall, immolating every last one of them.

Another cornerstone of Vlad's reign was his crackdown on morality, with a particular focus on maintaining female chastity. Adulteresses as well as unmarried girls and widows who deigned to have sex had their breasts hacked off or were impaled on a hot stake inserted into their vaginas and forced through their body until it emerged from their mouths. Even Vlad's mistress (so much for his own morality!) wasn't spared. After her purported pregnancy turned out to be either a lie or merely a false alarm, he slit her open from belly to breasts, and declared, "Let the world see where I have been." Vlad allowed her to wallow in her agony, contemplating what he saw as her falsehood as she suffered a painfully slow demise.

But Vlad's brutal treatment of his mistress wasn't personal; he was equally cruel to complete strangers, if he judged the women guilty of immorality. Before one man's unfaithful wife was impaled, she was skinned alive in Târgoviște's public square, and her skin was set aside on a nearby table for all to gawk over. A peasant woman was impaled for being an indifferent housekeeper after Vlad encountered her shabbily attired husband. To compensate the man for his loss, Dracula found the widower a new wife, but first he made sure to show her what he'd done to her predecessor for failing to properly look after her mate.

What did Vlad's own wife think of this? one wonders. Somewhere along the line, he did acquire a spouse, though historians differ as to her origin. She may have been a Moldavian noblewoman or she may have been a highborn Transylvanian. In any case, her opinion, if she dared to voice one, is as lost to posterity as her name, although she was reputed to be lovely, innocent, and kind. Their marriage was most likely an arranged (or forced) one, and it is doubtful that she had any choice in the matter.

Unsurprisingly, Vlad's method of ruling with an iron fist (or stake) didn't thrill everyone. The peace he had made with the neighboring Transylvanian cities of Brasov and Sibiu upon claiming the throne didn't last long. Within the year many of the citizens revolted against his tyranny. Most of the rebels were Saxon German craftsmen who had been accustomed to trading freely in Wallachia and who therefore objected strenuously to the high tariffs Vlad had imposed on their wares.

The Impaler decided to teach the Saxon upstarts a lesson. He stopped their carts at the borders and had the goods inspected. He made the items available to Wallachian merchants for next to nothing. And when the craftsmen objected, Vlad's troops descended on their villages like Cossacks, pillaging, looting, and burning them to the ground. The following year, 1458, he decreed that any Transylvanian villagers caught sheltering his enemies be mercilessly slaughtered.

The few Germans who somehow managed to survive the first wave of the 1457 onslaught were marched back to Târgoviște, where they were impaled. Those who were lucky enough to have evaded Vlad's grasp fled to Austria and other regions within the Holy Roman Empire. There, they spread stories of Vlad's brutality. One of these colorful narratives opens with the words: "Here begins a very cruel, frightening story about a wild bloodthirsty man Prince Dracula. How he impaled people and roasted them and boiled their heads in a kettle and skinned people and hacked them to pieces like cabbage. He also roasted the children of mothers and they had to eat the children themselves."

The Saxons had formulated a mighty revenge. They achieved it with the pen rather than the sword, and their efforts shaped and cemented Vlad Dracula's enduring legacy as a human monster. In a concentrated campaign to forever besmirch his place in history, the Germans continued to avenge Vlad's cruelty to their countrymen by printing and disseminating multiple pamphlets recounting the numerous acts of violence perpetrated by the Wallachian prince against those whom he perceived had wronged him in some way, whether they were German, Transylvanian,

Wallachian, Turks, Gypsies, nobility, or peasants. The little books, with lurid titles such as "The Frightening and Truly Extraordinary Story of a Wicked Blood-drinking Tyrant Called Prince Dracula," were incredibly graphic, and they became immensely popular. Some of the events recounted in the pamphlets are exaggerated, although Vlad's bloody deeds scarcely required the benefit of hyperbole. Most of the atrocities were factually verifiable, including his slaughter of hundreds of people at a time through impaling, boiling them alive, or immolating them. A victim's youth was no guarantee of leniency. On one occasion, Vlad had four hundred German boys burned alive after accusing them of spying.

The country that would eventually give us the grisly tales of the Brothers Grimm unstintingly depicted Dracula's barbarism in one of its many propagandist pamphlets, claiming "He devised dreadful, frightful, unspeakable torments, such as impaling together mothers and children nursing at their breasts so that the children kicked convulsively . . . until dead. In like manner he cut open mothers' breasts and stuffed the children's heads through and thus impaled both. He had all kinds of people impaled sideways: Christians, Jews, heathens, so that they moved and twitched and whimpered in confusion a long time like frogs."

Thanks to the printing press, the German pamphlets received widespread distribution during the fifteenth and sixteenth centuries, perpetuating the image of a blood-thirsty psychopath long after Vlad was dead and buried. According to another booklet, "He had some of his people buried up to the navel and had them shot at. He also had some roasted and flayed. . . . He had a large pot made and boards with holes fastened over it and had people's heads shoved through there and imprisoned them in this. And he had the pot filled with water and a big fire made under the pot and thus let the people cry out pitiably until they were boiled to death. . . . About three hundred gypsies came into his country. Then he selected the best three of them and had them roasted; these the others had to eat."

In 1459, Vlad was rumored to have nailed the hats (or turbans, since differing nationalities of the victims have been reported) to the heads of a foreign delegation when for some reason they angered him—possibly by refusing to remove their headgear in deference to their own culture and customs. The most popular version of the story casts the foreigners as emissaries from the Ottoman sultan, come to collect Vlad's annual tribute of boys and money. Evidently, the Impaler was not in a giving mood that day.

During the winter of 1459, Vlad launched what would be the most vicious raid of his reign thus far. On the hunt for an enemy, Dan III of Transylvania, he burned the town of Brasov to cinders, refusing to spare even its church. Then he impaled everyone he could find regardless of their age or gender. Surrounded by their dead and dying bodies, he sat down to enjoy a hearty dinner. An extant woodcut commemorates this grisly event. And perhaps this is where the legend of Vlad Dracula drinking the blood of his victims began—with the widespread assertion that he had dipped his bread in the blood of these massacred Transylvanians.

Having unsuccessfully led a revolt against Vlad, Dan III met a gruesome fate as well. Vlad caught up with him, and invited the man to his own funeral, where he made Dan recite his own eulogy and dig his own grave. Then Vlad beheaded him.

In 1461 Vlad decided to stage an attack against the Turks, cutting a bloody swath through Bulgaria, beheading and burning his victims. He kept meticulous tallies of the numbers of people he slaughtered in each town he ravaged. The total number of deaths in some places reached nearly seven thousand—probably close to the entire population of some of the villages. In the winter a surprise raid along the southern bank of the Danube considerably raised his body count. Vlad couldn't resist the urge to brag about his bloody triumphs to the Hungarian king Matthias Corvinus, the son of his late ally and sometime nemesis János Hunyadi. "I have killed men and women, old and young . . . 23,884 Turks and Bulgarians without counting those whom we burned alive in their homes or whose heads were not chopped off by our soldiers." As proof, he sent along samples of his handiwork: two sacks stuffed with heads, ears, and noses.

With a force of sixty thousand men-at-arms, the Turkish sultan, Mohammed II, launched a counterattack against Vlad in the spring of 1462. Vlad was outmanned militarily but he managed to repulse the sultan by repelling him. An unknown Turkish chronicler wrote of the sight that greeted the Muslims upon their arrival at the gates of the capital city of Târgovişte: "In front of the wooden fortress where he had his residence he set up at a distance of six leagues two rows of fences with impaled Hungarians, Moldavians, and Wallachians (and Turks, we may add). In addition, since the neighboring area was forested, innumerable people were hanging from each tree branch." An unnamed Greek chronicler of the day observed that "Even the emperor [the sultan], overcome by amazement, admitted that he could not win the land from a man who does such great things and above all knows how to exploit his rule and that over his subjects in this way."

And just in case Mohammed and his army weren't turned back by the sight of twenty thousand impaled corpses, Vlad poisoned his own principality's wells and burned the crops so the Turks would not find anything worthwhile to conquer.

The sultan turned back, but assigned one of his military leaders (who just happened to be Vlad's half brother, Radu, now a Muslim convert) to lead the Turkish forces in Wallachia. "Radu the Handsome" managed to convince the terrified Wallachians to abandon their bloodthirsty prince. This entailed fleeing the realm. People from every stratum of society, from boyar to peasant, took to the roads. Many of the latter joined Radu's army.

Radu declared himself prince of Wallachia and put Vlad on the run. The sadist was out of allies. He managed to reach Castle Dracula by the end of 1462, but Radu's forces followed him. What supposedly happened next may belong more to the realm of legend, or at least apocrypha, because the specific feat of archery at the core of the story is virtually impossible to achieve.

Vlad was purportedly tipped off that Radu's army was waiting for him. The informant was a former servant of Vlad's who was now a Turkish slave. This brave slave is said to have fired an arrow from the ground (near the army's camp, presumably) that managed to sail through just the right window (and medieval turrets have narrow arrow slits for windows), landing—*thwomp*—in the middle of a candle, as the *whoosh* of air extinguished the flame. The virtuous but unnamed Mrs. Vlad, noticing that the candle was out, went to relight it and discovered a note attached to the arrow shaft, warning Vlad that his half brother had the castle staked out.

Unwilling to be taken prisoner by Radu and the Turks, Vlad's wife allegedly exclaimed that she "would rather have her body rot and be eaten by the fish of the Argeş than be led into captivity by the Turks." Then she threw herself from the turret into the riverbed below. The area of the Argeş tributary where her body landed was nicknamed "the Princess River" or *Rîul Doamnei*, "the Lady's River."

Neither Vlad nor his wife had given much concern to the fate of their young son, not-so-charmingly named Mihnea cel Rău, "Mihnea the evil"—though in Vlad's family, perhaps the name was intended to be a compliment. After receiving the warning from his former servant, Vlad fled the castle with Mihnea and twelve of his retainers; but when the boy's horse was spooked by cannon fire, leaving the child clinging to his mane, Vlad pressed on and never looked back. His goal was to meet up with the king of Hungary, Matthias Corvinus, and demand the king's aid in exchange for having defended his territory in the past.

But Matthias didn't exactly welcome Vlad with open arms. Instead he threw him in prison, incarcerating him temporarily in a nearby castle. Some sources claim that Matthias had received false information that Vlad was secretly plotting against him. Whatever the reason, Vlad remained in Matthias's custody; and after making sure that the tales of Vlad's cruelty were disseminated far and wide, Matthias threw his support behind the new prince of Wallachia, Vlad's half brother, Radu.

Under heavy guard Matthias brought Vlad to the Hungarian city of Buda, where the Impaler spent the next twelve years as his prisoner in a fortress known as Solomon's Tower. To keep his talent for torture from becoming rusty, Vlad allegedly amused himself by brutalizing rodents and birds in his cell.

Accounts regarding the duration of Vlad's incarceration vary. His twentieth-century biographer Radu Florescu believes that Dracula actually spent only four years—from 1462 to 1466—in captivity and that over the dozen years he remained in Hungary he and Matthias reached an accord. A fifteenth-century Hungarian court chronicler, who noted that Vlad was rather popular among certain segments of society, wrote that by imprisoning him, Matthias had "acted in opposition to general opinion," and consequently reversed his decision to detain him. During Vlad's incarceration he received guests from all over Europe, who regarded him as a hero mostly for his vigorous and largely successful efforts to keep the Turks at bay.

So Matthias offered Vlad a deal: Convert to Roman Catholicism and marry into the Hungarian royal family and you will be released. It wasn't a difficult decision. Vlad renounced the Eastern Orthodox religion into which he was born, became a Catholic, and married Matthias's cousin, Countess Ilona Szilágy. Not much more is known of Ilona beyond her name and her immediate lineage. We don't know what she looked like or how she felt about being wedded to one of the fifteenth century's greatest monsters.

By 1474 Vlad had been released. With his second wife and their two young sons, he moved across the river to Pest, where they set up housekeeping. The older boy was named after his father, while the name of the second son has been lost to history. Ilona was also the stepmother to Mihnea cel Rău, Vlad's "evil" son by his first marriage.

The following year Vlad was back in the saddle, joining forces with Matthias and Vlad's Transylvanian cousin
Stephen to defeat the Turks in Bosnia. War began near
the start of 1476 and Vlad demonstrated that neither
imprisonment nor wedlock had diminished or dulled his
penchant for cruelty. He "tore the limbs off the Turkish
prisoners and placed their parts on stakes," according to
Nicolas of Modrussa, the papal envoy in Budapest.

It is from this legate to Pope Pius II that we have the only
surviving physical description of Vlad Dracula: "He was not
very tall, but very stocky and strong with a cruel and terrible
appearance, a long straight nose, distended nostrils, a thin
and reddish face in which the large wide-open green eyes
were enframed by bushy black eyebrows, which made them
appear threatening. His face and chin were shaven, but for
a moustache. The swollen temples increased the bulk of his
head. A bull's neck supported the head, from which black
curly locks were falling to his wide-shouldered person."

Fresh from his triumph over the Turks, Vlad deemed
that it was time to retake the throne of Wallachia. His half
brother, Radu, had died, replaced by a man named Basarab
Laiota. In the battle for the crown fought in November
1476, each side lost ten thousand men, yet Vlad emerged the
victor.

But not long afterward, on December 14, 1476, his luck
finally ran out. The forty-five-year-old Impaler was killed
near Bucharest during another skirmish with Basarab's
army. Two different accounts of his death have emerged.
In one, Vlad was beheaded and his head was, fittingly,
mounted on a spike and delivered to the Turkish sultan as
a trophy, while his body was buried in the nearby monastery at Snagov, which rests in the middle of an island. At the

time of Dracula's death, Snagov was a fortified complex like any other typical medieval town. The monastery may have had darker uses then, too. Decapitated skeletons with the heads placed in the hollows of their owners' abdomens were discovered in an area beneath the floor that Dracula may at one time have used as a prison and torture chamber. Local peasant lore includes lurid tales of prisoners being thrust through a trapdoor in the floor, where they'd immediately become impaled on the spikes erected below.

An alternative version of Vlad's demise has more credence. According to a remark made on a 2005 British television documentary about Vlad's life by his twenty-first-century biographer, the Romanian historian Matei Cazacu, the Turks did not decapitate their enemies. The alternate theory regarding the manner of Vlad's death therefore supposes that he was not beheaded but scalped, most likely via the eastern European and Asian technique of slitting the face and removing the skin, rather than slicing off the top of the head.

Facts support this method of execution, because what was believed to be Vlad's corpse (given the lore regarding the location of his burial) was discovered at Snagov by the grandfather of another of the Impaler's recent biographers, Radu Florescu. However, when the tomb was pried open, and the remains were exposed to fresh air and sunlight, within minutes they began to crumble to dust. The corpse's face had been covered with a cloth, suggesting that it may indeed have been hiding the grisly results of a scalping. The fact that there was a face at all (or, for that matter, a head) should eliminate the beheading theory. Also found inside the coffin was a woman's ring that once contained a stone. The jewel may have been stolen during the nineteenth century, when the tombs were vandalized and looted. Florescu surmises that the ring might have been a lady's favor, bestowed to Dracula before a joust. The remnants of a crown were also discovered beside the skull within the tomb purporting to be that of Vlad Dracula. While there is no conclusive evidence that Florescu did indeed locate Vlad's remains, enough of the elements tally to make the discovery a plausible one.

What happened to Vlad's wife Ilona Szilágy after his death remains lost to history. Since she was a Hungarian countess, presumably she remained at her home in Pest. According to Florescu, some historians believe that she is also buried in the tomb at Snagov. Vlad's son from his first marriage, Mihnea cel Rău, eventually became the (highly unpopular) *voivode* of Wallachia from 1508 to 1509; he was assassinated outside the cathedral of Sibiu in Transylvania on March 12, 1510. Vlad Dracula IV, Vlad's first son by Ilona, was still a boy when he joined the retinue of King Matthias Corvinus. His younger brother had been sent to live with the bishop of Oradea but was returned to his parents when he became terminally ill, and died soon afterward.

Vlad the Impaler was long dead by the mid-sixteenth century, when the Turks conquered Hungary. And until the late nineteenth century Wallachia, Transylvania, and Moldavia were under either Turkish or Russian rule, merging in 1881 to form the independent country of Romania.

Although Vlad was prince of Wallachia for only seven years, spread over the course of three reigns—1448, 1456 to 1462, and 1476—he may have been responsible for causing the deaths of as many as a hundred thousand people, the equivalent of one-fifth of the population of Wallachia at the time. Even if modern biographers estimate his actual body count at closer to forty thousand, that figure would account for one in twelve Wallachians, though Vlad's victims also included Turks, Transylvanians, Bulgarians, Hungarians, and Germans.

And yet, in one corner of the world—the very region where Vlad Dracula perpetrated his bloody atrocities—being a royal pain remains in the eye of the beholder. To many Romanians, as well as to the Russians, despite his vicious cruelty, Vlad was no worse than many medieval rulers, and in many respects, he was somewhat better.

Vlad was the type of ruler who kept his subjects in line through fear and intimidation rather than through love. Yet the man who so terrorized Wallachia's aristocracy was a champion of the craftsmen and the laboring classes. A Romanian Robin Hood, he reduced taxes and redistributed the boyars' property to his poorer subjects, a move that yielded a double benefit: It won Vlad support from the lower social strata while systematically weakening the economic power of the nobility.

Albeit violently, Vlad swept Wallachia of political corruption. And he was the only leader in the region brave enough to successfully take on the enemy Turks as well as the encroaching Hungarians. To this day he remains a local hero, rather than a villain, even gracing a Romanian postage stamp issued in 1996.

Ten years later, on a 2006 Romanian TV series broadcast, Vlad Dracula was voted one of the "100 Greatest Romanians." He didn't transform himself into a bat, didn't spend his days sleeping in a coffin, and probably never did drink the blood of his victims (or at least not much of it). Nevertheless, the real Vlad Dracula remains as immortal as his legend.

GEORGE, DUKE OF CLARENCE

1449–1478
and

RICHARD, DUKE OF GLOUCESTER

Later Richard III
1452–1485
KING OF ENGLAND: 1483–1485

*I*N THE ANNALS OF ROYAL HISTORY, RICHARD III IS PRE-
sented as one of the most rotten of all royals. When many
people hear his name, they immediately conjure the image
of the misshapen tyrant created with William Shakespeare's pen—a jealous kid brother and conniving, wicked
uncle who had members of his own family assassinated in
order to overleap them to the English throne. But Shakespeare's "history play" is a masterpiece of spin-doctoring
for maximum theatrical effect, and he was writing during
the reign of the Tudors (the first of whom, Henry VII,
had practically snatched the crown from Richard's corpse
in the heat of battle).

However, this time a good story didn't get in the way
of all the facts. Ricardian Society apologists (and stage
depictions) aside, it is a truth almost universally acknowledged that Richard III was not a nice guy. Even if he may

not have ordered the deaths of his little nephews, often referred to as the princes in the Tower (of London), Richard did commit several judicial murders, including those of some of his in-laws. And yet his early years provide little foreshadowing of the bastard he became.

On the other hand, Richard's next-oldest brother, George, Duke of Clarence, as immortalized by the Bard of Stratford-upon-Avon, is presented as a dope and a hapless dupe. In truth, Clarence, as he is known, was a serial traitor, conspiring a whopping four times against their eldest sibling, Edward IV, to topple him from the throne and place the crown on his own head.

Few kings have fomented as much controversy during—and long after—their lifetimes as Richard III. In the years that immediately followed his demise on Bosworth Field in 1485, chroniclers like the Tudor historian and statesman Sir Thomas More were quick to assign him myriad abnormalities, so that the body of the vanquished usurper represented the outward manifestation of a sick and twisted soul. "Little of stature, ill-featured of limbs, crook backed, his left shoulder much higher than his right, hard favoured of visage . . .; he was malicious, wrathful, envious, and from afore his birth, ever froward [meaning 'contrary' or 'disobedient']. It is for truth reported, that the Duchess his mother had so much ado in her travail that she could not be delivered of him uncut: and that he came into the world with the feet forward . . . and (as the fame runneth) also not untoothed. . . . He was close and secret, a deep dissimuler, lowly of countenance, arrogant of heart, outwardly companionable where he inwardly hated, not letting to kiss whom he thought to kill; dispiteous and cruel, not for evil will alway[s], but after for ambition, and either for the surety or increase of his estate."

This description of Richard can be found in *The History of King Richard III*, penned by Thomas More around 1513, some twenty-eight years after Richard's demise. It's a spot-on lesson in how to play Shakespeare's villain.

But precious little of it is true.

For starters, there is no evidence that Richard III suffered from any physical defect. The most famous portrait of Richard, which depicts him with his right shoulder somewhat higher than his left, was recently revealed through X-ray technology to have been altered; beneath the pigmented deformity is a pair of perfectly aligned shoulders. That said, by all contemporary accounts Richard lacked the physical stature of his handsome, six-foot-four-inch oldest brother Edward IV, and of his other surviving brother, the charismatic George, Duke of Clarence (a royal pain in his own right).

But just because Richard did not in fact resemble the "bunch-backed toad" of Shakespeare's imagination, the revelation of his actual appearance in no way discredits his catalog of misdeeds that began almost as soon as his brother Edward IV breathed his last.

Without a bit of background on Richard's predecessors, Henry VI and Edward IV, it's harder to develop an understanding of how Richard III came to be who he was, and why he and his older brother George, Duke of Clarence, turned sibling rivalry into a battle royal.

So, who *was* the real Richard? And how did he become a royal pain?

He was born at Fotheringhay Castle, the eleventh of twelve children (and the fourth son) born to Richard, Duke of York, and Cicely Neville. Only six of their offspring would survive past childhood. Small and slight with a bit of a dour personality, dark hair, and attractive features, including a strong jawline, Richard was said to have resembled his father. He had entered the world during a violent era, his entire life shaped by an ongoing dispute between the houses of York and Lancaster. Because of the Lancastrian and Yorkist emblems of the red and white rose respectively, this family feud would in the sixteenth century come to be known as the Wars of the Roses, a nickname that has stuck ever since.

When the future Richard III was born, the orb and scepter of England were nominally in the hands of Henry VI, the monkish and mentally deficient son of Henry V. The power behind the throne was wielded by a cadre of courtiers and by Henry VI's French-born wife, Margaret of Anjou, a tough termagant who led the king's forces into battle herself. The Lancastrian Henry VI had yet to father a child; consequently, the kingdom's future was on shaky ground. Descendants of two of Edward III's sons, Richard, Duke of York, and Edmund Beaufort, Duke of Somerset (a Lancastrian), both expected to be named as Henry's heir, each man assuming he had the greater claim than his cousin.

The popular choice, Richard, Duke of York, was the second-largest landowner in the kingdom, after the crown. And the elder Richard was after the crown in other ways as well. He made a grab for it in 1452, the year Richard III was born, but was captured and taken to the Tower. Only the rumor that the duke's ten-year-old son, Edward, was marching on London at the head of an army ten thousand strong secured his release.

Henry VI and Margaret of Anjou finally had a son in October 1453, but it didn't put an end to the family feud. In

1459 the Duke of York's army was trounced and his family was forced to flee the Welsh city of Ludlow. For their safety, young Richard and his brother George were placed in rather classy foster care (which was more like house arrest), first with their mother's sister, the Duchess of Buckingham, and then with the archbishop of Canterbury.

Richard was only eight years old when his father and second-oldest brother, Edmund, Earl of Rutland, were killed at the Battle of Wakefield on December 30, 1460, after the duke had made another attempt to usurp the crown. The elder Richard's severed head was displayed as a trophy by his enemies, sporting a mocking coronet made of paper and straw.

But the duke's oldest son, Edward, Earl of March, managed to finish the job his father had begun, deposing Henry VI. The pious, half-mad monarch and his tigress of a wife fled, first to Yorkshire and then to Scotland. In 1461 a triumphant Edward proclaimed himself king of England. Is it any wonder, then, that Edward's youngest brother, Richard, ended up the way he did? Usurpation was the family business.

Although Edward had forcibly seized the crown, he was welcomed by his new subjects with open arms because he was expected to usher in an era of good government. Edward IV was crowned in June, and at his coronation he made his brother George the Duke of Clarence. Richard was still only nine years old, but Edward made him Duke of Gloucester four months later. And even at such a young age, there was no love lost between Richard and George, who felt his baby brother was far too young to have been entitled to equal preferment. Grumbling and discontented with his lot, no matter how much King Edward awarded him, George would eventually try—four times—to snatch his brother's crown.

Until the latter months of 1468, Richard and George lived high on the hog in the north of England, where they had been sent to live with the family of Richard Neville, the 16th Earl of Warwick. Known as "the kingmaker" because his strategic and martial acumen enabled first Edward IV and then Henry VI to grab (or reclaim) the throne, Warwick was the Karl Rove of the Wars of the Roses.

Edward spent the first decade or so of his reign trying to retain the crown and thwart the challenges from Henry VI's Lancastrian supporters to reinstate the deposed monarch. Edward IV also had to defeat the turncoat Warwick. The earl had defected to Henry's side soon after Edward secretly married a widowed commoner, the scrumptious blonde Elizabeth Woodville, in 1464. Warwick had been in the midst of negotiating an important dynastic marriage for Edward with Bona, Duchess of Savoy, the sister-in-law of the French king, and didn't take too kindly to ending up with political egg on his face. Nor (after he'd busted his haunches to put Edward on the throne) did Warwick appreciate having to contend with the vast family of Woodvilles (plus Elizabeth's two sons from a prior marriage), each of whom now had to be given plum titles, offices, and royal preferment. The earl also resented Edward's desire to break free from his influence and become his own man.

The year of 1465 was a banner one for Richard. He was only twelve and a half years old when Edward appointed him Constable of England for life, in addition to awarding him numerous land grants. That July, the man formerly known as Henry VI was captured in Lancashire and brought back to London, where he was imprisoned in the Tower. For the next three years Warwick seethed as Woodvilles garnered the kingdom's highest honors. In 1468 he turned on the man he'd helped to achieve the throne; he staged a rebellion in concert with the hotheaded George, Duke of Clarence, who didn't get along with his older brother any better than he did with his younger one and was out only for himself.

Clarence, as he is most commonly known, was by this time the middle of the three surviving York brothers. Born in Dublin in 1449, he was three years older than Richard and seven years younger than Edward. Although he was good-looking and devilishly charming, his personality was a fatal combination of ambition, greed, envy, and dimwittedness; and he had a terrible case of wanting anything either of his brothers had, including estates, titles, offices, and the crown.

By the spring of 1468 the kingmaking Earl of Warwick had become so peeved by Edward that he decided to switch horses and make a different king. Clarence, more of a handsome jock than a canny politician, cheerfully allied himself with the earl against his own brother in the vain delusion that Warwick intended to set him on the throne. The following year, after Clarence and Warwick had sneaked across the Channel to continue plotting against Edward, in direct contravention of the king's wishes the hotheaded Clarence secretly wed Warwick's older daughter, Isabel.

Meanwhile, as Constable of England, the now sixteen-year-old Richard was dispatched to quash a Welsh uprising while Edward decided how to handle Warwick and Clarence. From then on, until Edward IV's death in 1483, Richard was an active principal participant in the governing of the kingdom, as an administrator, adjudicator, and military commander.

Clarence and his new father-in-law returned to England and took up arms against their sovereign. In what some historians view as a huge public relations gamble, in 1469 Edward allowed himself to be kidnapped by the conspirators. None of the followers of the rebellion wanted anything to do with executing their king, so Warwick and Clarence had no choice but to release Edward and beg to be reconciled to the royal bosom, despite the fact that they had captured and summarily executed the queen's father, Earl Rivers, and her brother John Woodville.

Although the mercy they requested was granted, it was immediately exploited: Warwick and Clarence fomented *another* rebellion the following year. And in the spring of 1470, it was Edward IV who was on the run, taking sanctuary in Burgundy with his sister Margaret of York, wife to the reigning Charles of Burgundy. Charles eventually agreed to help Edward raise an army and return to England, ostensibly to reclaim his dukedom of York.

That July, Warwick entered an alliance with Henry VI's exiled queen, Margaret of Anjou, agreeing to betroth his younger daughter, Anne Neville, to Edward of Lancaster, the once and future prince of Wales. On September 30, an abject Warwick knelt before Henry and begged his forgiveness. The Lancastrian monarch was formally restored to his throne on October 3. And on or around December 13, the fifteen-year-old Anne Neville and Edward of Lancaster, an arrogant and vengeful whelp of seventeen, were wed.

Henry VI's brief second reign, which lasted until he was again ousted by Edward IV on May 21, 1471, is known as the "Readeption." After the victorious Edward IV entered

London on that date (it was his second effort in as many years to reclaim the throne), Henry was taken to the Tower, where, in the presence of the highest-ranking nobles in the land, including Richard, he was put to death. It was Richard who had brought the writ of execution to Lord Dudley, the Constable of the Tower. Although Henry VI was personally harmless and politically ineffectual, Edward IV saw no alternative but to have him snuffed out so that no more rebellions could be raised in his name. The fifteenth century was full of sleepless nights.

The other threats to Edward's IV's crown were dead as well. The fair-weather Warwick had fallen on Easter Sunday, 1471, in the Battle of Barnet, where Edward's forces were commanded by the teenage Richard. Three weeks later, at the decisive Battle of Tewkesbury on May 4, Henry VI's arrogant teenage son, Edward of Lancaster (husband of Anne Neville), met the business end of several broadswords (one of which was likely in Richard's hands) when he was stabbed during a melee. With his demise went the Lancastrian hopes of regaining the crown.

Edward IV was as beloved as Henry had been despised for turning a deaf ear and a blind eye to the corruption that had bankrupted England's treasury. He'd spent the 1460s trying to keep the crown he had usurped, and he devoted the balance of his kingship (after the Readeption ended and Henry was killed) to stabilizing the realm in the wake of more than a decade of violence and uncertainty. At least, that was what Edward IV was up to when he wasn't wenching, gourmandizing, and keeping the queen almost perpetually pregnant.

Meanwhile, brother Richard continued to move onward and upward. After the Yorkist victory at Tewkesbury, he prepared to set off to secure the north for his brother. But before his departure he also secured Edward's permission to wed the now-widowed Anne Neville. The young couple's relationship began as a star-crossed one, with the villain of the story being none other than Richard's grasping older brother Clarence, who did everything in his power to thwart it.

Although it's one of the most compelling "love" scenes in Shakespeare's canon, Richard did not seduce Anne in the middle of the street over the corpse of her late father-in-law. But the real story of their courtship does rival the fictional one for juiciness. On his return from the north, Richard came to claim his betrothed, who was ostensibly living with her sister, Isabel, and Isabel's husband—the Duke of Clarence. But the wily Clarence, vengeful and manipulative, insisted that Anne was no longer in his household.

Richard then embarked on an exhaustive search for Anne, and as the story goes, he found her disguised as a kitchen maid in the London home of one of Clarence's supporters. Clarence had placed her there to hide her from Richard, with the expectation of controlling the girl's portion of the inheritance left by Anne and Isabel's father, the late Earl of Warwick. Upon liberating Anne from the scullery, Richard brought her to sanctuary at St. Martin le Grand in order to shield her from any efforts by Clarence or his adherents to harm or nab her.

According to Richard's mid-twentieth-century biographer, the sympathetically inclined Paul Murray Kendall, Anne's rescue from the kitchen carried no quid pro quo. Kendall views it as an act of chivalry for which Richard did not expect Anne to be beholden to him. She was still free to sunder their precontract of marriage if she'd changed her mind.

So, if Richard and Anne's relationship was not the product of a reptilian seduction in the middle of a London street, was it the opposite—a love match? That may be reading too much into it. In the fifteenth century, even people who'd known each other all their lives could not afford to marry for love. Marriage was a political and economic arrangement. In this case, Anne was an heiress and Richard was the favorite brother of the king.

Richard and Anne were kin—cousins through the Neville line, but more important, they had been childhood playmates and had spent many years in each other's company. Yet if there was no love at first, there was surely a bond of affection, as well as a new one of shared affliction—victims of Clarence's scheme to keep Anne under his thumb and deprive his brother of his intended bride. Of course, as the *other* brother of the king, Richard was the only man with enough clout to save Anne from Clarence's machinations.

Edward did not appreciate ending up in the middle of a fraternal spat and sought an equitable solution that each of his younger brothers could live with. Clarence ultimately relented, agreeing to let Anne wed Richard on the condition that Richard inherit none of her estates. Richard consented, and the king finagled a bit by redistributing some of Warwick's property that had reverted to the crown, so that Richard would receive the late earl's Yorkshire demesnes.

As cousins, Richard and Anne required a papal dispensation permitting them to wed. Until recently, scholars assumed that the pair was too impatient to wait for its arrival, that after finally obtaining Clarence's permission to marry Anne, Richard fetched her out of St. Martin le Grand

and they were married on the spot. However, according to
an article by Peter D. Clarke titled "English Royal Marriages and the Papal Penetentiary in the Fifteenth Century,"
published in 2005 by the Oxford University Press in the
English Historical Review, the necessary papal paperwork
indeed exists.

Unfortunately, their wedding date is unknown, although
it is believed to have been sometime around March 1472.
Richard was nineteen, and Anne, about as young a widow
as they come, was a couple of weeks shy of her sixteenth
birthday.

Early in 1473, Richard and Anne had a son whom they
named Edward; but he was a sickly boy (as some biographers believe Richard himself had been), and was to be the
couple's only child.

Around the same time, the treasonous Clarence, who
still retained visions of usurping the throne, allied himself
with the archbishop of York, George Neville, the brother of
the slain Earl of Warwick. Edward IV had the archbishop
arrested toward the end of April 1473. During the Readeption in 1470, when Henry VI had briefly regained the throne,
Parliament declared Clarence to be his heir *if* Henry's son,
Edward of Lancaster, and Anne Neville had no issue. Since
Henry VI's son was slain at Tewkesbury before he and Anne
had the chance to propagate, did Clarence, somewhere in
the dim recesses of his even dimmer brain, believe that *he*
should be wearing the crown?

Shallow and small-minded, and dissatisfied with his lot,
no matter how much he had, the man seemed congenitally
incapable of *not* committing treason. Even after his cohort,
Warwick, had gone to his heavenly (or hellish) reward,
Clarence, not at all the clueless victim of Shakespeare's

drama, was still plotting and scheming against his older brother. He became a widower in 1477 after Isabel Neville died (most probably of consumption), and began to look for a new wife. Having ideas above his station, he was keen to wed his niece Mary, the daughter of the Dowager Duchess of Burgundy (his favorite sister, Margaret). Marriage to Mary would also have placed Clarence in a better position to secure the English throne for himself. Unsurprisingly, Edward refused to grant permission for such a union.

Clarence by now avoided the court, blamed younger brother *Richard* for all his ills, and began extorting money from fellow nobles to fund his own war chest, neither too shy nor too proud to bully them into submission.

He lashed out at everyone and everything, leveling a charge against Ankarette Twynho, a former maidservant to his late wife, Isabel, accusing the woman of poisoning her, and using his royal status to intimidate a panel of jurors. Ankarette was found guilty and hanged, along with a man named John Thuresby of Warwick, who had been accused of poisoning Clarence and Isabel's newborn son. Clarence had convinced himself that the pair had been planted in his household by Edward IV and the Woodvilles for the express purpose of destroying his family. However, historians feel fairly certain that both Ankarette and John were innocent.

It appears to have been a season for witch trials. After two Oxford clerks were accused of sorcery, they pointed the finger at Thomas Burdett, a prominent member of Clarence's household. Burdett was arrested for disseminating treasonous documents and for using necromancy to plot Edward's death. Maintaining his innocence, he was nonetheless tried and hanged on May 19, 1477. But

Clarence himself failed to heed the warning. Remarkably, his treason escalated.

Intent on bringing down his older brother, he crashed a privy council meeting with a priest in tow who in 1470 had affirmed Henry VI's claim to the throne. Clarence insisted that the priest read aloud Thomas Burdett's avowal of innocence.

After amassing a group of supporters, Clarence then dispatched them to proclaim throughout the kingdom that Edward IV was a practitioner of the dark arts who had bewitched his subjects into following him—and in a super-stitious age, this was not such a far-fetched accusation. The duke maintained that he was Edward's next victim and that his older brother intended to destroy him "as a candle con-sumeth in burning, whereof he would in brief time quyte [require] him."

Frustrated that his accusations weren't catching fire, and his rage to rule so great that he had no scruples about tarnishing the pious and respectable image of their own mother, Clarence began spreading the rumor that Edward was illegitimate (a charge that Richard would conveniently employ once he became Protector of the realm) Clarence also leveled another charge—which Richard would eventu-ally adopt as well. He insisted that Edward IV's union with Elizabeth Woodville was invalid (and as a consequence, their children were illegitimate, and therefore ineligible to inherit the crown). Clarence insisted that at the time of Edward's marriage to Elizabeth, he had already been pre-contracted to wed another woman, Eleanor Butler (née Talbot). Never mind that Lady Eleanor had died nine years earlier, in 1468; by this time Clarence was desperate.

And when his arsenal of accusations failed to topple

Edward from his throne, Clarence committed the ultimate act of treason: He ordered his followers to take up arms against their sovereign, "to be ready in harness within an hour warning . . . to levy war against the king."

If Clarence hadn't been the king's kid brother, he surely would have been executed after his first attempt to stage a rebellion against the crown. Edward had been magnanimous in giving the duke every possible chance to mend his ways. But Clarence had twice joined forces with his late father-in-law, the Earl of Warwick, to dethrone Edward, in addition to conspiring against the king with Warwick's brother, the archbishop of Canterbury; now, *for the fourth time*, he was openly preparing to depose him.

Consequently, Edward had no alternative but to have his brother arrested and charged with high treason. Clarence was tried by Parliament in the fall of 1477 and found guilty. He spent the Christmas holidays in the Tower; and on January 16, 1478, Parliament met to consider the matter of attainting him, which meant that Clarence would be stripped of his title and property. However, his son, the developmentally disabled Edward Plantagenet, was permitted to remain the 17th Earl of Warwick, the title that was held by his executed maternal grandfather.

On February 7, in his office as high steward speaking on behalf of Parliament, the charismatic Duke of Buckingham—the second-highest peer in the realm, after Richard—pronounced the death sentence against Clarence. Although the Parliamentarians encouraged Edward to proceed with the former duke's execution, the king hesitated to shed his own brother's blood.

On February 18, 1478, the speaker of the Commons approached the bar of the Lords (they were not termed "house of . . ." until the sixteenth century) and demanded that it was time to act: *Now or never*, they insisted.

And so that day, as he languished in the Tower, the twenty-eight-year-old Clarence was liquidated. Literally. Although it's one of William Shakespeare's most memorable death scenes, most scholars believe that Clarence really *was* drowned in a vat of Malmsey wine (his favorite beverage), perhaps as a perverse last request. His daughter Margaret (later Margaret Pole, 8th Countess of Salisbury) always wore a wine cock (the faucet or spigot from a wine cask) about her wrist, and this unusual bracelet was accepted by her contemporaries as a tribute to her father, giving credence to the supposition.

Most historians believe that it was a difficult decision for Edward to execute his brother, despite the fact that Clarence had committed numerous acts of treason, including leading a rebel army against the crown and frequently attempting to depose him by violent means. Yet the queen undoubtedly urged her husband to abandon any ideas of clemency. After all, Clarence had been instrumental in the pitiless executions of her father and brother. In the words of a contemporary chronicler, Elizabeth Woodville believed "that her offspring by the king would never come to the throne unless the Duke of Clarence were removed." Little could she know that it was the king's *other* younger brother she should have feared as well.

Richard was among the realm's highest-ranking nobles to witness his brother's execution. His reaction is lost to posterity; although the pro-Ricardian biographers such as Paul Murray Kendall view Richard's obtaining of a license to set up two religious foundations, or chantries, soon thereafter as an example of his deep-seated grief. But the

Ricardians tend to find what they want to see. Richard never specifically named Clarence as one of the York family members for whom prayers should regularly be offered at the chantries. Additionally, the cost of such a bequest was so considerable that it was more likely that Richard had been saving up the money for quite some time in order to afford to make such a gift. And while he might not have cackled with glee (nor copiously wept) at Clarence's untimely demise, Richard was the one who most benefited from his death. Edward restored the office of Great Chamberlain of England to him (having previously rescinded it and given it to Clarence, who had griped about his perceived lack of preferment). Richard received some of Clarence's estates as well.

Soon after Clarence's death, Richard returned to the north, absenting himself from court for several months. According to Dominic Mancini, an Italian chronicler who visited England during 1482–1483, and who therefore had no home-turf ax to grind whether for or against Richard, "[T]henceforth Richard came very rarely to court. He kept himself within his own lands and set out to acquire the loyalty of his people through favors and justice. The good reputation of his private life and public activities powerfully attracted the esteem of strangers [foreigners]. . . . Such was his renown in warfare, that whenever a difficult and dangerous policy had to be undertaken, it would be entrusted to his discretion and generalship. By these arts Richard acquired the favor of the people, and avoided the jealousy of the Queen, from whom he lived far separated."

Richard and Elizabeth Woodville, Edward IV's queen, never got along. Of course, his brother Clarence's role in the summary execution of members of her family, and the possibility that in return Elizabeth encouraged her husband to carry out the judicial murder of Clarence, might have had something to do with it! Historians also believe that Richard felt shunted aside by all of the preferment showered upon the queen's vast family, favors that did indeed provoke his envy. However, no contemporary administrator or chronicler ever claimed that the Woodvilles didn't capably fulfill the obligations with which Edward IV entrusted them; and Richard received more honors and titles from his brother than did anyone else in the kingdom.

If the Duke of Gloucester was chewing on sour grapes over the perks awarded to his sister-in-law's relations, biding his time as he seethed with bitterness and jealousy, he hardly had anything to complain about. Nonetheless, once he'd secured the throne for himself, his revenge against the Woodvilles was extremely thorough. Clarence was not the only son of York to assassinate relatives of the queen. Richard would eventually murder Elizabeth's brother, as well as her younger son from her first marriage. He also tormented Elizabeth and her daughters, and may also have murdered her sons by Edward.

On April 9, 1483, Edward IV, so morbidly obese he could barely move, died of a fever at the age of forty. Because his oldest son (now Edward V) was only twelve, he named Richard, Duke of Gloucester, temporary Protector of the realm.

According to the terms of Edward's will, Richard was to fill the role of Protector until the coronation of Edward V; and the fifteenth-century Croyland Chronicler seemed to believe that it had been Edward IV's intention to see his son crowned as soon as possible after his death. Following the boy's coronation, the kingdom was to be governed by a regency council until Edward V reached his majority.

But the Woodville family had no intention of honoring the late king's wish, one that also had no legal force or authority. Worst-case scenario for the Woodvilles: They would quickly cobble together a regency council in which Richard would be allowed an equal role with others. Best-case scenario for them: His participation would be eliminated altogether.

We now come to the point in time when Richard truly revealed himself to be an arch royal pain. Having been named Protector, he was now so close to the throne, he could taste it. Why stop at being regent when with a bit of political sleight of hand he could reign in his own right?

Thus, it was in *Richard's* best interests to forestall little Edward's coronation for as long as possible, without letting on that he was doing so. Plans for the grand event proceeded apace, even as the date itself was continually postponed. Yet historian Rosemary Horrox contends that the boy's coronation did not take place as soon as possible after his father's death because the late king had left the kingdom's coffers empty on his demise and Richard, as Protector, had no money to spend on a lavish coronation.

Richard was in the north when Edward died, and consequently missed his brother's funeral. The Woodvilles took advantage of his absence from London to see a resolution passed by the privy council that would from the start replace Richard's protectorate with a regency council that would undoubtedly be packed with Woodvilles and their supporters. According to the contemporary chronicler Dominic Mancini, "[T]hey were afraid that if Richard took the crown, or even governed alone, they who bore the blame for Clarence's death would suffer death or at least be ejected from their high estate." Yet it's disingenuous to imply that the Woodvilles had been the impetus behind Clarence's execution. The duke had committed treason— four times; *Parliament* had judged him and found him guilty; the sentence for treason was death.

Resolution or not, a race against time was under way to see who could move first and with the greatest show of force behind them. It was a real-life game of chess to capture and control the barely adolescent king before the opposing faction could reach him. Edward V was living at Ludlow, where as Prince of Wales he had enjoyed his own household since he was a toddler. His governor was Elizabeth Woodville's oldest brother, the dashing and erudite courtier who had inherited his father's title, Earl Rivers.

Richard believed in the preemptive strike, sticking it to his adversaries before they had the chance to stick it to him. He moved swiftly, beating the Woodville faction to the punch—and then some.

The Protector's devious machinations were just beginning; one by one he began to eliminate the personal and political threats to his ascent.

On May 1, 1483, Elizabeth Woodville, the dowager queen, learned that her young son and his governor, Earl Rivers, had been waylaid the previous day by Richard and his cohort, the Duke of Buckingham, as they made their way from Ludlow to London for the youth's coronation. Richard had knelt before the boy king and with mock sincerity told the naive child that his mother's relatives had his worst interests at heart, adding that they were the same evil councilors and ministers who had surrounded his father in his last years and who had encouraged him to indulge in all manner of vice and excess. The Protector, an ironic name if ever there was one, impressed upon the boy that these malignant influences had to be removed for the good of the realm. In Richard's view, he wasn't kidnapping the king—he was *rescuing* him.

When Edward didn't quite seem to buy it, Richard upped the ante. He told the little king that these wicked councilors not only sought to deprive his nice uncle Richard of his office as Protector (which was partially true), but that they were plotting to kill little Edward himself—and that Earl Rivers was one of the ringleaders. Edward was overwhelmed by the barrage of frightening information his uncle was feeding him, and especially by this casting of aspersions against the man who had been his governor since he was a baby. Intimidated by Richard, the child ultimately agreed that the kingdom would be better off if it were governed in accordance with his late father's intentions, meaning that Richard should remain Protector.

Charging them with conspiring against him as Protector and for leading the late king into debauchery, on April 30 Richard arrested the dowager queen's brother Anthony Woodville, the 2nd Earl Rivers; Sir Richard Grey, her younger son by her first marriage; and another Woodville adherent, Sir Thomas Vaughan, who had been the treasurer in the boy's household. The men were brought to Pontefract Castle and imprisoned there.

Meanwhile, as little Edward was being escorted out of Wales, back in London the dowager queen's servants and other retainers were hastily scrambling to hide what remained of Edward IV's treasures so that Richard couldn't get his usurping hands on them. Fearing the worst, the dowager queen sought sanctuary at Westminster with the rest of her children, including Edward V's younger brother, the little Duke of York.

Richard began to amass adherents who would back the notion of crowning an adult, experienced administrator in preference to an untested, easily influenced child, reminding them how disastrous it had been for the realm during the minority of Henry VI—events that remained firmly entrenched in the minds of many men who had lived through them. But at some point (historians continue to debate over when Richard formed the idea), he decided that he didn't want to be a bookmark for Edward V, keeping the throne warm until the boy king's coronation. He wanted the crown for himself. However, to cloak his motives, Richard continued to maintain the pretense of planning for Edward's big day.

On Sunday, May 4, 1483 (the day the Woodvilles had originally scheduled for the coronation of little Edward V), Richard and Buckingham entered London with their adolescent "captive." Fearing reprisals from the Woodville faction (to whom the boy king was considerably closer than he was to Richard, a man the child barely knew), Richard had summoned military aid from his northern supporters, the better to checkmate the Woodvilles from raising arms against *him*. Edward V, clad in blue velvet, rode through the streets of London with great pageantry. Behind him rode Richard, garbed head to toe in obsequious black. But clattering along the cobblestones with the royal entourage were four cartloads of armor and weapons bearing the Woodville coat of arms—Richard's offer of proof that the dowager queen's party was indeed plotting against him.

That very day, acting as Protector, Richard summoned London's highest officers, clerics, and nobles and before them swore fealty to his nephew. He then called his first council meeting—bringing into the political tent (if only as a matter of lip service) Woodville supporters as well as those men who had been loyal to Edward IV, but were never too crazy about his wife and her family. It was the latter group who would comprise Richard's chief cadre of ministers. Thus, the transition from Edward IV's reign to Richard's (since Edward V never really reigned at all, except in name) was a fairly smooth one.

From the moment he became Protector, Richard's ambition knew no bounds. He would use every weapon in his arsenal from reason to intimidation to murder to ensure that the next coronation would be his own.

Writing his history from a monastery, the Croyland Chronicler was a contemporary of Richard's who may have been an eyewitness to many of the events of the day, and in any case was privy to certain information that has since been proven accurate. The Croyland Chronicler stated that "with the consent and good will of all the lords" Richard "was invested with power to order and forbid in every matter, just like another king . . ." and was given "*tutele* and oversight of the king's most royal person."

This is telling. "Tutele" is the root of our word "tutelage" and the person given "tutele" over a royal minor was his governor or teacher, responsible for the child's education and upbringing, as Earl Rivers had been for little Edward. But the person who would have had oversight of the minor was most often someone else, acting in loco parentis. When it came to his nephew, the rightful king, Richard made sure to be formally awarded both roles, which meant that he could control all access to the boy.

It was generally agreed that Edward V's temporary

residence at the palace of the bishop of London was far too ascetic and unsuitable for a king. So Richard cheerfully accepted the Duke of Buckingham's suggestion to move the boy to the Tower of London—which at the time was one of the capital's four royal residences as well as a prison. Sometime between May 9 and May 19, Edward was ensconced in the apartments of state. For having Richard's back, Buckingham was rewarded with numerous judicial and administrative offices throughout the entire kingdom.

As time was of the essence, Richard became the consummate multitasker, taking down his perceived enemies on all fronts. That spring he denounced Edward's favorite mistress, Jane Shore, for sexual immorality; and in an event that unwittingly made her a folk heroine, he had the bishop of London command her to parade through the streets in the manner of a penitent—clad only in her white shift and kirtle, carrying a candle and reciting psalms with a conical "dunce" cap perched on her head. This Jane did with as much dignity as she could muster, much to Richard's dismay. The king then imprisoned her at Ludgate on charges that she had employed sorcery and witchcraft to aid and abet her royal lover—allegations that of course could not be proved.

Richard would also accuse Jane of carrying on illicit and passionate affairs with two of Edward IV's kinsmen and supporters—lords Dorset and Hastings. In a proclamation dated October 23, 1483, Richard denounced Dorset for harboring "the unshameful and mischievous woman called Shore's wife in adultery." However, Hastings, who some historians believe became Jane's next protector, was not even in England during the time he was allegedly bedding her.

And in any event, Richard had sent Hastings to the block on June 13, 1483. The charges of harlotry with Dorset and Hastings were likely a smear campaign, one that bears the fingerprints of Richard's cabal of courtiers. The accusations are now considered baseless, but at the time, Jane's countrymen and -women gave them credence and she was roundly denounced as a whore.

As Richard continued to insist that he was planning Edward's coronation, setting a new date of June 22, England was on the brink of turmoil. There was no constitution at that time. With Edward V still a minor, the realm could easily descend into chaos in the absence of a strong governor. As for the day-to-day political machinations during Richard's protectorate, everyone was winging it. In addition, various factions were already seeking to control and influence their barely adolescent new monarch.

Spreading the word that the Woodville faction intended to do him harm, on June 10, 1483, Richard appealed to his loyal northerners to rise up and come to his aid. He dispatched a letter that read:

> We . . . pray you . . . come unto us to London . . . with as many as ye can defensibly arrayed, there to aid and assist us against the Queen, her blood adherents, and her affinity, which have intended, and daily doth intend, to murder and utterly destroy us and our cousin the duke of Buckingham, and the old royal blood of this realm. . . .

He was lying. No Woodville plots to assassinate Richard have ever been uncovered. Although it was a dog-eat-dog world, there is no historical proof that the Woodville faction ever intended to dispose of Richard. True, they

wanted to relegate him to a minor role on a regency council, but they didn't wish him dead.

Was this just a clever excuse to assemble an army? What
was Richard's real motive in amassing as many troops as
possible? Was it to rattle enough spears to intimidate the
Woodville faction into standing down, or was it to engage
them in combat?

A proposal to extend indefinitely the duration of the
protectorate was presented to Parliament. Some saw it as a
pragmatic step. Others who were closest to the Protector
himself were all too aware of Richard's ulterior motives.

On June 13, 1483, in the middle of a privy council meeting, Richard accused William, Lord Hastings, Edward
IV's boon companion and still England's Lord Chamberlain, of treason. Jealous over the preferment Richard
showed to Buckingham, and fearing that the Protector
never intended to see his nephew crowned but was instead
plotting to usurp the throne, the 1st Baron Hastings had
defected to the Woodville faction. Richard had sniffed out
his treachery and was now prepared to snuff out his life.

Before the Lord Chamberlain could say a word in his
own defense, he was seized and dragged to Tower Hill,
where he was summarily beheaded. When the public became
alarmed, Richard made certain that the event was conveniently spun: Hastings, they were told, had been caught
plotting against the life of the young king, and had paid
the ultimate, and appropriate, price for his treason. And
yet, Richard's conscience was disturbed enough by the
execution of the talented and capable Hastings to ensure
that the baron's widow, Katherine, would inherit his property and that his son would assume his late father's title,
with the assurance that it would never be attainted.

Having secured official control over the young king, Richard wanted to keep tabs on Edward's younger brother as well. So he insisted that the nine-year-old Duke of York be released to attend his brother's coronation. Richard also maintained that Edward had been lonely in the Tower without his little brother to play with. But the wary Elizabeth Woodville refused to let her other son emerge from sanctuary into his uncle's clutches. Ricardian historians such as Paul Murray Kendall tend to paint the dowager queen as the villainess while portraying Richard as a pragmatic, if ineloquent, politician, a stickler for law and order, and loyal to the memories of his two dead brothers. And in Richard's view, Elizabeth was keeping her own son hostage.

A delegation of clergy and lay lords descended on Westminster and encouraged the dowager queen to relinquish her younger son, but she remained adamant about keeping him in sanctuary. After she was threatened with force and informed that guards would violate the sanctuary and snatch the boy from her if she persisted in withholding her consent, on June 16, 1483, Elizabeth finally agreed to release him. With tremendous reluctance and a heavy heart, she allowed the archbishop of Canterbury, Thomas Bourchier, to escort the little Duke of York to the Tower to join his brother. Elizabeth Woodville knew, somehow, that she would never see either of her sons again.

The little princes were not the only relations whom the queen would never see again. She lost another son that month, as well as a sibling. At Pontefract Castle on June 25, Elizabeth's brother Earl Rivers, her son Lord Richard Grey, and Sir Thomas Vaughan were beheaded. The act was completely unlawful because Richard had not yet *formally* been named Protector when he'd had the men arrested and therefore he lacked the authority to detain them, let alone to execute them. Is it any wonder that the dowager queen was so reluctant to trust her deceitful brother-in-law?

The two princes now lived in the Tower, where they were seen romping in the gardens and shooting at archery butts like any other twelve- and nine-year-old boys of the era. Meanwhile, Richard rode through London attired and arrayed as though he were already king, and the real king's coronation date had once again been postponed.

A seedling that had been germinating in Richard's mind was about to sprout. By now he was planning to usurp the throne. But in order to bolster his own legitimate claim to the crown (a very tough sell, regardless of his military and administrative résumé), Richard needed to destroy the viability of all other heirs and claimants to the throne. Only if he became the last person with a rightful claim could he secure the key support of Parliament, the privy council, and the clergy, in an age where archbishops were considered princes of the Church with widespread influence over their flocks.

Richard ruthlessly trotted out all the tricks that Clarence had once used to prop up his own claim. Willing to throw their mother under a proverbial bus, besmirching her honor and reputation if it would help him gain the throne, Richard declared that the late Edward IV was illegitimate, conceived while their father was away at war, and citing the lack of family resemblance to prove his point.

But when few gave credence to this assertion, Richard tried another angle. He sought to have Edward IV's marriage to Elizabeth declared invalid on the grounds that before the late king met Elizabeth, he had entered into a precontract with the widowed Lady Eleanor Butler. A precontract was considered as binding as an actual marriage, rendering any subsequent union bigamous unless the precontract was sundered. Although Eleanor had died in 1468, Richard dredged up Bishop Stillington of Bath and Wells, the cleric who had allegedly witnessed Edward's promise to wed her. Richard also renewed the charges of witchcraft against the dowager queen's mother, Jacquetta Woodville, who had died in 1472, claiming that Jacquetta had used sorcery to enchant the late king into marrying her daughter.

The matter of the precontract with Lady Eleanor Butler was the only issue that was awarded any serious credibility. Yet, during Edward's lifetime no one had ever questioned the validity of his marriage to Elizabeth or the legitimacy of their children, or doubted that their firstborn son was the true prince of Wales. But if Edward's royal marriage could be judged invalid, then his children would be ineligible to inherit the throne. And after the royal children were retroactively made bastards, there would be only one Yorkist claimant to the throne still standing: Richard, Duke of Gloucester.

For bonus points, Richard insisted that the 17th Earl of Warwick—Clarence's developmentally disabled son, who had been living in his household—was also ineligible to ever inherit the throne because his father had been attainted— meaning that the king had stripped him of his lands and title. That contention sounds good; however, it's untrue.

But Richard had managed to bully and intimidate everyone from clergy to courtiers to councilors. He'd already demonstrated a willingness to execute anyone who got in his way. No one wanted to be next.

So, in the last days of June 1483 the privy council

awarded formal credence to Richard's claims, drafting a writ that would allow the usurper to place the crown on his own head. On June 25, in a formal document issued by Parliament known as the Titulus Regius, Elizabeth Woodville's marriage to Edward IV was declared null and void—which meant that all of their children were illegitimate, and therefore barred from inheriting the throne. Elizabeth was deprived of the title of queen mother, to be known thereafter simply as Dame Elizabeth Grey.

After being presented with the writ at Baynard's Castle in London, Richard gave an Oscar-worthy acceptance speech, dripping with faux modesty. He didn't deserve such an honor, he insisted—but if the kingdom needed him, well, he couldn't possibly decline, although the responsibility would be a weighty one.

Buckingham delivered a rousing oration, enumerating all the reasons that Richard should be acclaimed as king of England. But the *Great Chronicle* recorded that only a minority of the crowd shouted, "yea, yea," and that they did so "more for fear than love."

On June 26, 1483, the Duke of Gloucester usurped the throne, proclaiming himself Richard III. Edward V and his younger brother, Richard, Duke of York, were "progressively removed from men's sight," according to contemporary chronicler Dominic Mancini; and by the autumn of 1483 the princes were never seen or heard from again.

And on July 6, Richard was crowned with great pomp and splendor before an illustrious assemblage of England's peerage, including Henry Tudor's battle-ax of a mother, Margaret Beaufort. Like his big brother, Richard had usurped the crown, but unlike Edward IV, Richard had won it with more craft and stealth than might.

But precisely because he had achieved his heart's desire by underhanded means, Richard struggled to *maintain* the throne throughout his entire reign. Desperate to retain what he had so unrightfully seized and never content with his triumph, he grew much more vindictive and vengeful than he had been as Duke of Gloucester, cloaking his every misdeed behind the power of the crown. During the summer of 1483, just weeks after Richard's self-aggrandizing coronation, his most stalwart supporter, the Duke of Buckingham (a descendant of Edward III's youngest son), turned against him. The duke was among the leaders of a revolt that would be nicknamed "Buckingham's rebellion," although the uprising was fomented by several members of the southern nobility, encompassing a geographical swath that stretched from Kent to Cornwall and from the River Thames to the Severn on the Welsh border.

The *Chronicles of London* contains a contemporary account of the uprising. "In this year many knights and gentlemen, of Kent and other places, gathered them together to have gone toward the duke of Buckingham . . . which intended to have subdued King Richard; for anon as the said King Richard had put to death the lord chamberlain [Hastings] and other gentlemen, as before it is said, he also put to death the two children of King Edward, for which cause he lost the hearts of the people. And thereupon many gentlemen intended his destruction."

Richard managed to quash the rebellion in only a fortnight, beheading a total of ten traitors and attainting ninety-six others. On October 15, 1483, Richard formally proclaimed Buckingham a rebel. He was convicted of high treason on November 2 and beheaded in the Salisbury marketplace.

In late July 1483, while Richard was on progress, he'd

gotten wind of an attempt to free the two young princes from the Tower. After his two nephews disappeared from view sometime later that summer, there was widespread belief not only throughout England, but abroad, that the princes had been murdered and that Richard was complicit in their deaths.

Not the way to win hearts and minds. But he tried. The Tudor-era chronicler Polydore Vergil explained how Richard tried to reverse his subjects' negative opinion of him: "Because he could not now reform the thing that was past, he determined to abolish the note of infamy wherewith his honour was stained, and to give such hope of his good government that henceforth no man should be able to lay any calamity that might happen to the commonwealth to his charge. . . . He began to take on hand a certain new form of life, and *to give the show and countenance of a good man*, whereby he could be accounted more righteous, more mild, better affected to the commonalty . . . and so might first merit pardon at God's hands."

However, the bad press never abated, no matter how greatly the members of Parliament and others, including Elizabeth Woodville, lived in fear of Richard's reprisals. On March 1, 1484, he managed to coax the dowager queen and her daughters out of sanctuary and bring them to court, only after publicly swearing an oath to protect them from harm and to ensure that all five daughters made good marriages. But Elizabeth would never forget that Richard had ordered the execution of her brother and one of her oldest sons, and she certainly blamed him for the young princes' disappearance from the Tower.

Vengeance makes bedfellows as strange as politics does; and after an unsuccessful attempt to raise an army against

Richard, the former queen formed an alliance with the Yorkists' age-old enemies, the Lancastrian claimants to the throne. She brokered a deal with Henry Tudor, who was living in exile on the Continent. Henry was the grandson of Catherine de Valois—daughter of King Charles VI of France, and the first wife of England's Henry V. If Henry would agree to a precontract to wed Elizabeth of York (the eldest daughter of Elizabeth Woodville and Edward IV), then the dowager queen vowed to place whatever might and influence she had behind his claim to England's throne. So, on Christmas morning, 1483, Henry Tudor knelt in the cathedral of Rennes and promised to wed Elizabeth of York.

It stands to reason that Elizabeth Woodville never would have entered such a bargain, agreeing to support someone else's plans to seize the throne, if she believed that her sons were still alive. After all, each of them had a greater claim to their father's throne, being boys, than any of their sisters had.

Aware that the Woodville faction was conspiring with Henry Tudor to topple him from the throne, Richard began to shore up his support. He could still count on aid from the north because the nobles remembered him as a capable and magnanimous steward of the region.

But there was one thing that remained beyond Richard's control: death. On April 9, 1484, his only son, Edward, who had been invested in a grand ceremony the previous summer as Prince of Wales, died at the age of eleven. Richard and Anne were distraught. Not only was the boy gone, but with him all hope of Richard's creating a dynasty. A contemporary chronicler, describing the effect of the child's death on his parents, wrote, "You might have seen his father and mother in a state almost bordering on madness by reason of their sudden grief."

Queen Anne died at the age of twenty-eight the following March, having wasted away from heartache and
consumption after the death of her son. Contrary to
Shakespeare's plot, Richard did not have her murdered.
He was genuinely grief stricken at her loss, although
rumors did persist that he had poisoned her in order to be
able to wed his own niece, Elizabeth of York, as a way of
further cementing his claim to the throne.

But those rumors seem baseless. Richard had declared the
children of Edward IV illegitimate, so it's unlikely he would
turn around in the space of a few months and marry a girl
he had officially declared a bastard and therefore ineligible
to sit on the throne (as would be her progeny). Additionally, Richard was fully aware of the precontract of marriage
between Henry Tudor and Elizabeth of York, which in the
fifteenth century was as valid as a marriage itself. Therefore for Richard to snatch Elizabeth from her betrothed
only to wed her himself would have been viewed as bigamy.
And considering that it was within his purview to bestow
his nieces' hands in marriage, it's also notable that Richard
didn't give Elizabeth of York to one of his own supporters:
additional proof that he acknowledged and respected the
girl's precontract.

How ironic that what Richard had so willfully endeavored to destroy—the legality of Edward IV and Elizabeth
Woodville's marriage based upon a prior precontract—
would be what came back to bite him. But it certainly
established his acceptance of the premarital understanding
between Henry Tudor and Elizabeth of York.

So, absent an heir and all out of ruses to bolster any
legitimate claim to the throne, Richard went about the business of governing and prepared for Henry Tudor's inevitable

invasion. Both sides spent the winter of 1484–1485 shoring up support.

On Sunday, August 7, 1485, Henry Tudor landed a few miles west of Milford Haven in Wales and began his march eastward, prepared to confront Richard wherever their armies intersected. Three weeks later, on August 22, in the Battle of Bosworth in Leicestershire, as the opposing forces clashed for two hours on Ambien Hill and Redmore Plain, Richard met his bloody end, the last English king to die in battle. He was thirty-two years old and had reigned for two years, one month, and twenty-eight days.

Henry snatched the crown from the dead king's crested helm (some sources say it was dislodged by his stepfather, the first earl of Derby, Thomas Stanley, who placed it on Henry's head), proclaiming himself Henry VII. The age of the Tudors had begun.

Richard's naked corpse, his neck encircled with a felon's noose, was tossed unceremoniously over the back of a packhorse and brought to Greyfriars Chapel in Leicestershire for interment. Good riddance to a brat, brute, and bad seed, say most historians, but staunch members of the Richard III Society are quick to assert that even in death, Richard remained a hero to the citizens of York who remembered his wise and astute governance. They mourned him sincerely, attesting in the city's civil records, "King Richard, late mercifully reigning upon us, was . . . piteously slain and murdered, to the great heaviness of this city."

His twentieth- and twenty-first-century apologists cite certain accomplishments as evidence that he wasn't such a baddie after all. Some scholars, particularly the Ricardians, who often seek to sanitize the awful reputation Richard has retained over the past five centuries, seem to agree that Richard was a loyal husband. As proof, they point to his outsize prudery vis-à-vis his brother Edward's massive libido, and his opinion of the courtiers who helped the king procure and enjoy his paramours. Of course, Richard was hardly a monk, having fathered two children out of wedlock when he was still a randy teen: his son, John Pomfret (also known as John of Gloucester); and his daughter, Katherine Plantagenet, born before his marriage to Anne.

Another Ricardian argument is that while the Duke of Clarence was always a thorn in Edward IV's side, both personally and politically, during Edward's reign Richard was a stalwart, capable steward. Although both younger brothers had been made dukes and received substantial land grants after Edward became king, despite Clarence's seniority as the middle brother, it was Richard whom Edward trusted as a military commander and as an administrator. And it was Richard, not Clarence, whom Edward made his viceroy in the north of England. There, the young Duke of Gloucester proved himself a most favored son of York. The more time Richard spent in the north, the more renowned he became for his good governance, forgiving tax payments and suppressing the illegal building of fishing weirs—a system of wicker nets known as "fish garths."

So, is Richard III's reputation as a royal pain a deserved one?

Well! If you can find it in your heart to subtract all of his numerous acts of treachery, you could try to argue that he had in fact been a fairly good king. He was intolerant of corruption, instituted tort reform, and munificently provided for the widows and families of executed traitors.

He was kind and generous to his two (pre-Anne) illegitimate children. His daughter, Katherine, married well and
his son John was made Captain of Calais in 1485.

Richard had a happy and, by all accounts, faithful marriage; and he spent substantial sums building chapels and
castles and patronizing the arts, particularly musicians and
choirs. He did, however, award the lion's share of royal preferment to his trusty northerners, which left the southern
nobles seething with enough resentment to foment a rebellion within weeks of his coronation. To the detriment of his
reign, he never did secure their support.

Thomas More, the Italian-born Polydore Vergil, and
other writers of the Tudor era, including William Shakespeare, had their own agendas, and these have largely
shaped our perception of the deeds and personality of
Richard III. It is a skewed image, because Richard proved
himself a well-liked and exceptionally competent and fair
administrator during his years in Yorkshire. But the Ricardians of recent centuries do protest too much. Richard was
neither hero nor saint. In a bloody and violent age, at best,
he was no *less* and perhaps only a bit *more* brutal than
many of his brethren.

But—and there's always a "but."

There are simply too many strikes against Richard III
to absolve or exonerate him.

In addition to the other crimes he is well known to have
committed, it's hard to ignore the heartrending mystery
regarding the fate of the princes in the Tower, which has
continued to puzzle and fascinate us for more than five
centuries.

Members of the Richard III Society and other Ricardians
seek to acquit their hero by suggesting that others, most

specifically the Duke of Buckingham and the exiled Henry Tudor, had motive (and Buckingham also had opportunity) to dispose of the princes. But none of their arguments, while intriguing, hold water; and because Richard had the most to gain from the princes' demise, he remains the primary suspect. Surely, with all the rumors of their deaths swirling about during the summer of 1483, if the children had been alive, Richard would have taken pains to produce them, in order to burnish his tarnished reputation. And if the boys had, as some Ricardians believe, been secretly smuggled to safety elsewhere in the kingdom, undoubtedly some loyal adherent to their mother would have informed her.

Dominic Mancini, the Italian-born chronicler, departed the English court just days before Richard's July 6 coronation. He surmised that the princes were already dead by then. "After Hastings was removed, all the attendants who had waited upon the king were debarred access to him. He and his brother were withdrawn into the inner apartments of the Tower proper, and day by day began to be seen more rarely behind the bars and windows, till at length they ceased to appear altogether. A Strasbourg doctor, the last of his attendants whose services the king enjoyed, reported that the young king, like a victim prepared for sacrifice, sought remission of his sins by daily confession and penance, because he believed that death was facing him. . . . I have seen many men burst forth into tears and lamentations when mention was made of him after his removal from men's sight; and already there was a suspicion that he had been done away with. . . ."

And in January 1484 the chancellor of France, Guillaume de Rochefort, proclaimed at a meeting of the Estates-General, "*Regardez, je vous prie, les événements qui après la mort du Roi Édouard sont arrivés dans ce pays. Contemplez ses enfants, déjà grands et braves, massacrés impunément, et la couronne transportée à l'assassin par la faveur des peuples.*" In other words, de Rochefort said (possibly with a soup-çon of schadenfreude), "Look, I beg you, at the events that occurred in this country after the death of King Edward. Consider his children, already big and brave, massacred with impunity, and the crown passed to their assassin by popular acclaim."

Although France was England's age-old nemesis and invariably gained political mileage from the faux pas of the Anglos, the chancellor had "a learned and rather staid per-sonality." He was not a propagandist, and historians con-tend that he would not have made such a declaration had he not been privy to certain specific, and reliable, information about the princes' deaths. Guillaume de Rochefort's source may very well have been Dominic Mancini.

What amounted to regicide (because the older prince was rightfully King Edward V) was the talk of Europe, and medieval historians were quick to condemn Richard for the boys' deaths. The *Great Chronicle*, a contemporary document, states that "[S]ome say they were murdered atween two feather beds, some say they were drowned in Malvesey [Malmsey], and some say that they were sticked with a venomous potion." All of those scenarios are very dramatic, but perhaps the importance of the assertion is not *how* the princes were murdered, but simply that they *were* murdered.

Shakespeare drew his research from the writing of Sir Thomas More, who was only five years old when Richard III died at Bosworth. In *Richard III*, one of the assassins hired to dispose of the princes is named James Tyrell. While

Shakespeare's play is comprised of one part invention, two parts imagination, and a heady dose of propaganda, there really was a James Tyrell who served in Richard's court, and who eventually committed treason against Henry VII after serving him for a few years. On the scaffold, Tyrell confessed to killing the princes. Most modern historians don't believe him, maintaining that he was more than likely covering up for the actual murderer, and his admission would conveniently end the search for the killer(s). Nevertheless, Tyrell's deathbed confession serves only to deepen the mystery.

Ricardians like to refer to the dowager queen's willingness to quit the sanctuary of Westminster and come to Richard's court as an exoneration of any complicity he might have had in her sons' deaths. But records indicate she hardly did so eagerly. On the contrary: Richard's men arrived at Westminster and threatened Elizabeth Woodville with violence (as they had previously done when Richard had demanded custody of the little Duke of York) if she and her daughters refused to come forth of their own volition. And if the dowager queen believed Richard capable of killing her little boys, surely she'd fear him enough to comply with his wishes, especially as he had promised in the presence of the privy council to protect her and her daughters and to arrange good marriages for the girls.

Although his reign was brief, Richard's shadow upon the stage of history looms larger than those of many monarchs who wore the crown far longer. The controversy over whether he was responsible for the death of his nephews may continue to rage for another five hundred years, but Richard was most assuredly a usurper and a murderer; and he circumvented the laws of the land on multiple occasions as Duke of Gloucester, as Protector, and as king of England. Even if Richard's conduct can be explained, or clarified, as a product of his time (after all, both Edward IV and Henry VII were usurpers and murderers as well), on balance, his murderous misdeeds far outweigh his fish garths!

IVAN IV

"Ivan the Terrible"
1530–1584
RULED RUSSIA: 1533–1584

*I*F IVAN IV HAD ENJOYED A HAPPY CHILDHOOD, WOULD he have entered the annals of history as "Ivan the Not So Terrible After All"?

In Russia the tyrant is known as "Ivan Grozny," which translates to Ivan the Awe-Inspiring/Awesome/Fearsome/ Terrible (as in "terrible swift sword" from "Battle Hymn of the Republic"). And even today, Russians can be quick to point out that little matter of semantics.

Ivan the Awesome? Well, not if your definition of "awesome" comes from Funk and Wagnalls, the slacker dude dictionary. Regardless of what may get lost in translation, Ivan's brutality cannot be dismissed. He *did* do truly terrible things, not only by our own modern definition but even by the standard of sixteenth-century Russia's extremely violent culture—in which case, "Ivan the Fearsome" is indeed a well-deserved moniker. And his spectacularly violent career (as both autocrat and royal psychopath) scores him a perfect trifecta within this volume's subtitled cast of brats, brutes, and bad seeds.

In Ivan's day, about a hundred and fifty noble Russian families, known as the boyars, owned most of the land, held most of the government's highest offices and military posts, and shared power with Moscow's grand prince. Eight or nine million people paid rent to live and grow crops on the boyars' vast estates. Ivan's grandfather, Ivan III, had brought all of the boyars under control; nonetheless, they were accustomed to governing their own lands without interference from the grand prince. Ivan's father, Vasily III, consulted them on important decisions. But Ivan's unhappy and brutal childhood forever shaped the way he viewed the boyars. When it was time to grasp the reins of power, he decided that Russia should be an autocracy. His reign changed the course of history.

After twenty years of marriage, in 1525 Ivan's father Vasily forcibly shoved his barren first wife, Salomonia, into a convent. Needless to say, she was not terribly pleased with this turn of events, and being a temperamental person herself, she resisted. With all her might. Salomonia kicked and screamed and had to be beaten on the way out the door. To add an odd tidbit of historical context in terms of rulers operating in seemingly parallel universes for even the briefest space of time, Vasily's banishment of Salomonia occurred right about the time that half a world away England's Henry VIII had fallen in love with Anne Boleyn and was toying with the idea of putting aside his first wife, Katherine of Aragon, "for the curse of sterility" as his advisers put it.

As Vasily contemplated a divorce from Salomonia, he was allegedly cursed for his actions by Mark, the Patriarch of Jerusalem. Mark prophesied, "If you do this evil thing, you shall have an evil son. Your nation shall become prey to terror and tears. Rivers of blood will flow, the heads of the mighty will fall, your cities will be devoured with flames."

But Vasily wasn't buying Mark's mumbo jumbo. Instead,

he ostentatiously flouted the prophecy and found himself a nubile babe who would bear him a baby. Circumventing tradition, he engendered another scandal by choosing for his second wife Elena Glinskaya, forgoing the traditional "beauty pageant" that was held when Russia's sovereign decided to marry. Vasily had been smitten with "the beauty of her face and her young age," and decided that she was The One without needing to hold a competition. Approximately twenty years old at the time of her wedding on January 26, 1526, Elena was beautiful, educated, cultivated—and a Catholic. In order to appear younger for his trophy wife, the forty-six-year-old Vasily had shaved off his beard, practically an act of sacrilege in his culture.

Although they considered themselves enlightened, the bridal couple was as superstitious as all Russians of the era. The eighty black marten or sable pelts placed over their seats and at the base of the numerous candles during the three-day wedding festivities were intended to ward off evil spirits. But the sheaves of grain placed in and around the bedchamber didn't bring the newlyweds the expected luck in the fertility department. It took more than four years for Elena to become pregnant, but finally on August 25, 1530, in the midst of a terrible thunderstorm, Ivan was born at the Kremlin. Although Vasily claimed paternity, rumors spread that Elena's child had been fathered by her lover, the handsome Prince Telepnev-Obolensky.

Ivan's coming was ill-starred. After his birth, the khan of Kazan, a realm on Russia's border, warned the Russian boyars, "A sovereign has been born to you and he already has two teeth. With one, he will devour us; but with the other, he will devour you!"

Once again, Vasily doesn't seem to have blinked. He

raised Ivan in Moscow's Kremlin, a walled city within a city boasting three separate palaces, as many cathedrals, five churches (plus a chapel), a treasury, government offices and council chambers, bathhouses and storehouses, prisons, and even a mill sponsored by his consort, where silk and cloth of gold were loomed. On the face of it, it's hard to imagine a cushier life.

In 1532, Elena bore Vasily another son, the developmentally disabled Yuri. But the following year Vasily developed a leg ulcer that turned into a hideous boil. The prince was bled and the oozing sore was treated with poultices of honey, wheat flour, and boiled onions—which only increased the pus-filled discharges. Finally the wound was doused with vodka, and Vasily was dosed with a laxative of seeds, which weakened him further. He soon developed blood poisoning, dying on December 4 at the age of fifty-four, after begging on his deathbed to be made a monk. After brazenly ignoring so many religious prophecies, in his final moments Vasily may have been hedging his bets, hoping that adopting the pure soul of a monk would speed him on the highway to heaven.

As Vasily breathed his last, and passed his throne to his oldest son, a council of seven boyars was already in place to act as regents, guiding little Ivan's government and military decisions until he reached the age of fifteen, when he would claim the throne on his own. But Ivan's mother, Elena, who now openly consorted with the Grand Equerry, Prince Telepnev-Obolensky, was the real power behind the throne, setting her young son an example of how to deal with dissidents and detractors. Elena had her late husband's two brothers, Yuri and Andrei, arrested and incarcerated. Yuri starved to death in prison, but Andrei was captured in the process of instigating a revolt, so Elena had proven herself to be more prescient and astute than paranoid.

But she wasn't immortal. On April 3, 1538, Elena was seized with painful convulsions and dropped dead; her demise was so sudden that many suspected poison.

Elena's death sparked a war between two noble families, the Belskys and the Shuiskys. The goal of each faction was to seize control of the throne, turning little Ivan into a mere figurehead or puppet prince. When Ivan was seven years old his nanny, Agrafena Cheliadnina, the sister of his mother's lover and the only stable force in his life, was packed off to a convent; he never saw her again. According to Ivan, the Shuiskys proceeded to steal his parents' belongings while he and his younger brother, Yuri, who was a deaf-mute, were kept in deprivation and poverty. The boys were left with nothing to wear but ratty garments, and were trotted out all dressed up only on ceremonial occasions.

Ivan himself described the conditions that he and Yuri endured after their mother's death and their treatment at the hands of the greedy and competing boyars:

"Our subjects saw their desires fulfilled: they received an empire without a master. Paying no attention to us— their sovereigns—they rushed to conquer wealth and glory, falling upon one another in the process. . . . As for my brother Yuri and me, they treated us like foreigners or beggars . . . lacking both food and clothing! We were allowed no freedom. . . . Many were the times when I was not even served my meals at the appointed hour! And what of my father's treasure that was mine by right? It was all looted. . . . The sons of boyars carried off that treasure, they melted it down to make vessels of gold and silver; they engraved their parents' names on them as if they had been hereditary possessions!"

Prince Ivan Shuisky even appropriated Vasily III's bedroom in the Kremlin, crudely and ostentatiously resting his dirty foot on Ivan's father's pillow as he lectured the boy. Ivan later wrote, "He . . . adopted toward me a contemptuous attitude." The young prince privately swore revenge.

The religious leader of the official Church of Russia was known as the metropolitan. One night when Ivan was eleven, the current metropolitan, a priest named Josef (who was a Belsky supporter), came tearing into his bedroom, his robe ripped and spit upon, demanding Ivan's protection from the Shuisky family members who were pursuing him. The boy was in bed and had no idea what to do when the Shuiskys burst into the room, began to beat the priest to a pulp, and then dragged him away. The only reason Ivan may not have been the Shuiskys' next victim was that they needed him as a figurehead. He was the hereditary prince.

Neither the Shuiskys nor the Belskys ever established a firm grip on the government. Ivan remained inside the Kremlin, sheltered, scared, and clueless about what went on outside its impenetrable walls. The council of boyars kept him surrounded by guards and servants, most of whom were spies for the two competing families. He had no friends, because any playmates might be a source of influence. "I was never free to do anything. I could never do what I wanted or what a boy should," Ivan wrote.

In 1542, Ivan developed a friendship with a powerful boyar named Feodor Vorontsov. Prince Andrei Shuisky, who had the upper hand at the time, grew anxious about Vorontsov's potential influence on the youth. So Shuisky and his men pummeled Vorontsov to a bloody pulp and then sent him to prison. It was the proverbial last straw for the twelve-year-old Ivan. That Christmas he hosted a feast and invited the leading boyars. In the middle of the meal, Ivan rose and gave a speech accusing the noblemen of taking advantage of his minority. The pursuit of their own corrupt agendas, illegally appropriating lands for themselves, and imprisoning people without provocation had destroyed the country. And the worst offender was Andrei Shuisky.

Ivan ordered Shuisky's immediate arrest, but there would be neither prison nor deportation. Andrei was beaten to death by the palace guards and fed to the hungry hounds outside. However, the bloodbath was just beginning. Thirty boyars with close ties to Andrei Shuisky were summarily hanged. Ivan was seizing control of the country and of his destiny. And while his vengeance might seem justified, one can only pause at the viciousness of the acts ordered by a twelve-year-old boy. Ivan had metamorphosed from brat to brute with alarming velocity.

Ivan matured quickly in more ways than one. By the time he was thirteen he already had an imposing physical presence: six feet tall, broad shouldered, and barrel-chested. His small, piercing blue eyes missed nothing. His long hooked nose lent him an air of hawklike majesty. He had lanky brown hair and, as he went through puberty, grew a long, reddish beard. Whether it was because he had seen so much brutality in his young life or that he'd gotten a taste of it after taking care of the Shuiskyites, he developed a taste for killing things and watching them die. He'd rip the feathers from the bodies of live birds, pluck out their eyes, and slit their bellies—fascinated by their pathetic throes of agony. As an entertaining pastime, he'd toss cats and dogs off the ramparts of the Kremlin. Most of us would be tempted to describe this callous behavior with a single word: psychopath.

In 1546 both the Shuiskys and the Belskys lost their bid to control the throne. Instead, the reins of power were grabbed by another rival faction—Ivan's mother's family, the Glinskys. As Ivan considered them allies, the Glinskys' ascension freed him to enjoy his teenage years in an attempt to make up for all the fun he'd missed during his childhood. So, while the Glinskys ran the government, Ivan and his friends ran amok on horseback through the streets of Moscow, horsewhipping and riding roughshod over peasants and their vending stalls outside the Kremlin walls. Torturing cats and dogs had been entertaining, but trampling peasants afforded Ivan the chance to take his sadism to the next level.

Although Ivan and his pals enjoyed behaving like thugs and vandals, he considered himself a religious man. He remained superstitious throughout his life, hiring and heeding fortune-tellers. But in an age when most men, and even some rulers, were illiterate, Ivan recognized that in order to be a proper leader, reading and writing were just the tip of the iceberg. He decided to educate himself, employing teachers and learning songs and prayers through rote memorization. He gave himself a practical education as well, learning the way of the world through eyewitness experience. According to Ivan, "I adopted the devious ways of the people around me. I learned to be crafty like them."

Ivan had an insatiable thirst for information, questioning everyone from artisans to ambassadors to priests to ministerial secretaries about their work. He traveled widely, ostensibly to familiarize himself with his realm, although he spent more time fighting and fornicating than sightseeing. And at every location he demanded feasts, gifts, and other tributes—largesse that the villages and towns could ill afford to sponsor.

But Ivan's selfishness and his monstrous sense of entitlement were the least of his sins, and perhaps the easiest for his subjects to deal with. More difficult to endure was his rage. Throughout his life, Ivan demonstrated an emotional instability and a hair-trigger temper. One never knew when he was going to lose control and summarily order the removal of a friend's tongue or some similar act of savage butchery. He was slow to trust and quick to assume betrayal.

In December 1546, the sixteen-year-old Ivan summoned his theology tutor, Metropolitan Makary, and announced that he had decided to marry. Makary astutely dissuaded Ivan from considering a foreign princess for his bride because he doubted that any of them would want to come to a country that had been at war for ten years with the Tartars of bordering Kazan, and which remained riddled with civil strife.

Although it was the custom in Russia for the sovereign to hold a beauty pageant to choose his wife, Ivan's father, Vasily, had circumvented the process when he remarried, selecting Ivan's mother, Elena, before the thousands of eligible Russian virgins could be assembled for a lineup. Ivan would ultimately marry eight times, but the first time around he followed the traditional route. An exhaustive search was conducted throughout the realm with some candidates as young as twelve (an appropriate marriageable age for centuries; the girl was old enough to have gotten her first period, but young enough to have avoided physical temptation). The girls were made up in traditional Russian fashion, with white lead foundation and red circles of rouge on their cheeks. The cosmetics were not intended to enhance their features, but rather to conceal them from the prying eyes of lascivious men. One wonders whose idea of a "beauty contest" this actually was, with the competitors' charms so effectively concealed.

The initial selection of virgins was made by Ivan's regional representatives, who had to winnow out the number of possibilities from a thousand entrants. The semifinalists were housed twelve to a room in a building adjacent to the palace, where they were routinely subjected to visits and interviews by the sovereign and were scrutinized by a group of duennas who poked and prodded and attested to their general good health and the veracity of their virginity. After the series of interviews, Ivan reduced the number of contestants to a manageable dozen or so.

The winner of "Who Wants to Be the First Czarina?" was Anastasia Romanovna Zakharina, whose father, a boyar, gave his name to the Romanov dynasty. Instead of a crown (which she would eventually receive) and a dozen roses, she was awarded a handkerchief embroidered with gold and silver threads and embellished with pearls.

On January 16, 1547, at Moscow's Cathedral of the Assumption, the sixteen-year-old Ivan was crowned as grand prince of Vladimir and Moscow, czar and monarch of all the Russias, in a ceremony conducted by the new head of the Russian Orthodox Church, Metropolitan Makary. It was the first time the term "czar" (also spelled "tsar"), which derives from the Roman title *caesar,* or emperor, was used to denote sovereignty. Yet according to Ivan's biographers Robert Payne and Nikita Romanoff, he was not formally permitted to use the title of czar until 1561—and only after he paid the Greek patriarch Iosaf of Constantinople three times the sum originally agreed upon for the privilege.

At his 1547 coronation Ivan wore a centuries-old conical fur-trimmed crown known as the Cap of Monomakh (meaning "one who likes to fight in single combat"), and was given a few splinters of wood said to have belonged to the true cross on which Jesus Christ was crucified.

Ivan wed Anastasia in the cathedral on February 3, 1547, less than three weeks after his coronation. They stood side by side before the altar on a carpet of red damask bordered by black sable pelts. At the end of the ceremony the bridal couple participated in a ritual familiar to many Jews; they each took a sip of wine from a glass that Ivan then crushed under his heel.

The royals' bedchamber was stuffed to the gills with fertility symbols, including sheaves of wheat. The bed itself had been sprinkled with handfuls of loose grain. Ivan's marriage was consummated as one of the bride's brothers, Nikita Zakharin, slept beside the bed of state. Just outside, Ivan's uncle, the Master of the Horse Mikhail Glinsky, rode about the courtyard below the bedroom with an upraised sword in his fist: phallic symbolism meets bodyguard.

On the following morning, Anastasia and Ivan visited their respective bathhouses for a ritual cleansing. Nikita Zakharin and Ivan threw pails filled with cold water on each other. One assumes that some honored female relation did the same for Anastasia. Then the newlyweds sat down to a hearty breakfast of kasha.

The English explorer Richard Chancellor, who first visited the Russian court in December 1553, wrote that Anastasia ruled her "young and riotous" husband "with [gentleness] and wisdom." Ivan evidently adored her and nicknamed her his "little heifer." It soon became common knowledge that Anastasia was the only person in Russia capable of taming the imperial mood swings. Chancellor remained in Russia for some time, and is a reliable eyewitness. (He eventually brokered a trade agreement with Russia on England's behalf; and after Elizabeth I became queen in 1558, Ivan entered into a lengthy correspondence with the English monarch.)

Among his other unpleasant traits, Ivan was a paranoid ruler. One can only suppose that he'd witnessed so many horribly violent political incidents during his childhood that it might have been difficult for him to maintain any psychological equanimity. On the other hand, there were those small birds he liked to torture as a teen and the cats and dogs he'd lobbed from the Kremlin's ramparts. In any case, early in Ivan's reign he summarily ordered the beheading of the leaders of fifty arquebusiers, or musketeers, who had brought him a petition protesting his oppressive measures. Ivan later claimed he'd mistaken the armed men for an assassination squad.

One of the victims was his former boyhood buddy, Feodor Vorontsov. Vorontsov's demise set a dangerous precedent. Throughout his reign, Ivan thought nothing of executing his favorite courtiers and advisers (and in the most brutal manner he could devise) when he perceived they had turned against or in some way betrayed him. Ivan believed that he ruled by divine right and was therefore closer to God than other men, which both justified and excused all of his excesses: alcoholism, rape, torture, and murder.

And yet, as certain as he was that God was in his corner, Ivan had such a superstitious nature that sometimes a perceived "omen" could save his potential victims. In

1547, a group of citizens from Pskov came to Moscow to protest Ivan's rule and were literally saved by the bell. As a punishment for their criticizing the way he ran the country, Ivan ordered his guards to douse them with alcohol and light the men's beards on fire. No sooner had the orders been given than a messenger galloped up to the czar to announce that the enormous bell in the Kremlin had suddenly fallen. Ivan saw the event as a divine sign and released his prisoners.

While his first wife, Anastasia, was alive to manage and mollify his temper, Ivan actually demonstrated some excellent leadership skills, especially for one so young and with so many millions of subjects under his rule. He organized workers and tradesmen into guilds and implemented tax reform, curbing some of the excessive power wielded by the wealthy boyars who owned the lion's share of Russia's real estate. Lest these acts be mistaken for beneficence, it soon became all too apparent that Ivan's objective was to consolidate power under the aegis of the crown.

On June 21, 1547, disaster befell the capital when Moscow was destroyed by fire. Nearly two thousand people were killed and thousands more became homeless. Rumors spread that the Glinsky family was responsible for the conflagration. They were accused of ripping out human hearts and soaking them in water, and wherever they then sprinkled the water, flames had risen up. An antiboyar riot turned against the Glinskys directly. Ivan's uncle, Yuri Glinsky, was killed in the cathedral where he had sought shelter from the mob.

After the angry throng marched on Ivan's home in Moscow, he ordered the summary execution of the leaders. The Glinskys' grasp on the reins of power had been destroyed, and Ivan was compelled to acknowledge that his own rule was a tenuous one. It was time to cement his authority. The czar created a Chosen Council, composed of a select, trusted cadre of advisers. To Ivan's credit the council included a trio of men who were anything but sycophants: Metropolitan Makary; Father Sylvester (a no-nonsense priest from Novgorod who didn't mince words when it came to criticizing Ivan's use of brutality to subjugate his subjects); and the kindhearted Aleksei Adashev, known for his sympathetic care of lepers. The Chosen Council's goal was to reform government, although Ivan's concept of "reform" was to further strengthen his autocracy.

With the council's advice, Ivan enacted a series of laws and measures designed to leach power from the boyars and the Orthodox Church and concentrate it instead in the person of the czar. "Starting from this day, I shall be your judge and your defender," he told the people of Moscow. Ivan promised tax relief, and punishment of corrupt government officials. He ordered his laws to be uniformly followed throughout the realm (in the past, outlying areas under the control of powerful boyars tended to ignore the ruler's decrees). If the Church wanted to increase its real estate holdings, it had to apply to the crown. Literate priests were ordered to open schools. Ivan's goal was to rival the courts of western Europe, which were far more progressive and enlightened.

Another of Ivan's aims was to expand his empire westward; he had his eyes on Poland, Lithuania, and Sweden. His greatest threats, however, lay to the south and to the east, where the brutal Tartar khans ruled khanates (kingdoms). Every spring, Tartar horsemen astride sturdy ponies thundered into Russia, wreaking havoc. Unleashing death from their quivers, they plundered villages, raped women, and kidnapped children, especially blue-eyed blondes, and sold them into slavery in Asia and the Mediterranean, where their fair coloring fetched high prices.

Ivan mustered an army of *streltsy*, or shooters—an early form of riflemen or musketeers—to combat the Tartar archers. He hired them for their marksmanship, unconcerned with whether they were commoners or came from the nobility. With his eye not just on defense but on offense, Ivan set as his target Kazan, the capital of the khanate of the same name, a city on the Volga of a hundred thousand citizens that was the size of London at the time. The czar intended to conquer the kingdom and add it to his empire, converting its Muslims to Christianity. It seemed that the doomsday prophecy uttered by the khan of Kazan to Ivan's father at his birth was coming true.

By 1552, Ivan had already attacked Kazan three times without success. On his fourth try, when he found the city walls to be impenetrable by his cannons, he cut off the water supply. His army dug two large tunnels under the walls and set off explosives inside them on October 2, 1552. That day, Ivan was hit with a bout of nerves, and spent the day praying while his army attacked Kazan. His aides-de-camp finally convinced the czar to saddle up so that he could inspire his troops—which he did, as long as his horse was stationed on a hilltop high above the fray. Ivan was never a courageous fighter; if there was any risk of injury to his own person, he was particularly craven. However, by the early afternoon his men had conquered Kazan, slaughtering thousands. The khan, Yediger Makhmet, and his family were captured and brought in chains before Ivan, where they prostrated themselves and begged for his mercy. The czar spared them, but most of Kazan's citizens weren't so lucky. However, it would take five more years before Ivan could add the region *around* Kazan to his empire, and Russia still remained threatened by the Tartars in the Crimea, at his southern borders.

On his return journey to Moscow, Ivan was greeted with the news that his beloved Anastasia had given birth to a son, Dmitri. She'd already borne him a daughter, Maria, but a girl could not inherit the throne. With Dmitri's birth, Ivan had his heir.

To commemorate his great victory in Kazan, Ivan commissioned a glorious cathedral to be built within the Kremlin walls on the site where Saint Basil, a *yurodivy* or holy fool, was buried. Later known as the Cathedral of Basil the Blessed, during Ivan's lifetime the edifice—constructed of multicolored bulbous domes, ribbed, covered in shingles resembling the scales of a fish, and faceted like jewels—was called the Cathedral of the Intercession of the Holy Virgin. According to one of Ivan's twentieth-century biographers, Henri Troyat, the cathedral was intended to be "an act of mystical madness." It was important to Ivan to select a Russian architect for the project, to prove to the world that his empire boasted as much talent and ingenuity as the West; his choice was a man named Postnik Yakovlev.

Paid for by the conquered inhabitants of Kazan, the cathedral took six years to build, and even at the commemoration, the central spire had yet to be completed. Legend has it that Ivan asked Yakovlev if he could ever again design a cathedral quite as beautiful, and when the architect enthusiastically responded in the affirmative, the czar had him blinded so he could never duplicate his masterpiece. With so many verifiable atrocities attributed to Ivan, there's no need to invent any. This anecdote is apocryphal; the fully sighted Yakovlev went on to design several more cathedrals, including one in Kazan.

St. Basil's was a spectacular monument to Ivan's triumph over Kazan, but he was not able to enjoy his victories for very long. Toward the end of 1552 and into the new year the conquered Kazanites rose up in violent rebellion against the czar's tax collectors. Ivan began to wonder whether he should have heeded the boyars who'd told him to leave some troops stationed there after his military victory.

His elation at having an heir lasted less than a year as well. In March of 1553, Ivan became too ill to rule and left Moscow to recuperate. In his absence some of his Chosen Council members had backed the succession of his cousin, Prince Vladimir Staristsky, over the czar's infant son. Before Ivan returned to Moscow he insisted on duplicating a trek his mother had made when she was pregnant with him, embarking on an arduous pilgrimage to various holy sites, including the monastery of Saint Kirill (Cyril) to commune with the pious hermit, or *starets*, there. Although the source of the warning is attributed to different people, depending on the historian relating the incident, Ivan was told that if he insisted on traveling to Saint Kirill with his wife and baby, the boy would never return to Moscow alive.

As Ivan was about to board the ship for his return voyage to Moscow, Dmitri's nurse stumbled on the wobbly gangplank and the nine-month-old czarevitch flew out of her arms and tumbled into the river, where he drowned. However, according to Ivan's biographer Henri Troyat, the infant died of a cold he'd caught during the journey. Seeking someone to hold accountable for the death of his heir, the czar blamed his old friend and trusted adviser Aleksei Adashev, whom Troyat credits with cautioning Ivan about his son's fate.

In June 1553, little Dmitri was buried in Moscow at the feet of his grandfather Vasily III. But Ivan wasted no time begetting another heir. Nine months later, on March 28, 1554, Anastasia gave birth to another son, whom they named Ivan.

And that year on August 25, his twenty-fourth birthday, the czar received another fabulous gift: He learned that the Tartar kingdom of Astrakhan to the south had fallen to Russia the previous month. It was welcome news, but it wasn't enough; Ivan wanted access to the Baltic, which would mean control of wealthy port cities and lucrative trade routes. He decided to annex Livonia (where Latvia and Estonia are today). Although his two closest advisers, Father Sylvester and Aleksei Adashev, had cautioned against waging war against Livonia, in January 1558, forty thousand Russian troops invaded, seizing the port city of Narva, which gave them immediate access to western vessels laden with merchandise. But Livonia would prove no easy conquest. The Danes, Swedes, and Poles threatened to join forces with Livonia against the Russians, and the war dragged on for more than two decades.

More bad news arrived on the domestic front. Anastasia had given Ivan six children, three girls and three boys, but only two of them had lived past their second birthday: Ivan, and his younger brother, Feodor. Feodor's birth in 1557 had weakened Anastasia and she had never fully recovered. Her specific ailment remained undiagnosed and the imperial couple resorted to prayer and the worship of special icons. But the saints weren't listening. In November 1559, after journeying with Father Sylvester to the monastery of Mozhaisk, Anastasia was seized with a sudden illness; neither doctors nor medicine were within reach. Her condition worsened during the following months. In July 1560, while she was bedridden, a fire

broke out in the Kremlin. Fearing the flames were growing nearer, Anastasia panicked and left her bed. Ivan had
her transported to the royal residence at Kolmenskoye, a
few miles away, but the czarina remained delirious and
feverish, imagining that the fire was on the verge of con-
suming her and her young children. On August 7, 1560,
she died. Her age at the time is unknown, although if
Anastasia had been Ivan's age, she would have been about
thirty. Perhaps she was a few years younger. It is doubtful
he would have chosen a bride older than he was. She was
buried in the Ascension Convent in the Kremlin.

Ivan's grief knew no bounds. He sought solace in drinking copiously and accusing his boyar enemies of poisoning
Anastasia. Several men were punished for the purported
crime, although Ivan had no firm proof of it beyond his
suspicions. However, according to Isabel De Madariaga's
2006 biography, *Ivan the Terrible: First Tsar of Russia*, late-
twentieth-century forensics may sustain his allegation.

During Anastasia's illness, Ivan lost much of his pro-
found, and genuine, religiosity. According to one of his
confidants, Prince Andrey Kurbsky, "The Tsar came to
detest the narrow pathway laden with sorrows which leads
to salvation through repentance. Instead he ran joyfully
along the broad highway that leads to Hell. Many times I
heard from his own lips—when he was depraved he would
say these things in the hearing of all: I must make my
choice between this world and the other world! He meant:
the broad highway of Satan or the sorrowful pathway of
Christ." Kurbsky noted that Ivan "embarked on all sorts
of things in an ungodly manner," beginning his awful
walk on the wild side when he realized that his beloved
wife was dying.

After Anastasia's death, Ivan became more paranoid than ever. Any inclinations he might have had to act as a righteous ruler evaporated. Instead he became a bloodthirsty despot, seeing spies and foes everywhere. These perceived enemies included his two most trusted advisers on the Chosen Council. Ivan charged Father Sylvester and Aleksei Adashev with witchcraft and placed them on trial. Neither man was permitted to speak in his own defense, and it was a foregone conclusion that they would be found guilty. Adashev was imprisoned and died two months later; Father Sylvester was exiled to a remote island off the Arctic Circle, where he also died mysteriously within a matter of weeks. Known allies of both men, including Adashev's twelve-year-old nephew, were executed as well.

In August 1561, Ivan remarried. His bride was a seventeen-year-old Circassian princess, Kocheney Temrjukovna, a Muslim beauty who took the name Maria when she converted to Russian Orthodoxy. Ivan had fallen head over heels for her exotic Asiatic looks and decided to marry her on the spot, forgoing the traditional beauty pageant. But the new czarina was detested by the Russians for having an aggressive personality and for never fully assimilating into their culture. They accused her of being a witch and manipulating the czar. Ivan, too, was soon disappointed in his choice, finding his wife uncouth and uneducated, and—perhaps worse—uninterested in raising his sons by Anastasia.

Historians generally tally Ivan's spouse count at seven, but he actually made eight trips to the altar. His second wife, Maria Temrjukovna, died in 1569, leaving no surviving children. She was so unpopular with the Russians that Ivan suspected poison again—his fallback position because he always needed someone to blame for every ill that befell him.

He called another bridal beauty pageant and surveyed two thousand virgins. From this lineup, he chose Marfa Sobakina, a merchant's daughter, wedding her on October 28, 1571. But she was ill when they married and died just sixteen days later. It had almost been a double wedding; on November 3, the seventeen-year-old czarevitch was married to the first runner-up, Eudoxia Saburova.

Naturally, Ivan needed somewhere to place the responsibility for young Marfa's death, so he accused the late czarina's brother of killing her and impaled the man on a pike. For good measure, Ivan also executed a handful of others.

According to the Russian Orthodox Church, a man could marry no more than three times; but Ivan insisted to the bishops—when he sought their permission for an unprecedented fourth wife—that the marriage to Marfa had never been consummated. That's hard to swallow, given the czar's rampant priapic urges, but no one was about to gainsay him.

On April 29, 1572, Ivan wed wife number four, Anna Koltovskaya. But Anna was banished to a convent three years later for failing to conceive a child. Wife number five was another Anna Vasilchikova—who lasted from 1575 until 1577, when she succumbed to illness.

Ivan's sixth spouse, the perky and voluptuous Vasilissa Melentieva, whom he married in 1577, was similar to Henry VIII's fifth wife, Kathryn Howard, in that she was caught cheating on her royal husband. Astonishingly, given Ivan's temper and reputation for brutality, Vasilissa got off more lightly than her English counterpart. Dispatched to a convent and shorn of her hair, Anna at least got to keep her head, although she was forced to witness her lover being impaled to death on a spear in the courtyard below her window.

Ivan's seventh wife was Maria Dolgorukaya, but on their wedding night the czar discovered that she wasn't a virgin after all. Betrayed and humiliated, he sought revenge. And this time he had no one but himself to finger for the demise of his wife. On the following morning, Ivan ordered Maria to be tied up inside a carriage and driven to the river, where she was drowned. The czar took an eighth and final bride in 1580. Maria Nagaya, who survived him, was the daughter of a court dignitary. She bore Ivan a son who lived to the age of nine, when he was assassinated in 1591.

None of his subsequent wives succeeded in tempering Ivan's behavior the way his first czarina, Anastasia, had done. In fact, as time went on, his contemporaries observed that Ivan just became more and more brutal. His paranoia grew as he saw spies and conspiracies at every turn, and his customary excesses of liquor and women grew even greater. With all of this overindulgence came an increased desire to punish those who had done him wrong, the more brutally, the better.

Some years were worse than others. In 1563, for example, Ivan suffered a number of setbacks. Vasily, his infant son by his second wife, Maria, died, as did the czar's sweet-tempered deaf-mute younger brother, Yuri. With little use for Yuri's wife hanging around, and perhaps to rid himself of any reminders of his brother, Ivan shoved his kind, pious sister-in-law into a convent, but when she didn't appear appropriately grateful, he had her murdered.

During his second marriage Ivan had begun to carry a steel-tipped staff wherever he went, striking people at will, and occasionally killing them. The czar would become so violent that he "foamed at the mouth like a horse," according to his contemporary Daniel Prinz von Bruchau. Prinz left a colorful description of Ivan's appearance at the time. "He is very tall and physically powerful, though somewhat tending to fat. He has large eyes which are perpetually darting about observing everything thoroughly. He has a red beard with a somewhat black coloring and wears it rather long and thick. But like most Russians he wears the hair of his head cut short with a razor."

Metropolitan Makary had also died in 1563, replaced by a priest named Afanasy, who was not afraid to criticize Ivan, warning him that "no Christian tsar has the right to treat people like animals." But Afanasy was far from the only source of resistance. Ivan's cruelty had already engendered a backlash, and by 1564 his support among the ruling classes had significantly dwindled.

So on December 3, Ivan pulled a publicity stunt, packing up all his household goods, jewels, wardrobe, and furniture on sleighs. Everything was taken to the remote, fortified Alexandrova Sloboda (the word *sloboda* means "large village"), a hunting lodge about sixty miles from Moscow. On January 3, 1565, Ivan sent letters to the leading boyars and clergymen of the capital, accusing them of the basest forms of corruption. "With a heavy heart," he added, he was resigning his throne to seek life elsewhere, "wherever God may lead him." In another letter to his subjects, which was read aloud to the gathered commoners in the Kremlin square, Ivan told them that he had no quarrel with them, but they would get far worse treatment under the boyars than they had ever received from him.

Naturally, this engendered a public outcry along the lines of "bring back the czar!" and rumors spread among the people that the boyars had driven him away, countered by other tales that the masses planned a retaliatory attack on the boyars. The nobles urged Ivan to return, giving him carte blanche to punish any corrupt evildoers among their ranks.

Ivan's stunt had worked. But when the thirty-four-year-old czar returned to Moscow, he was a shadow of his former physical bulk. His hair had fallen out in clumps, his features were sunken, and his skin was sallow. His eyes had a crazed, glazed look about them.

Things were going to be different around Russia from then on. Ivan divided his territory into two regions. He would rule the *oprichnina*—the "land apart." The balance of his realm, to be known as the *zemschina*—would be ruled by the boyars, subject to the czar's jurisdiction. Ivan created a team of special forces called the *oprichniki*—the men apart—policemen and personal bodyguards who swore undying loyalty to him. The home base for these licensed marauders was Alexandrova Sloboda, where the men lived monastic lives, robed in black cassocks and addressing one another as "brother." They worshiped as ascetic monks did—with long hours and limited personal possessions.

As marauding horsemen, garbed head to toe in terrifying black, they hung from their saddles the severed head of a dog (emblematic of the *oprichnikis'* constant vigilance over the country), and a broom (for sweeping away the enemies of the czar). These police, chosen from six thousand nobles, were personally handpicked by Ivan and had free rein to plunder and ravage at will, uprooting wealthy families at their whim and appropriating their real estate. During the particularly cold winter of 1565,

Ivan's *oprichniki* displaced some twelve thousand land-owners and their families, creating an army of homeless.

The *oprichniki* were responsible for carrying out Ivan's judicial assassinations in whatever form he ordered them to take place. In one such instance, Prince Simeon Rostovsky, who had long been a thorn in the czar's side for several reasons, including his opposition to Ivan's first marriage, was taken to the frozen Vetluga River, where a hole was dug in the ice. One of the *oprichniki* leaned down from his horse and, with a single swipe of his saber, beheaded the prince, dumping the body into the hole and returning the head to Ivan. The czar wagged his finger at the decapitated append-age, scolding, "Head, head—you with your crooked nose—you were very thirsty for blood while you were still alive, but now that you are dead, you will quench your thirst in water!" He gave the prince's head a swift kick and com-manded that it be dumped into the river.

The *oprichniki* also brought Ivan's victims to Alexan-drova. As a small boy, Ivan had learned how to treat captives from observing the way his mother dealt with her enemies. She would have been proud of her son's modus operandi at Alexandrova. A German translator of the era explained that "a man invited by the tyrant to Alexandrova sets out feel-ing that the Day of Judgment has arrived because no one returns from there." At Alexandrova, Ivan devised par-ticularly brutal, albeit creative forms of torture and execu-tion: flaying the skin off a man's back by boiling him alive; roasting him in a giant frying pan; subjecting victims to the knout (a long horsewhip particular to Russia); plucking off one's nails with pincers; sawing a naked body in two by friction from a length of rope; and various other methods of hacking and dismemberment. For after-dinner sport, Ivan's favorite *oprichnina* executioner, Maliuta-Skuratov, would round up some serving women, have them stripped naked and publicly whipped, and then sent into a pit to run after squawking chickens while his *oprichniki* shot arrows at them. Most of the women had already been raped.

It was commonly believed that Ivan once sewed a man into a bearskin and tossed him into an arena, where he was set upon by hungry hunting dogs. The czar was also known to send his victims into the arena gladiator-style—dispatching seven monks armed with spears to fight against seven bears. Needless to say the score was bears 7, Russians 0.

Eyewitnesses noticed that the odors of roasting and rotting flesh, of blood and urine and excrement emitted under the most gruesome circumstances, gave the czar a perverse, almost sexual thrill. Ivan would take a break from gourmandizing and washing down the numerous courses with wine, vodka, and kvass to instigate a little torture session. Afterward, flushed with satiety and "beaming with contentment," he would "talk more cheerfully than usual," before heading off to church where he, a true believer, would pray devoutly, utterly free of guilt or compunction for the mutilation and murders he had just witnessed or participated in.

One eyewitness, Albert Schlichting, spent considerable time observing Ivan's behavior in the dungeons of Alexandrova Sloboda. According to Schlichting, "The tyrant habitually watches with his own eyes those who are being tortured and put to death. Thus it happens frequently that blood spurts onto his face. He is not in the least disturbed by the blood but on the contrary he is exhilarated by it and shouts exultantly: '*Goida! Goida!*' [Hurrah] and then all those around him shout: '*Goida! Goida!*' But whenever the tyrant observes someone standing there in silence, he immediately suspects that he is sympathetic to the prisoner, and asks why he is sad when he should be joyful, and then orders him to be cut to pieces. And every day people are killed at his orders."

Schlichtling counted about twenty judicial murders a day in Alexandrova Sloboda and also remarked that Ivan intentionally left the corpses unburied, because the stench itself was a deterrent to others.

To visiting foreign ambassadors Ivan showed an entirely different face: courtly, cultured, and charming. A modern FBI profiler would probably peg him as a textbook psychopath. Yet for all his brutality, Ivan must have had a conscience, because he didn't sleep well, employing three blind men to tell him bedtime stories every night until he drifted off into the Land of Nod.

In 1567, the thirty-seven-year-old Ivan, who had become something of an Anglophile, conceived of the idea of espousing himself to England's thirty-four-year-old Virgin Queen, although he was still married to the czarina Maria. Elizabeth I prevaricated, as she did whenever the topic of her marrying was raised by anyone. Although privately she considered Ivan a nutcase, Elizabeth refused to refuse him outright because she was just as interested as Ivan was in negotiating a trade agreement between England and Russia.

Ivan cheerfully considered putting Maria aside to marry Queen Elizabeth, but that issue was mooted on September 1, 1569, when Maria died. Ivan suspected poisoning. Again. Needing a scapegoat to blame for her death, he executed his own cousin Prince Vladimir Andreyevich and his entire family. Ivan trumped up a conspiracy in which some of his minions bribed a palace cook to accuse Vladimir of attempting to poison him. Ivan then fed poison to the prince; his wife, Eudoxia; and their two young sons and blithely watched them convulse and die. Then he ordered Vladimir's mother, Princess Euphrosyne, to be removed from the convent where he had previously banished her and had her drowned in the river.

After learning that the king of Sweden had been overthrown by his people, Ivan began to fear for his own throne. He wrote to Queen Elizabeth and asked her to grant him asylum in England, if it became necessary for him to flee Russia. And he surrounded himself with additional bodyguards. His paranoia increasing, Ivan would stab anyone who displeased him with the bayonetlike point of his metal-tipped staff. When a peasant's horse bolted and ran across the road in front of him, followed by the distraught owner, Ivan had them both chopped up into pieces and tossed into a swamp. He listened to informants of all stripes and acted on their tips, regardless of whether the intelligence was genuine or invented. According to his German translator, Ivan delighted "in listening to informers. He does not care whether their information is true or false if it provides him with an opportunity to destroy people."

As one might expect, all this mental instability led to Ivan's sabotaging his own ability to rule effectively. For one thing, he was executing some of his most skilled military commanders with scant evidence of wrongdoing. And in the absence of qualified leadership, Russia suffered some of its greatest defeats in the Livonian wars.

In 1570, the losses in Livonia triggered Ivan's greatest single act of brutality. He accused the leaders of the city of Novgorod of treason and sacked the city. Ivan's death squad, the *oprichniki*, slaughtered thousands, subjecting the citizens to slow deaths by myriad forms of torture: flogging with the knout or whip; hacking off limbs and ears; slitting noses; castrating; disemboweling; boiling or roasting people alive; as well as tying their freezing bodies to sleighs and dumping them into the icy river. Entire families were murdered together; the czar's butchers never spared women and children. Between fifteen and eighteen thousand souls perished, and the Volkhov River was choked with dismembered corpses and bits of human remains.

While Novgorod's embers still smoldered, in February 1570 Ivan's army decided to attack the nearby city of Pskov, stationing themselves outside the city walls. When Ivan entered Pskov, he was confronted by a *starets*, or holy man, one of the ascetic hermits whose spirituality and clairvoyance was given great credence by Russians of all social castes. This particular *starets*, named Mikula, verbally attacked Ivan from the safety of his house, shouting, "Ivan! Ivan! How much longer will you shed innocent blood? Enough. Go home! Or great misfortune will befall you!"

Ivan entered the *starets*'s dwelling, where Mikula offered him a piece of meat.

Ivan declined it. "I am a Christian. I do not eat meat during Lent," he insisted.

The holy man responded, "You do much worse! You feed upon human flesh and blood, forgetting not only Lent, but God himself!"

According to legend, the skies darkened and the air resounded with thunder. Taking it as a religious omen, Ivan spared the residents of Pskov, ordering his troops to withdraw.

On July 25, 1570, Ivan celebrated his return to Moscow by setting up a spectacular torture arena in the Kremlin's Red Square. Seventeen gallows were erected along with an enormous frying pan suspended over a pile of logs that would provide the fuel for a massive human parboil. Ivan staged another bloodbath, viciously executing some three hundred of his former favorites, including many of his comrades in debauchery, having falsely accused them of giving the inhabitants of Novgorod advance warning of the attack. Some men had their skin flayed off like an eel's, by alternate immersions in boiling and freezing water. Others were hanged, had their throats slit, or were hacked to pieces or impaled on spears. Additional murders were conducted indoors: When the widow of one of Ivan's victims refused to reveal where her late husband stored his treasure, the *oprichniki* stripped her naked and made her sit astride a thick rope, which tortured her into submission. Prince Telepnev suffered an agonizingly slow death while being forced to watch the murderers rape his mother. The wives of eighty of Ivan's prisoners were drowned in the Moskva River while their husbands' corpses lay rotting in the sun, suffering the added indignity of being denied a Christian burial.

This litany merely scratches the surface of Ivan's cruelty; it is beyond the scope of this chapter to enumerate all of the murders he ordered or committed or to describe every method of torture he devised.

By 1571, it was clear that the unchecked brutality of the *oprichniki* had done far more harm than good. The lands they had seized had gone unworked, resulting in unemployment, crop failure, and starvation, and with them came epidemics of cholera and bubonic plague. The invading Tartars (this time an army of forty thousand) had help from Ivan's many enemies within Russia. His disorganized forces could not stave them off. Many soldiers simply gave up, retreating from Alexandrova to Moscow. They joined the ranks of thousands of refugees who had taken to the roads leading into the capital. Ivan prepared to flee north to the White Sea with a cadre of his most trusted bodyguards.

The enemy reached the gates on May 24, 1571, and the Crimean khan, Devlet, torched the capital. Within six hours, the entire city of Mosow had been reduced to piles of smoking rubble. The Tartars returned to the Crimea with thousands of Russian captives.

The following year, Ivan combined the forces of his two regions, the *oprichnina* and the *zemschina*, and managed to repulse the Tartars' annual invasion. But in the fall of 1572 he finally disbanded the *oprichniki*. As cruel in their repudiation as he had been in their support, Ivan made it an offense punishable by a public whipping to even mention the word.

With his own brand of whimsy, Ivan decided in 1575 to abandon his throne again, appointing Simeon Bekbulatovich, a Christian Tartar, as his successor. Simeon never received the czar's crown, however. The reason for this odd power shift might be explained by Ivan's belief in the prediction that he would die that year. However, his rationale behind selecting the unknown and untested Simeon is anyone's guess. Ivan began referring to himself by his proper name, Ivan Vasilyevich, or by the nickname "Little Ivan of Moscow," and made a grand show of humbly petitioning Simeon anytime he wanted something.

But the fortune-tellers were wrong; Ivan survived, and the following year he was back on his throne. Simeon was given a plum administrative job and retreated into the annals of history.

The 1570s were inauspicious years for Ivan. The Livonian

war dragged on. Sweden joined forces with Lithuania and Poland to repel any Russian onslaughts. The combined forces were led by the charismatic Stephan Báthory (the uncle of the "Blood Countess," Elizabeth, or Erzsébet, Báthory, whom we'll meet in a later chapter). Short and stocky, with a low forehead, high cheekbones, and a long, pointed nose, the forty-three-year-old Stephan had begun his political career in obscurity, rose to become the *voivode*, or military commander (often translated as a prince or duke) of Transylvania. He was crowned king of Poland and Lithuania on December 12, 1575, through popular election by Polish nobles. Ivan had always detested (as well as distrusted) him. If a king could be elected, what did that bode for an autocracy? Not only that, Báthory refused to call Ivan "czar," referring to him as the "grand prince" in his correspondence.

Stephan Báthory began winning the Livonian War. He tormented Ivan after the czar complained that Báthory was denigrating the corpses of his Russian soldiers, writing, "You accuse me of abusing the dead. I do not abuse them. You, however, torture the living. Which is worse?" Báthory asked rhetorically.

The lengthy Livonian War exacted a huge price from Russia. To afford it, Ivan borrowed from the nobles. They in turn worked the peasants even harder to increase production so they could afford to fund the conflict. Exhausted and starving, many of them ran away from their overlords, taking to the roads. According to an Italian visitor at the time, "No one lives in [the villages]. The fields are deserted and the forest growth over them is fresh."

The peasants' desertion caused the predictably furious Ivan to enact new laws governing their existence. Instead of quitting the farms after the harvest every November in order to seek new employment, as of 1581 their rights to leave a landowner were restricted by the czar. The peasants would become serfs, enslaved to the land in perpetuity. Serfdom would not be abolished until 1861.

Ivan added Siberia to his empire in 1583 after negotiating with the leader of the Stroganovs, a family of wealthy Russian landowners who organized an army of cutthroats to invade Siberia. He threatened to execute the Stroganovs, but was persuaded to change his mind by the outlaws' leader, who showed the czar a passel of stunning furs and offered him Siberia if he would specifically spare the Stroganovs. Ivan accepted the deal.

Ivan's distrust of everything on two legs extended to his relationship with his own heir. Although by then the czarevitch (twenty-seven years old in 1581) wasn't exactly a child, his father mistrusted him as well as all of his friends. The younger Ivan was well educated, intelligent, charming, popular, and as much of a psychopath as his papa. He also dared to openly disagree with his father. The czarevitch reveled in brutality and debauchery, and yet he devoted many of his leisure hours to writing a life of the gentle Saint Anthony. But his interest in a mild-mannered martyr did not make the younger Ivan a nice guy, by any means. The czarevitch remained in every way the polar opposite of his younger brother Feodor—a sweet-tempered young man with none of the psychotic quirks of the two Ivans. Unfortunately, Feodor was developmentally disabled or "simple," and therefore was considered unfit to rule.

Depending on the scholar, there are discordant versions of the demise of the czarevitch. In one iteration, the two Ivans were sitting in the Kremlin palace on the evening of November 14, 1581, along with the czarevitch's very pregnant spouse, Elena. Things came to a head when the czar decided to criticize his daughter-in-law for not being properly dressed. Elena was the czarevitch's third wife, the first two having been dispatched to convents; evidently she was wearing only one dress instead of the traditional three—and it was a flimsy garment at that. In his outrage, Ivan smacked Elena so hard with the back of his hand that she fell over backward in her chair. Her husband took her side, although it's not clear whether he saw the attack or confronted his father after hearing that the czar had dared to strike his pregnant wife. The czar became so enraged at his son's temerity that he brained him with his metal-tipped walking staff. The czarevitch crumbled to the floor in a bloody heap, the victim of a cracked skull. Doctors could not save him and he died five days later on November 19. Not too long afterward, Elena miscarried, expiring soon after that—although that's only one version of the story. In a conflicting recitation of events, after Elena miscarried, she retired to a convent and was awarded the income of an entire town in perpetuity, living out her days with this undesired largesse.

Nevertheless, a single moment of rage had cost Ivan the Terrible his entire dynasty. The czar "tore his hair and beard like a mad man, lamenting and mourning," according to an unnamed witness. He clawed at the walls with his fingernails and cried out his son's name.

This act of infanticide profoundly changed Ivan. Focusing on the carnage he had wrought during his reign, he began to make a list of all the people he had executed or had otherwise caused to be murdered. Sometimes he didn't even know (or remember) the names of his victims, so he wrote "with his wife," or "with his sons," or "names known only to God." The list ran to more than three thousand names. He pardoned each of the people post-mortem, sent copies of the list to monasteries, and asked the monks to pray for his victims.

In 1582, while Ivan was married to Maria Nagaya, his eighth wife, he revisited the notion of espousing an English-woman, and became fixated on a distant relation of Queen Elizabeth's named Mary Hastings, the daughter of the Earl of Huntingdon. First, however, he required proof of her beauty in the form of a portrait. Depending on the source, Elizabeth and Mary either seriously considered Ivan's proposition and his assurance that he would cheerfully put aside his present wife, as she was only a commoner's daughter, *or* the two Brits never remotely conscienced the idea of packing Mary off to Moscow to wed a bloody tyrant. What *is* certain is that Queen Elizabeth dithered and delayed as usual, claiming that Mary was recuperating from smallpox and was there-fore unfit to sit for a portrait. For years afterward, Mary's friends mockingly called her the "Empress of Muscovy."

By then, the czar's health had been deteriorating for years. He endured increasing immobility in his joints and spine, evidently suffering from a very painful form of arthritis. Servants carried him about in a chair. A bowel complaint bloated his body and caused it to stink. Even his testicles were swollen. According to Jerome Horsey, an English diplomat and explorer who spent considerable time at Ivan's court, the czar had begun "grievously to swell of the cods, with which he had most horribly offended above fifty years altogether, boasting of a thousand virgins he had deflowered and thousands of children of his begetting destroyed." Given the fact that Ivan began to take advan-tage of what he believed to be his royal prerogatives when he was in his midteens, the estimation of "a thousand virgins" may not be much of an exaggeration.

Toward the end of his days, Ivan's favorite pastime was to be carried into his treasure room, where he would spend hours amid his jewels, telling his visitors about the individual healing properties of various gemstones. In the early months of 1584, when a comet appeared in the sky with a tail in the shape of a cross, he was certain that it foretold his imminent demise. Ivan was wrong, in that he continued to live out the year, but his health diminished further during the winter of 1584. He consulted dozens of fortune-tellers from Lapland, which at the time was known for its talented prognosticators. Sixty of them were asked by Ivan's BFF of the moment, Bogdan Belsky, to provide daily updates on the czar's condition, and they seemed to agree that he would die on March 18, 1584. Ivan (or Bodgan—historians disagree on the source of the warning) threatened to execute all of them if he didn't expire on cue.

The czar spent that day as he did any other. "According to the fortune tellers, today is the day I should draw my last breath. But I feel my strength reviving. So let the imposters prepare for death themselves!" he told an aide. As the evening wore on, he gleefully looked forward to killing the bevy of astrologers—who warily reminded him that the day wasn't over yet.

According to legend, as Ivan set up his chess pieces, the king and queen collapsed prophetically. Moments later the czar slumped over his chessboard with a loud cry of anguish. He was carried to his bed, and like his father had done in his waning minutes, Ivan survived just long enough to be made an instant monk (but only temporarily, so that he could die a humble man), before he shuffled off his mortal coil.

Ivan had reigned for fifty of his fifty-three years. To some, he was considered an empire builder for seeking to annex lands to the south and east (such as Kazan) and to the west (such as Livonia); but to most, he was little more than a remarkably cruel despot. Ivan's only surviving son, the affable (and euphemistically referred to as "simple") Feodor, became the next czar—and the puppet of his own council of advisers, particularly his brother-in-law, Boris Godunov. After Feodor's death in 1598, the Romanov dynasty came to power. They would rule Russia until Czar Nicholas II was deposed in 1917; Nicholas and his entire family were assassinated in 1918.

So, how "terrible" was Ivan? And was he measurably worse than some of his erstwhile successors, or even than other sovereigns of the era? For example, Edward VI, Mary I, and Elizabeth I of England were known to have burned religious heretics alive. But none of Ivan's contemporaries *institutionalized* brutality to such an extent or committed mass murder of whole cities and towns, as well as of entire families. And none of them tortured, maimed, and murdered their enemies for the sheer pleasure of watching them die. For viciousness and vindictiveness, Ivan trumped them all.

In 1944, the Latvian-born film director Sergei Eisenstein brought Ivan's life to the silver screen in the first part of a cinematic trilogy. (Part one was released in 1944, part two in 1958, and part three in 1988.) Eisenstein was criticized by the Soviet dictator Joseph Stalin for not showing a complete portrait of the czar (even though he lived to see only the first of the film's three parts). "Ivan the

Terrible was cruel," Stalin admitted to Eisenstein. "You can show he was cruel. But you must show why he needed to be cruel." To provide a bit of perspective, Stalin made "Ivan Grozny" look like a rank amateur in the slaughter department, responsible for the deaths of (depending on the source) anywhere from three million to sixty million Russians, excluding those who died in famines during his iron-fisted tenure.

On April 23, 1953, a few weeks after Stalin's death, Ivan's corpse was exhumed. Threads of the monk's cassock still clung to the skeleton. The bones were examined and found to contain traces of quicksilver and arsenic—not necessarily an indication of poisoning, as Ivan was very ill for some time before his death and many medications of the era contained those elements. Movie cameras recorded the event and after the scientists were satisfied, the despot's remains were covered with sand and the coffin was resealed, allowing Ivan to enjoy a peace he never accorded to his victims.

And for what it's worth, the remains of the czar can repose in eternity, safe in the twisted knowledge that there was one thing he achieved that Stalin never could. Mass tortures and corpse counts aside, Ivan the Terrible will forever be considered Russia's greatest royal pain.

LETTICE KNOLLYS

1543–1634

*I*MAGINE THAT YOU ARE THE QUEEN OF ENGLAND, THE most powerful woman in the world, with everything at your fingertips, your every desire, every whim, made manifest. Then imagine that someone you grew up with, almost but not quite like two cherries on a single stem—imagine that more than anything in the world, she wants to be you. She shares your peach-colored skin and russet hair. And she shares your blood, though she is not the daughter of a king, as you are. But she wants people's heads to turn in a double take when her silk gowns rustle down the corridors at court, because in looks and manner she is Your Majesty's doppelgänger, dressing herself in the sort of finery that only queens can afford. She can ape your wardrobe, but she can never wear your crown. She can't be you, so she steals your man.

What could be more cloying or annoying than the copycat royal pain, who usurped not with the sword, but with sexuality and psychology? War was declared and waged right under the queen's nose, with an entire court to witness it. For the combative Tudor cousins Lettice Knollys and Queen Elizabeth it was the boudoir, and not a place like Bosworth Field, that became a battleground.

Elizabeth I was the daughter of Henry VIII and Anne Boleyn. Lettice Knollys's mother was Lady Catherine Carey, the daughter of Mary Boleyn Carey, Anne's older sister—making the two feisty and formidable redheads first cousins once removed. Therefore, technically speaking, Lettice Knollys was not a royal because she was neither the parent, sibling, nor offspring of a monarch. But she was such a royal pain, a thorn in her cousin Elizabeth's side, that she warrants inclusion in this volume. Of course, there are people, including sixteenth-century contemporaries of the key players in this drama, who believe that Catherine Carey, born sometime around 1524, was a royal by-blow, the bastard child of Mary Boleyn and Henry VIII, which would technically make Lettice one-quarter royal.

Soon after Elizabeth ascended the throne in November 1558, Lettice's parents were awarded prominent positions at court. Catherine Knollys (Mary Boleyn's married daughter), became one of Elizabeth's senior ladies of the bedchamber, and Lettice's father, Francis, was made vice chamberlain of Her Majesty's household. Then in her midteens, Lettice, too, was appointed to a plum position at court as a gentlewoman of the queen's bedchamber.

In December 1560 she wed Walter Devereux, 2nd Viscount Hereford, who would be made 1st Earl of Essex in 1572. Lettice left court after her marriage and bore Devereux five children in quick succession, reappearing at court in 1565, when she was very pregnant with her son Robert.

And here's where part of the scandal begins: Even in her delicate condition, Lettice completely captivated the Earl of Leicester—the queen's favorite, Robert Dudley. Surely it tickled Lettice on several levels to have captured his fancy. The very fact that Dudley was so adored by Elizabeth meant that all eyes at court were upon him. And if Dudley was watching Lettice, then everyone at court was watching her, too.

The Spanish ambassador, Diego Guzmán de Silva, who found Lettice to be one of the prettiest women at court, cheerfully sent his employer a dispatch announcing that Dudley was utterly smitten with Her Majesty's gorgeous cousin.

Suddenly, the redheaded viscountess was no longer the third bedchamber woman on the left, but the beauty about whom every tongue at Whitehall was buzzing. It undoubtedly thrilled her. After all, her name was being spoken in the same breath with her cousin the queen's!

Ten years separated the two women, and it may be safe to assume that every time Elizabeth looked at Lettice, she saw a younger, prettier, and equally proud version of herself. Lettice possessed the same dark sparkling eyes as her late great-aunt, Anne Boleyn, and the abundant auburn hair, rosebud pout, and flawless, pale complexion of the Tudors, an enviable bonus in an age of smallpox. She was seductive and knew how to use her charm to maximum effect. But among her less adorable qualities were vanity, envy, arrogance, and possessiveness—attributes that perhaps made Lettice appear even more identical to Elizabeth. Lettice had also inherited the Boleyns' ambitious streak and saw the queen as a cousin, not as a boss. Consequently, she refused to show the deference due Elizabeth as her sovereign. In Lettice's mind, the two women were equals. It was a war she couldn't win, but it would never deter her from trying.

Elizabeth wished to be magnanimous to Lettice because she was the daughter of two of her most faithful courtiers, but her young cousin's behavior made it difficult to like her, let alone to be kind. And when the queen caught wind of Dudley's infatuation with Lettice, she castigated him for his disloyalty to her. So Dudley endeavored to cool his ardor, but he couldn't keep away from Lettice for long.

Her favorite's apparent infatuation for her look-alike kinswoman was particularly vexing to Elizabeth, because of her relationship to the parties involved. And the fact that the sexual tension between Lettice and Dudley was not only noticed by all, but was the talk of the court, infuriated the queen no end. Elizabeth was practically legendary for demonstrating precious little sympathy for other people's romantic entanglements. Frankly, she discouraged them entirely; messy relationships got in the way of people's duties and responsibilities at court. They were also a perpetual reminder of her own choice to be England's bride instead of sharing a warm bed with a spouse of her own. And Lettice's outrageous flirtation with Dudley—particularly when she was married to someone else and carrying her husband's child—rubbed metaphorical salt into Her Majesty's wounded ego. Small wonder that Elizabeth was reluctant to surround herself with a bevy of beautiful waiting women. It was vital that everyone in the kingdom, the world at large, and within her royal court acknowledge that she was the queen bee, and the sun around which every other planet revolved. To hold the throne and command everyone's respect, she knew there could be no distractions, or the attention they claimed would dilute her authority. All eyes must be on her at all times; the prescribed function of her courtiers was the single-minded responsibility to serve her.

Elizabeth engaged far fewer female attendants than any

of her predecessors had done. She passive-aggressively discouraged courtiers from bringing their wives to live with them at court, by requiring them to endure cramped and unpleasant lodgings. The few married women in the royal household had obtained the queen's permission to wed; and even so, Elizabeth considered their wedlock an unnecessary and unwanted intrusion, and made it clear that their domestic arrangements irked her. They were at court to serve her—not a husband. The single females would also have to receive Her Majesty's permission to marry; if they wed without it, they did so at their peril. And yet, deliberately raising the topic of matrimony, Elizabeth would tease her waiting women, often to the point of torment. According to her godson, Sir John Harrington, "She did oft aske the ladies around her chamber, If they lovede to thinke of marriage"—and woe betide the lovestruck girl who answered honestly that she dreamed of becoming a bride.

Although everyone feared the queen's legendary Tudor temper and quaked at the possibility of incurring her wrath, because humans are human, secret marriages were made. Worse still, clandestine liaisons were furtively enjoyed under the royal eaves of various palaces, despite Elizabeth's efforts to enforce strict morality at court. Even if a woman didn't become pregnant, her amorous secret would soon be revealed. Times had not changed since one of Henry VIII's courtiers had observed, "There is nothing done or spoken but it is with speed known in the court." Even the queen herself acknowledged her complete want of privacy, remarking, "I do not live in a corner. A thousand eyes see all I do."

As to the queen's personal morality, no one has ever been sure. It's another of history's great unsolved and highly debated mysteries as to whether her "virgin queen" persona was sincere or merely a magnificent public relations scam. Most specifical, although one can speculate on the ramifications involved, no one can state for certain whether Elizabeth ever allowed herself to consummate her notorious flirtation with the companion of her youth and lifelong favorite, Robert Dudley, Earl of Leicester. Did she frown upon extramarital liaisons only to distract attention from her own? Or was she as pure as she claimed? At an early age, Elizabeth had forsworn the state of wedlock. It was none other than her childhood friend, "sweet bonny Robin" (as she had nicknamed young Robert Dudley), who was sitting beside the eight-year-old Elizabeth, then a former princess stripped of her birthright and legitimacy, when she resolutely announced that she would never marry. Her mother's fall from her father's favor was lesson enough in the fickleness and cruelty of husbands. And when little Elizabeth uttered her famous remark she had just lost another stepmother, after Henry executed his fifth wife, Kathryn Howard. Elizabeth had also seen her half sister Mary fall under the spell of the undeserving Philip of Spain, too deeply in love with her husband to acknowledge that he was, like their father, false in love as well as in politics.

As queen, Elizabeth only begrudgingly permitted her waiting women to wed. She had a long history of punishing attendants who contracted secret marriages, particularly if they'd been careless enough to get themselves pregnant first. Bess Throckmorton had the temerity to succumb to the formidable charms of Sir Walter Raleigh, wedding the adventurer and bearing his baby. Bess was dispatched to the Tower, as was Sir Walter. Yet he was released months before his wife was liberated. And after Bess was freed, she was never again welcome at court.

One of Elizabeth's gentlewomen of the bedchamber, Anne Vavasour, gave birth to the Earl of Oxford's child in the maidens' chamber. The infant's squalling revealed Anne's secret and she was sent packing to the Tower when she was scarcely postpartum.

In general, the queen came down hardest on the women whose marriages threatened Elizabeth's security on the throne, or who had somehow crossed or angered her. By these lights, no one would transgress as greatly as Lettice—although there was a first runner-up in the How to Massively Provoke the Wrath of Her Majesty sweepstakes.

Another lady-in-waiting—though far less brazen than Lettice—would eventually incur Elizabeth's enmity for secretly wedding a courtier. Not only did Lady Douglas Sheffield marry without the queen's consent, but she, too, fell for the one man who was off-limits: the Earl of Leicester.

Also more naive than Lettice, Douglas started out with more than an unfortunate first name. In 1560, she left court to marry the 2nd Baron Sheffield. She bore him two children, but the baron died at the age of thirty in 1568. The twenty-six-year-old Douglas returned to court and was awarded the position of gentlewoman extraordinary of the privy chamber (which really meant that she was a sort of understudy, tapped to fill in for an unavailable attendant).

However, being "a lady of great beauties," according to one of her seventeenth-century descendants, Gervase Holles, Douglas was conspicuous enough to catch the eye of Robert Dudley.

Despite his protestations of undying fidelity to Elizabeth, the earl clearly had a roving eye and a libido that needed constant care and feeding. Douglas, her head undoubtedly turned by the attentions of such a well-placed man at court, encouraged Dudley's flirtation; most sources date the commencement of their clandestine affair to the early 1570s. But nothing could remain a secret at court for very long, and by 1573, their liaison was the subject of widespread gossip, particularly as the earl was also seen flirting with Douglas's nineteen-year-old sister, Frances Howard. One day Queen Elizabeth noticed the sisters quarreling and was dismayed to discover that the cause of their tiff was a sibling rivalry for Dudley's affections.

Douglas was content for a while to remain the earl's secret mistress, but eventually, she fell deeply in love with him and, quite understandably, wanted more from their relationship. Dudley, however, was hedging his bets. Not only did he wish to keep their liaison under wraps in order to avoid the queen's inevitable wrath, but he was still holding out hope that Elizabeth would finally change her mind about remaining a virgin (or at least a spinster), and consent to marry him.

Responding to his paramour's insistence that he make an honest woman of her, the earl wrote Douglas a letter, reiterating the conditions he had laid down from the start with regard to their affair. "I have, as you well know, long both liked and loved you," Dudley told Douglas. However, if he agreed to *marry* her, he would be hazarding "the ruin of my own house," and "mine utter overthrow." Referring to Elizabeth, the earl added, "If I should marry, I am sure never to have favour of them that I had rather yet never have wife than lose them."

Douglas didn't want to hear that the queen was more important to her lover than she was; but Dudley gave her a choice: to continue the status quo and remain his mistress, or to end the affair. Douglas eventually got what she wanted when she was convinced that she was pregnant with Dudley's child. She wed the forty-year-old earl in the presence of three witnesses (all of whom would later deny everything) sometime between November 11 and Christmas Day, 1573. Although the reason for the trip to the altar may have been just a false alarm, almost exactly nine months from the "I do's," Douglas (who left court before her belly began to show) gave birth to a son whom they christened Robert.

Dudley was on progress with the queen at the time. His congratulatory letter to Douglas signed "your loving husband" subsequently disappeared. And the earl began referring to the boy as "my base [illegitimate] son," although he would leave most of his property to him, which Dudley might not have done if he had really considered the child to be a bastard.

In any event, the earl didn't act very married. In 1575 he renewed his pursuit of Elizabeth, urging her to once again consider his suit. As always, she equivocated, refusing to give him a firm answer.

Throughout her reign, the queen toyed with the prospect of wedding a foreign prince, or espousing one of her own subjects, but it was all politics and prevarication. She fully intended to keep the French, the Spanish, the Swedes, Mary, Queen of Scots, and even her own parliament relegated to the role of marionettes, dangling them on a string while she pretended to be considering a match. But the Earl of Leicester, Robert Dudley, remained the love of her life. She heaped him with honors, risking her reputation (and consequently her own value on the marriage market) to spend hours alone with him. But it came with a price. Dudley's job was to worship and adore her and her alone. In that respect, he betrayed her three times by wedding other women. The last Countess of Leicester would be Elizabeth's own envious cousin, Lettice Knollys.

Morality was clearly not Dudley's strong suit. He seemed to want it all, and believed he could get it. So while poor Douglas was relegated to being proverbial chopped liver, Dudley set his sights on the kingdom's biggest catch. However, during the mid 1570s, as the queen continued to forestall his marriage proposals (which he couldn't really make in earnest or it would have been bigamy), instead of focusing his attentions on his new wife (Douglas) and their young son, the earl turned in another direction entirely. Perhaps he reasoned that if he couldn't have Elizabeth, her look-alike cousin Lettice might make an appealing substitute.

There was just a bit of a hitch: at the time, Lettice Knollys was also married—to Walter Devereux, the 1st Earl of Essex. However, Lettice's marriage to the Earl of Essex, while fruitful, was not a particularly happy one. She was reported to have felt relieved in 1573 when her husband embarked upon a diplomatic mission to Ireland that would keep him there for two years. Essex's absence gave his wife ample opportunity to flirt with the Earl of Leicester.

Just how much Lettice knew about Dudley's relationship with Douglas is unclear. But it's certain that she encouraged his attentions and pressed her advantage with him. She was unhappily married; he was hot and popular, and, more to the point, if she could snag the court favorite, her own prominence would increase. Before long, although it looked to the world like Dudley was still wooing the queen, it was

Lettice who was warming his bed. Signs that he was passionately involved with the queen's doppelgänger were his magnanimous gift to Lettice of a passel of deer from his seat at Kenilworth Castle and a standing invitation to Lettice and her sister Anne West, Lady De La Warr, to hunt there at any time. By the summer of 1575 Lettice was a regular fixture at Kenilworth (just as, centuries later, Camilla Parker Bowles would assume the role of chatelaine at Prince Charles's Highgrove estate while he was still married to Diana).

In November Lettice's husband, the earl of Essex, returned to England to discover that he had been cuckolded by Dudley. The extramarital affair was the talk of the court, and false rumors were spreading that in Essex's absence Lettice had already borne her lover two children. But there would be no duels at dawn. Instead, in 1576 Essex accepted a return posting to Ireland, where he died of dysentery that September. The Tudor rumor mill being what it was, gossip circulated that Dudley had poisoned him.

Lettice was lucky in that Dudley's less than savory reputation actually worked in her favor, because it gave her the ability to take full advantage of what her cousin Elizabeth had to assiduously avoid. People were always willing to believe the worst about the Earl of Leicester. His first wife, Amy Robsart, whom he had married in 1550, died a decade later after a mysterious fall down a short flight of steps. Although a royal court of inquiry exonerated him of any blame, it was still widely assumed that Dudley had been complicit (perhaps with the queen herself) in his wife's swift and strange demise so he could clear his path to matrimony with Elizabeth.

But whether Dudley was involved (and Amy might indeed

have expired after what was just a freak household accident), he became the Elizabethan equivalent of kryptonite. As a result, the queen could never consider marrying him because their union would always be suspect—the denouement of Amy's convenient death. This left the door open for Lettice to swan in and pick up the radioactive pieces. Perhaps Elizabeth was somewhat relieved that his wife's odd demise scotched any notions of a match with Dudley—but in no way did the queen embrace the idea of his marrying anyone else. And just because Lettice may have believed that the earl's baggage made him ripe for the plucking, that didn't mean that she'd receive carte blanche to nab him.

She might have captivated Dudley, but the scales had fallen from her husband's eyes. The ailing Earl of Essex concluded that his wayward and adulterous wife was an unfit mother, and his dying wish was that their children should be removed from Lettice's custody and placed in the care of one of his relatives, the Earl of Huntingdon. As an added parting shot, in his will Essex left Lettice his estates, which he knew were mired in debt. Unsurprisingly, the queen refused to grant any financial aid to the libidinous cousin who was stealing her beloved bonny Robin.

Essex's death in September 1576 made Lettice legally available, but to her consternation Dudley evinced no interest in meeting her at the altar. Of course, he was also married to Lady Douglas Sheffield at the time, no matter how much he sought to deny it.

But just as Douglas had been, Lettice was not content to remain Dudley's mistress while he continued to angle after the biggest fish in the kingdom. Proud of her extraordinary beauty, her kinship to the queen, and her status as the Countess of Essex, she knew she was quite the catch herself—except for that little issue of her lingering debts. She couldn't exactly go out and get a job, so she desperately needed a man to assume her encumbrances. And the man she'd been shagging fit the bill perfectly. Plus, the fact that the Earl of Leicester was the queen's acknowledged favorite made him all the more desirable. How delicious it would be to get her debts discharged while sticking it to Elizabeth by stealing her man!

As his ongoing flirtation with Lettice finally blossomed into a full-blown affair, Dudley realized that he needed to ditch Douglas if he wanted to hold on to the queen's gorgeous cousin. He would begin by contending that his marriage to Douglas had never been legal.

Writing decades after the event, Douglas's descendant Gervase Holles maintained, "According to the nature of all men who think basely of their prostitutes, after he had used hir body sometime and got a base sonne . . . of hir, [he] rejected hir."

One day in 1578, Dudley arranged a meeting with Douglas in the gardens of Greenwich Palace, where he offered her the astronomical sum of £700 (more than $242,000 today) to walk away from their relationship and deny that they'd ever been lawfully married. Additionally, he wanted custody of their son.

Douglas became understandably hysterical. But eventually—and possibly in fear of her own reputation—she capitulated, accepting Dudley's bribe, as well as his offer of a consolation prize: to find her another husband.

The earl was tremendously relieved. With Douglas heading out of sight, their marital indiscretion would also be out of mind—Elizabeth's mind. Douglas's departure from his life also left Dudley free to concentrate on his romance with Lettice Knollys.

However, bestowing her sexual favors, particularly as it was generally surmised that the queen withheld them, wasn't getting Lettice any closer to the altar. So, relying upon Dudley's honor as a gentleman, the less-than-ladylike Lettice employed the oldest trick in the book. She made certain she got pregnant. Dudley and Amy Robsart had never had children; and Lettice knew that the earl was tired of Douglas and desperately wanted a legitimate heir, as he considered their son to be a bastard.

Just as Lettice had hoped, her lover caved as soon as she informed him of her pregnancy. She married Dudley in a secret ceremony at Kenilworth in the spring of 1578—with the precondition that the earl sever all ties with Douglas Sheffield. Once Dudley had complied with Lettice's demand, her next move was to insist on a formal wedding ceremony with witnesses present to attest to its legality. But Dudley had his terms, too: The marriage would have to remain a secret, because "it might not be publiquely knowne without great damage of his estate." No kidding.

Dudley was able to secure a few days' leave from Elizabeth's entourage in order to prepare his house for the wedding. He arrived at his estate in Wanstead, Essex, on September 20 and immediately contacted his chaplain, Humphrey Tyndall, informing the cleric "that he had a good seazon for borne marriadge in respect of her Majestie's displeasure and that he was then for sondry respectes and especially for the better quieting of his own conscience determined to marry the right honourable Countess of Essex."

The bride's father, Sir Francis Knollys, was one of the

witnesses at her second wedding ceremony. Being all too "acquainted with Leicester's straying loves," Sir Francis recognized that it was in his best interests to see his daughter legally wed. So on September 21, 1578, wearing "a loose gown" to conceal her swelling belly, the fecund Lettice married Leicester in a morning ceremony conducted in one of Wanstead's cozier chambers. Her brother Richard remained by the door, acting as a lookout. The ceremony took place almost two years to the day from Essex's death, although the formal period of mourning had not deterred Lettice from engaging in a passionate premarital affair with the bridegroom.

The queen arrived at Wanstead with the court two days after Lettice and Dudley's wedding and the newlyweds acted as though nothing extraordinary had happened. Dudley fawned over Elizabeth as much as he always did, and she was none the wiser—at least for the time being.

Although some sources believe that news of the marriage was whispered around court within two months of the nuptials, it's difficult to imagine that if everyone else had heard about Lettice's marriage, the queen wasn't aware of it as well. Yet if Elizabeth *had* known about her cousin's union with Dudley, she would undoubtedly have had a volatile reaction to Lettice's presence at court over the holidays, and no such explosion is recorded.

A smug Lettice attended the court's Christmas festivities in 1578 and presented her sovereign and rival with "a greate cheyne of Amber slightly garnished with golde and small perle." As for the pregnancy that tricked Dudley into popping the question, there is no further historical note about it; Lettice may have miscarried or delivered a stillbirth. She must not have appeared enceinte in December or Elizabeth surely would have noticed. Still, it's *possible*, though far-fetched, that Elizabeth didn't get wind of Lettice's marriage for a full year. According to her biographer William Camden, she was informed of it by Jean de Simier, the representative of the duc d'Anjou, her prospective bridegroom at the time. Alison Weir is among the historians who believe that Dudley himself may have privately disclosed his marriage to the queen as early as April 1579, because he left court soon afterward, ostensibly to take the waters in Buxton. However, that decision might not have been his own; considering it the ultimate betrayal, Elizabeth may in fact have banished him after hearing that he'd wed her rival.

The "Tudor cub," as the queen referred to herself, emitted a mighty roar when she discovered the couple's treachery, announcing that she would send Dudley to "rot in the Tower."

Lettice was unfazed by her cousin's rage; instead, she obnoxiously trumpeted her new status as Countess of Essex right under the queen's envious nose. But when she ostentatiously arrived at court arrayed in finery that rivaled the queen's, her chutzpah engendered a catfight. Elizabeth literally (and publicly) boxed Lettice's ears for daring to cross her—and then flaunting her triumph. "As but one sun lighten[s] this earth, [she] would have but one Queen in England," Her Majesty thundered, livid enough to make the witnesses to this altercation quake in their boots. After berating and humiliating Lettice, Elizabeth demanded that the "flouting wench" quit her sight and never darken a royal doorstep again.

The queen had been enraged at the news that Lettice had wed Dudley, but her ire exponentially intensified when she discovered that her precious Robin had *also* married Lady Douglas Sheffield, and that *they* might *still* be legally united. She became even more livid at the fact that she had not been informed of the situation when it arose, and her network of spies should have discovered it. Elizabeth had learned of the Dudley-Douglas union well after the fact via an anonymously penned letter—probably written by Lettice, who remained intent on crushing any potential rivals and ensuring, undisputedly, that she was the earl's one and only lawful wife. After receiving the tip-off letter about the nature of Dudley's liaison with Douglas, Elizabeth commanded the Earl of Sussex to conduct an inquiry for the purposes of determining whether the Earl of Leicester had indeed committed bigamy.

Although Douglas might have testified that *she* was Dudley's lawful wife, she was too terrified of the potential consequences of doing so to admit it. So she merely told Sussex that she'd "trusted the said Earl [Leicester] too much to have anything to shew to constrain him to marry her."

The queen was frustrated that Douglas would not implicate Dudley. Yet an act of vengeance turned into one of kindness (depending on how you look at it). Elizabeth insisted that their son, young Robert Dudley, be given over into her care as a royal ward. True, Douglas was no longer allowed to raise her own son, but as a displaced lady-in-waiting she understood the politics of the court and would have acknowledged that the sacrifice would have a handsome payoff. Her boy would be accorded tremendous royal preferment, which was what all courtiers spent their lives striving to achieve. One also wonders what it cost Elizabeth emotionally to take under her exalted wing the son she never could have with her beloved bonny Robin. The boy grew up to be an accomplished soldier who would have made his father proud.

Precious little took place in a royal court that did not have political undertones and ramifications. The queen's magnanimous offer to take Douglas's child into her protection was made partly in revenge against Lettice, whom she now referred to as the "she-wolf" for sinking her teeth into Dudley—the one man at court who was, at least tacitly, off-limits.

The she-wolf became persona non grata at court. Her crimes? Selfishness and arrogance; betrayal of her royal kinswoman; daring to set herself up as a rival to the highest person in the land—one who had no peer by virtue of her sovereignty. Lettice's role as a lady of the bedchamber was to cater to Elizabeth's every need and whim, but she sought instead to make *herself* the star, unwilling to sublimate her own desires to those of the queen. Consequently, Lettice endured an informal exile in the Essex countryside, and had to content herself with periodic visits from her husband, whom Elizabeth kept busy at court.

The queen condescended to forgive Dudley as long as he pretended that his marriage to Lettice had never occurred. Reminding her "sweet bonny Robin" which side his bread was buttered on, the queen wrote to him, "Whosoever professeth to love you best taketh not more comfort of your well doing or discomfort of your evildoing than ourselves."

Lettice gave birth to Leicester's son, Robert Dudley, Baron Denbigh, on June 6, 1581, and the earl immediately nicknamed the boy his "noble imp." In 1583, on the mistaken assumption that Elizabeth had forgotten all about their wedding, Lettice and Dudley began living together openly. However, soon after the earl moved to Leicester House, he discovered that the queen remained just as angry "about his maryage, for he opened up the same more plainly then ever before."

But Lettice and Leicester were not to enjoy their marital idyll for long. Their son, the little Baron Denbigh, died at Wanstead on July 19, 1584, a few weeks past his third birthday. The earl took a leave of absence from the court, returning to Wanstead for several weeks "to comfort my sorrowfull wyfe." Although the queen remained livid with Lettice and Dudley, she did send them a letter of condolence.

Lettice's mere existence so irked Elizabeth she didn't even need to be present to provoke the royal wrath. Even in her exile, Lettice managed to send the envious sovereign into a paralytic frenzy at the mere mention of her name.

Ironically, the two kinswomen were more alike than not; however, one of them had the added advantage of being queen of England. The other woman behaved as though she were. Vain, ruthless, and endlessly ambitious, Lettice desperately wished to be accorded the preferential treatment she felt was her due as Countess of Leicester and as the monarch's cousin. In the words of an unnamed courtier, "She now demeaned herself like a princess and vied in dress with the queen," arraying herself in regal splendor and traveling everywhere with an ostentatious entourage. Lettice's arrogance, her sense of entitlement, as well as her aspirations, were boundless. The colossal gall she displayed in her eagerness to draw attention to herself and away from the queen was tantamount to an act of disloyalty. The same courtier noted of Lettice, "Yet still she is as proud as ever, rides through Cheapside drawn by 4 milk-white steeds, with 4 footmen in black velvet jackets, and silver bears [Leicester's device] on their backs and breasts, 2 knights and 30 gentlemen before her, and coaches of gentlewomen, pages, and servants behind, so that it might be supposed to be the Queen or some foreign Prince or other."

Naturally, this outsize display, designed to rankle the queen, achieved the desired effect. Lettice had publicly humiliated her—risky behavior indeed.

Elizabeth's wrath increased in February 1586 after she heard the rumor that Lettice planned to join her husband in the Netherlands, where he'd been posted in 1585 to serve as Governor-General. Evidently, Lettice had no intentions of traveling light, but rather "with suche a train of ladies and gentylwomen and such ryche coches, lytters, and side-saddles, as hir majestie had none suche, and that ther should be such a courte of ladies as shuld farre passe [far surpass] hir majestie's courte heare."

The queen was seething. According to Dudley's factor at court, "This informacyon dyd not a lytle sturre hir majestie to extreme collour [choler] and dislike." He added that upon hearing that Lettice was outfitting an entourage that rivaled her own royal train, Elizabeth had released a string of "great othes [oaths], that she would have no more courtes under hir obeisance but hir owen [her own], and wold revoke you from thence with all spede."

Dudley's brother, the Earl of Warwick, warned him that "Her malice is great and unquenchable." The magnitude of the queen's ire was corroborated by her secretary William Davison, who told Dudley that the rumors regarding Lettice's extravagant travel plans "did not a little encrease the heat of her majesties offence against you."

Only when the tales turned out to be "most falce," and little more than malicious gossip, was Elizabeth mollified. But Lettice remained a pariah and would never be forgiven for what the queen perceived as the deepest possible betrayal short of political treason.

On September 4, 1588, just weeks after England's naval triumph over Spain's armada, Dudley died at Cornbury in Oxfordshire, possibly from a malarial infection. Elizabeth was utterly devastated and took to her bedchamber for days. The earl had appointed Lettice to be the executor of his estates; therefore, any legal wrangling over the distribution of his property became her responsibility. Robert Dudley, the earl's "base" son by Douglas Sheffield, was one such claimant. He had inherited Kenilworth, but the home's adjoining manors comprised part of Lettice's jointure as Leicester's widow.

Lettice was also saddled with her late husband's massive debts, amounting to about £50,000 (more than $16 million today), half of which was owed to the crown. Under the circumstances, Elizabeth had no intentions of forgiving so much as a farthing. To satisfy a mere fraction of Dudley's encumbrances, the queen demanded Leicester House and commanded Lettice to hand over a quantity of jewels.

Lettice complied. She'd been metaphorically bloodied, but remained unbowed. And like a cat (or perhaps more specifically, a cougar), she landed on her feet. Rather than grieve and mope about after Dudley's death, Lettice, who was described by a contemporary as having "a light, easy, healable nature," swiftly found herself another man. In July 1589 she took a third husband—a boy toy twelve or thirteen years her junior named Christopher Blount. Blount had been Leicester's Master of the Horse. He was also a hell-raising friend of her oldest son, Robert Devereux, who was now the 2nd Earl of Essex.

No stranger to scandal when it came to picking men,

Lettice had once again set tongues wagging; even her own son tsk-tsked over his mother's "unhappy choyce." The rumor mill churned up lurid tales that Lettice had become Blount's lover in 1587 and had poisoned Leicester so that she could wed her young stud.

Even with Dudley dead and buried, Lettice remained the target of Elizabeth's rage, and the cousins' games of brinkmanship continued. If Lettice could find herself a hot young guy to wear on her arm, Her Majesty could do the same. And Elizabeth's choice would really push Lettice's buttons and punish her for her arrogance. Who better than Lettice's own son, Robert Devereux, the 2nd Earl of Essex? The fifty-something queen took her handsome young cousin under her wing when he was in his late teens. Essex became the monarch's new favorite, in many ways replacing Dudley, his late stepfather, in her affections. Lettice was forced to bite her tongue and tamp down her ego with the recognition that the sovereign was able to give the young man something his man-stealing mother never could: power, prestige, and the indulgent, lavish attention of a queen.

Charming and hotheaded, young Essex was quite the philanderer, even though in 1590 he had clandestinely wed the young widow of Sir Philip Sidney. It's no wonder that the new favorite kept his nuptials a secret; predictably, Elizabeth became furious when she ultimately found out about it, viewing his wedlock as a personal betrayal, but she soon forgave him. Her male courtiers rarely suffered the penalties she meted out to the ladies of her court, Lettice's banishment being the ultimate case in point.

In January 1598, Lettice, who had spent the past two years rusticating at her Staffordshire estate, Drayton Bassett, heard that the queen might be willing to welcome her back to court. So she made haste for London and settled in with her son at Essex House (formerly Leicester House, restored to young Essex by the queen) to await Her Majesty's invitation.

It was the event of the decade for the courtiers, who eagerly anticipated the reunion of the two formidable red-headed cousins. According to Rowland Whyte, "The greatest newes here at Court is an expectation that my Lady Lester [sic] shall come to kisse the Queen's hands. Yt [it] is greatly labored in, and was thought shuld have bene yesterday, but this day a hope is yt will be."

But the summons from sovereign to "she-wolf" was not forthcoming.

Four days after he wrote his first announcement, Whyte offered an update: "Her Majesty will not yet admit my lady his [Essex's] mother to come to her presence, having once given some hope of yt."

Was Elizabeth deliberately tormenting Lettice, or had she changed her mind about seeing her?

Finally, a summit was arranged for March 1, 1598, on neutral ground, at the home of Lady Chandos. A "great dinner" was prepared in anticipation of the meeting, and Lettice was ready to tender the queen a peace offering, to wit, a "faire jewel of £300" (worth approximately $67,000 today).

But "upon a soddain [sudden] she [Elizabeth] resolved not to goe, and soe sent word." Essex was so livid that the queen had once again humiliated his mother that he tried to gain access to Her Majesty while he was still in his night-dress. His entrance to the queen's chamber was refused and he went back to bed in a snit.

Angry at being played for a fool, Lettice was on the verge of returning to Staffordshire when she received the long-awaited and much-desired call. The courtiers were undoubtedly disappointed that both of the women assumed their best behavior in each other's presence. Rowland Whyte observed that "My Lady Lester [sic] was at Court, kissed the Queen's hands and her brest, and did embrace her." Elizabeth kissed Lettice as well, and their interview ended.

However, the royal embrace was *not* the kiss of peace. Lettice remained unforgiven, and when she asked to kiss Elizabeth's hands a second time, the monarch curtly rebuffed her. A few days later the queen was overheard referring to Lettice with "some wonted unkind words." The young Earl of Essex attempted to intercede, but Elizabeth brushed him off, brusquely insisting that she had no desire "to be importuned in these unpleasing matters."

But Lettice wasn't about to give up easily, and continued to press for the queen's formal recognition and reconciliation. She sent Elizabeth a dress worth £100 (more than $22,000 today), but the queen, refusing to be bribed into granting Lettice her favor, deemed the gift inappropriate. In the year 1599, Lettice once again petitioned her cousin for an audience, but this time it was not for her own sake; she was pleading for clemency for her son. The hotheaded Earl of Essex, having successfully secured a commission to command a military expedition in Ireland, had mucked everything up by flouting Elizabeth's orders and negotiating an ill-advised treaty with the enemy.

Essex had been forbidden to return from Ireland until the queen commanded him to do so, but he violated her orders and sailed for England. After two trials he was eventually found guilty of treason and incarcerated. In February

1600, Lettice moved into a residence with a view of the prison. Although it was rumored that mother and son could see each other from their respective windows, the queen refused to permit Lettice to visit him.

The dowager countess eventually moved into Essex House and the earl was released, but by then he had been stripped of public office and his only source of income, a monopoly on sweet wines, was rescinded by the queen. Broke and angry, he stewed and seethed at Essex House, as his mood shifted "from sorrow and repentance to rage and rebellion." In 1601, he began to stockpile weapons at Essex House and amass supporters for what would be the ultimate act of treason. In a spectacularly arrogant and misguided move, Essex tried to raise an army against the queen, intending to topple her from the throne. One of his coconspirators was his drinking buddy and Lettice's young husband, Christopher Blount.

Essex and Blount were sent to the Tower. This time Lettice did not ask her cousin for clemency on her son's behalf. She surely realized that such a suit would be fruitless; not only did Elizabeth continue to despise her, and would therefore be disinclined to pardon Essex, but the earl had brazenly committed treason, and the punishment for it was death. On February 25, 1601, Lettice lost her beloved son. On March 18, her young husband was also beheaded.

Essex's execution broke Elizabeth's heart as well as Lettice's. Once again, the two cousins had something in common: the love of the same man, and the aching void left by his demise. But they never met again. And Lettice never again wrote to the queen requesting Her Majesty's permission to return to court. According to Elizabeth's principal secretary, Sir Robert Cecil, "for her marriage with him [Leicester]" Lettice "was long disgraced with the Queene" and their rift was a permanent one.

In the wee hours of the morning on March 24, 1603, Elizabeth died. Lettice outlived her by thirty-one years, a lifetime in itself in the seventeenth century. She died a wealthy woman at the age of ninety-three on Christmas Day, 1634.

At her request, Lettice was buried at St. Mary's, Warwick, "by my deere lord and husband the Earle of Leicester." Reposing beside him for all eternity, which Elizabeth (who was interred at Westminster Abbey) could never do, it was Lettice Knollys who had the last, celestial, laugh.

ERZSÉBET (ELIZABETH) BÁTHORY

"The Blood Countess"
1560–1614

T HE "CRIMES" COMMITTED AGAINST THEIR FAMILY MEM-
bers and their subjects by the royals profiled in this book
run the gamut from arrogance to zealous slaughter. But
there is one "pain" who took such pleasure in inflicting it
on the most innocent of victims that her conduct can be
described only as criminally insane.

She made the Marquis de Sade look like Mother Teresa.
In an age when her English counterparts were engaged in
such ladylike pursuits as plying their needles or playing the
virginals, Erzsébet Báthory was employing red-hot pincers
and bathing in virginal blood.

Erzsébet Báthory is technically not royalty in the manner of western European kings and princes, but she earns
her chapter in this book because the terminology used to
describe central European rulers is somewhat different.
What was known as the kingdom of Hungary during most
of Erzsébet's lifetime was ruled by a sovereign, yet within
this kingdom were principalities (such as the principality
of Transylvania), wherein local nobles or *voivodes* oversaw
their own demesnes, similar to the structure of a medieval
feudal society. Erzsébet Báthory was a countess within the

kingdom of Hungary; and on her lands, her word might as well have been law, even if local officials existed to keep the peace.

The Báthorys were one of the elite Hungarian Protestant families whose members became *voivodes*; in fact, Erzsébet's maternal grandfather, Stephan Báthory, had been a *voivode* of Transylvania.

Erzsébet's parents, György and Anna, were cousins from two different branches of the family tree. Like most members of the nobility, the Báthorys prided themselves on the purity of their line, and of course rampant inbreeding often leads to insanity. Unsurprisingly, Erzsébet's family had its share of mentally deranged relations. She came by her brutality honestly—or at least genetically. Her aunt Klara was a bisexual sadomasochist with a specific talent for flagellation; one of her uncles was into devil worship; while Erzsébet's brother was merely a libidinous drunkard. Her own predilections appear to have been a fatal combination of nature and nurture.

Because of her noble rank, it was beneath Erzsébet's dignity, even as a child, to be scolded for anything she did; consequently, she grew up vain, willful, and arrogant. She would also become quite a beauty: tall, raven haired, and voluptuous, with fair skin and catlike amber eyes. Desperate to appear as fashionably pale as possible, she slathered herself with various unguents and herbal concoctions that would yield the desired pallor, particularly on her face and hands. She usually dressed in white, her gowns and headdresses encrusted with Venetian seed pearls.

Although western Europe had emerged from the Dark Ages into the comparatively enlightened and cultured Renaissance, much of the central and eastern areas of the continent had yet to cast off the brutality and superstition of the Middle Ages. Hungary was still a feudal society. The nobles owned the serfs or peasants who worked their lands and toiled within their castles and manors, although independently governed towns and villages would emerge during Erzsébet's lifetime. The Báthorys, governing Ecsed (now only a small village in present-day Hungary), were so powerful that for years local officials, including clerics, dared not challenge their authority.

When Erzsébet was a little girl in Ecsed she was permitted to witness a public execution where a Gypsy (the malfeasor) was stuffed into the freshly slit belly of a horse (while the completely innocent beast was still alive), and sewn into the warm, bloody cavity. The tortured horse writhed in pain and tried to rid itself of its unwelcome burden, while the Gypsy struggled in vain to free himself from the horse's gut. Both expired in due course, but not until they'd provided an afternoon's entertainment with their highly gruesome display.

Perhaps Erzsébet inherited her predilictions, or experiences like this may have bred in baby Báthory her taste for gruesome torture. In any case, she lived in an especially violent culture and came from a particularly demented family with a ghoulish cast of role models. Witnessing this unique form of execution, Erzsébet might have assumed that no form of torture was so grim as to be unpalatable.

She was *never* quite right in the head, however. At the age of four or five, Erzsébet began to experience epileptic seizures as well as the violent mood swings of a classic manic-depressive. She also suffered from brutally painful migraines. Though her temper was fierce, her noble birthright shielded her from chastisement, let alone punishment,

164 ♒ LESLIE CARROLL

for any bad behavior. Thus, she was able to get away with tormenting her playmates, servants, and pets.

In 1570, at the age of nine, Erzsébet was contracted in marriage to a youth six years her senior, Ferenc (pronounced Franz) Nádasdy, the son of a neighboring count, who would in time inherit the title in his own right, although the Nádasdys were not considered to be quite as illustrious or as powerful a family as the Báthorys. The couple's formal betrothal was announced the following year. According to the custom of the time, Erzsébet was sent to reside with her future mother-in-law, where she would learn how to manage a household. There, she may have been as unsupervised as she was at Ecsed, because it was rumored that in 1574 she gave birth to an illegitimate daughter fathered by a peasant boy. The child, if there ever was one, was purportedly smuggled away by a trustworthy local woman, who was paid handsomely to take the baby to Wallachia and never to return during Erzsébet's lifetime.

Before Erzsébet could get herself into further trouble, on May 8, 1575, in the presence of forty-five hundred guests she was married to Ferenc Nádasdy in the palace at Varannó in Hungary. Erzsébet was fourteen years old; her bridegroom was twenty. At the time Ferenc was already a war hero known for his feats of athletic prowess off the battlefield, although even his mother admitted that her boychick was "no scholar." Upon wedding Erzsébet, Ferenc made the rare move of adopting his bride's surname as his own, because it would greatly enhance his prestige to be thought of as a Báthory. Their marriage united two of Hungary's greatest families, though unlike the Báthorys (who were known to be psychotic), the Nádasdys were believed to be respectable, conservative, and even pious. Yet Ferenc, a fearsome general and the scourge of the enemy Turks, was somewhat afraid of the intensity and formidability of his adolescent bride. Even as a child growing up in his family's home, Erzsébet had unnerved him during his infrequent return visits for rest and recreation.

Ferenc wouldn't be the first to marry a younger, smarter wife. Erzsébet was much better educated than her husband, able to read and write in Greek, Latin, German, and her native Hungarian. Nevertheless, it's always good for spouses to have common interests, and in the case of Erzsébet and Ferenc, they shared a particularly unusual one: Both were sadists.

Ferenc's temper was notorious. His favorite parlor trick was to toss a pair of Turkish prisoners in the air and catch them on the points of his swords. As a warlord he didn't spare the rod, savagely flogging and beating both adversary and underling, and earning himself the swaggeringly cool nickname "the Black Hero of Hungary." His wife's sobriquet was equally insouciant; in due time she would be known throughout Europe as "the Blood Countess."

After a brief stay at Nádasdy Castle in Sárvár, Hungary, where Erzsébet whiled away her hours as Ferenc studied in nearby Vienna, the couple took up residence in the thirteenth-century Castle Csejthe (pronounced "Chach-teetz-eh," it's also spelled Čachtice), a gloomy fortress perched high in the Little Carpathian Mountains near modern-day Trenčín, Hungary. It had been a wedding gift from the Nádasdy family to their teenage daughter-in-law. The castle, or the picturesque rubble that remains of it, is located in present-day Slovakia.

While Ferenc was off butchering his enemies the Ottoman

Turks, his young wife developed an odd way of relieving her boredom. No embroidery or dancing lessons for Erzsébet. She didn't even curl up with a good heretical tract. Instead, she satiated her libido in numerous extramarital affairs, even performing sex acts in front of her household with an exceptionally well-endowed manservant.

Aunt Klara began popping over to school her niece in *her* preferred methods of entertainment: flagellation, lesbian orgies, and various forms of sadomasochism. Klara was abetted by a loyal retainer named Thorko who introduced the beautiful young Erzsébet to the occult, piquing her interest in mixology. Erzsébet grew adept at concocting sundry drugs, brews, and potions; and in her husband's absence her various houseguests included self-proclaimed sorcerers and seers, warlocks, witches, and alchemists.

She was obsessed with her own beauty and needed constant affirmation of it. The countess would sit before her mirror for hours at a stretch, murmuring incantations to preserve her looks. If this behavior sounds familiar, Erzsébet Báthory was very likely the model for the inordinately vain wicked queen in *Snow White*, who in the early versions of the tale commands a hunter to take her young, virginal rival into the forest, cut out her heart, and return with it as proof of the girl's dispatch.

Before long, black magic and torture were Erzsébet's favorite ways to pass the time. She became especially fond of a set of silver pincers that could clip and claw off chunks of someone's flesh. The device had a particular allure because it was so versatile: It could be heated until it was as hot as a branding iron, or attached to a sturdy whip, turning it into an effective flaying tool.

While Ferenc was out massacring Turks, Erzsébet decided that blondes had more fun; so she used cinder water and distilled herbs to bleach her black hair the same flaxen hue that was all the fashion in Venice among both noblewomen and courtesans. She also amused herself with a variety of Italian sex toys. While her biographers don't go into specifics, the Italians of the sixteenth and seventeenth centuries were known throughout Europe for their dildo manufacturing.

Erzsébet liked to collect recipes, too, writing to her husband at the front about a particularly effective procedure she'd learned from one of her handmaidens. "Dorka has taught me a lovely new one. Catch a black hen and beat it to death with a white cane. Keep the blood and smear a little of it on your enemy. If you get no chance to smear it on his body, obtain one of his garments and smear it."

Like most sadists she learned that the best victims were the weak. And the peasant girls employed at Castle Csejthe were fair game and fertile fodder for Erzsébet's and Klara's gruesome hobbies. The countess's preference was for strapping blondes no older than eighteen; perhaps the sturdier girls resisted the various tortures with more vigor, making the hideous games more "sporting." For a few years, the town of Csejthe, "where the people were even more stupid than elsewhere," according to Erzsébet, supplied a steady stream of gullible girls, handed over by their trusting parents who were eager to gain favor with the countess.

Five of Erzsébet's most loyal and trusted servants ensured that the girls who survived the tortures, or made it safely through another day after their fellow slaveys and sculleries were murdered, would keep quiet about what they had seen or heard. Girls who were deemed too voluble had their mouths sewn shut.

Everyone in Hungary, regardless of rank or proximity, lived in terror of the powerful Báthorys. Still only an adolescent herself when she began torturing peasant girls, Erzsébet took advantage of a serving wench's merest misstep, using it as an excuse to punish her. She often devised tasks that were nearly impossible to accomplish, just so she could torture someone. But rebukes and slaps were for sissies. If a girl was suspected of theft, she was commanded to strip naked and was then tortured by the application of red-hot coins pressed against her bare skin. Sometimes the countess opted to go organic: The girls were whipped with stinging nettles after being beaten with some other device. And even if a servant girl hadn't misbehaved she might still end up as the day's entertainment. Mutilation was frequently on the menu. Girls were placed into cages fitted with internal spikes that impaled them everywhere as the cage tightened, resulting in an agonizing and bloody death. Pincers and tongs, heated until they glowed, were used to tear off bits of flesh. Scalding irons branded their tender skin. Erzsébet even perfected a technique of tearing a girl's head apart by tugging the sides of her mouth until they ripped and her neck snapped in two.

The countess was said to have achieved sexual ecstasy during these torture sessions, squealing in girlish delight at the sights and sounds of her victims' agony. She enjoyed whipping them from the front, just so she could see the pain and terror on their faces. Sometimes for kicks and giggles Erzsébet would slather a girl with honey and tie her to a tree, leaving her to the mercy of insects and other wildlife with a sweet tooth.

One day Ferenc discovered such a victim, but was satisfied by his wife's explanation that the girl was being punished for her disobedience. As long as the household was
smoothly run, the tired Turk-killer didn't want to hear
about how hard it was to get good help nowadays.

The countess's water torture involved stripping the girls
naked, dousing them with liquid, and then leaving them
in the frigid mountain air to freeze to death. Her "star-
kicking" game was a trick she learned from her warrior
husband; Ferenc used it on soldiers who were too lazy to
get out of bed in the morning or who may have been having epilectic fits. Bits of oiled paper were inserted between
her victims' toes and set aflame. Erzsébet had endless
hours of fun watching the hapless young women trying to
kick off the burning paper, which, thanks to the piping-
hot oil, was stuck to their skin, searing it as well. If that
became boring, she could always burn the girls' genitals
with a hot poker or candle wax. Oiled paper, set alight,
worked well when she placed it between a victim's legs so
that it would scorch her pubic area. Other instruments of
torture included razors, torches, and knives.

Sometime after Ferenc's death, the widowed Erzsébet
commissioned a mechanical device called the "iron virgin."
It resembled a beautiful naked girl with real hair (taken
from one of her flaxen-tressed victims), painted red nip-
ples, pubic hair, and movable eyes. The iron virgin even
had teeth, extracted from one of the tortured girls. If one
pressed on the figure's jeweled necklace the mechanized
arms would rise and tightly clasp the victim to her chest
as five knives emerged from the hollow cavity behind the
machine's breasts, slowly impaling the victim (usually a
young virgin herself) and stabbing her to death.

Ferenc died on January 4, 1604, at the age of forty-nine, possibly from a wound he received in battle. He and Erzsébet had been married for twenty-eight and a half years. She had spent their first decade together doing her best to avoid becoming pregnant, but between 1585 and 1598 the couple sired five children. The three who survived infancy, Anna, Katerina, and their son, Pál, were placed in the care of governesses, a common practice at the time.

Ferenc's death left Erzsébet facing the specter of her own mortality. Given her well-established penchant for torture, it's no surprise that she would endeavor to confront the gremlin of growing older in a truly ghoulish fashion. She was now a lonely widow in her early forties, losing her looks and intent on staving off the aging process. Traditional cosmetics weren't doing the trick. Even a glamorous new wardrobe failed to deflect attention from her epidermal flaws. As her rage to preserve her vanishing youth literally turned to bloodlust, the countess's games became even more sadistic.

Erzsébet now convinced herself that torture and mutilation had an additional, and healthful, benefit. One day, a hapless servant accidentally pulled the countess's hair while she was drawing a section of her tresses through a mesh hairnet studded with pearls. The girl received such a resounding slap that her nose bled, splashing on Erzsébet's hands (or face, depending on the source of the anecdote). After regarding herself in a mirror, Erzsébet was convinced that her skin looked much more youthful where the virgin girl's blood had spattered her.

A self-proclaimed local sorceress who called herself Darvulia (real name Anna), and was known as "the witch of the forest," had by then become one of Erzsébet's cohorts. Darvulia suggested to the countess that bathing in the blood of virgins would be as beneficial as a fountain of youth. So Erzsébet lured as many peasant girls as she could to Castle Csejthe, as well as to her other properties, including a town house in Vienna, to ensure that her new beauty regimen, as well as her preferred form of entertainment, remained uninterrupted. According to historian Margaret Nicholas, Darvulia and her confederate procuresses (aging widows who were well paid for their services) roamed the region after dark in search of fresh victims.

At the castles the girls were systematically slaughtered, their blood collected in vats and buckets for the courtesan's ritual baths, taken at the mystical hour of four a.m. If a victim was particularly beautiful, Erzsébet was reputed to have imbibed her blood.

It is a sad comment on the culture of sixteenth-century Hungary that countless young peasant women went missing and the authorities never bothered to search for them. No one dared speak out against the Báthory family, even if they had their suspicions; and other members of the nobility were loath to betray one of their own. Erzsébet wasn't even discreet about cleaning up after herself, and few others might have been around to mop up the gore, since her supply of domestics eventually dried up, so to speak. Rotting corpses and mutilated bodies dotted the castle's hallways and corridors. The stench was appalling.

After more than three decades of wholesale kidnapping, torture, and mutilation, Erzsébet ran out of peasants. She managed to purchase the service of a few more by telling their families that their daughters were being given the opportunity to serve the illustrious Báthory family. Naturally, the countess neglected to inform them that it was as a moisturizer.

But in 1609 came a stroke of fortune. Darvulia had disappeared into the woods one night, never to return. Her position was filled by a woman known as Erzsi Majorova, a local widow who had become one of Erzsébet's confidantes. Erzsi, who was skilled at manufacturing potions and poisons and writing incantations, had been concocting anti-aging remedies for Erzsébet, but the countess's mirror didn't lie; nothing was foolproof at staving off the ravages of time. After Erzsébet threatened to kill the sorceress for failing her, Erzsi, thinking quickly, informed the countess that she'd been doing it all wrong for years. No wonder she was getting wrinkles and crow's-feet, aging despite her best efforts! She'd been using peasants! The way to ensure a permanently youthful complexion was to bathe in the blood of virginal *aristocrats*!

So Erzsébet cleverly advertised for young women of the minor nobility to attend a sort of finishing school at Castle Csejthe, accepting twenty-five girls at a time to learn "the social graces appropriate to their class." The young ladies were indeed finished—but not in the way their families had anticipated. Finally, after several young noblewomen permanently disappeared, people began to notice; the rumors even reached Vienna, the epicenter of the Holy Roman Empire.

Evidently, the complaints had started years before, when from time to time Emerich Megyery, the tutor to the countess's son, Pál, had spoken up. In addition, some of Erzsébet's relatives seem to have been privately aware of her crimes, but dismissed any mention of them as malicious gossip and idle supposition, as well as the superstitions of unlettered peasants.

For so long Erzsébet had literally gotten away with murder

because she owned Castle Csejthe and could do what she pleased on its grounds. But Csejthe itself was a free village, governed by local councilors. And every once in a while, someone dared to speak out against the dark doings they believed were going on up at the castle.

As early as 1602 a courageous Lutheran minister named Janós Ponikenusz complained to the local and Viennese authorities. Ponikenusz had long suspected some ghoulish scenario after Erzsébet had asked him to discreetly bury a number of bloodless bodies; one of them belonged to Ilona Harczy, a girl he recognized because she used to sing at the church and he had been touched by the extraordinary beauty of her voice. The countess demanded that Ponikenusz's eulogy refer to the fact that Ilona had been killed for disobedience. The priest refused. By then, he had also noticed something unusual written in the parish register by his late predecessor, the Reverend Andras Berthoni. Alongside the usual list of births, deaths, weddings, and christenings was an entry recording the mysterious burial of nine female corpses on the same day.

In 1610, four broken bodies of adolescent noblewomen were discovered on the opposite side of one of the castle's walls, where they had been unceremoniously tossed.

At long last, the local officials agreed to hear the priest's allegations against Erzsébet. No one of note had cared about dozens, if not hundreds, of missing peasant girls; but the disappearance of so many aristocratic young ladies bore investigation. Thanks to Janós Ponikenusz and Emerich Megyery, the evidence of Erzsébet's atrocities eventually reached King Matthias II of Hungary.

Although Matthias had undoubtedly heard tales of Erzsébet's brutality, he had dithered for years before agreeing to confront it. According to some sources he had been financially indebted to Erzsébet's late husband, Ferenc, and was loath to stir up trouble because the Báthorys might suddenly demand payment. However, it finally became convenient to take the matter in hand, because he had made it a cornerstone of his reign to curb the power of the nobility. By bringing the Blood Countess to justice, Matthias would make an example of the Báthorys to any nobles who might be getting too big for their breeches.

In December 1610, eight years after Janós Ponikenusz first spoke up about the dark doings at Castle Csejthe, King Matthias and one of Erzsébet's cousins, the lord palatine of Hungary, Count György Thurzó, paid a visit to Csejthe to spend the Christmas holidays with the countess. Erzsébet sensed that the men suspected her of something, so she tried to poison them with a cake baked using some of her bathwater. Since she routinely bathed in the blood of her virgin victims, the ingredients may have been truly nauseating. Those who partook of the dessert suffered violent stomach pains afterward, but Matthias and Thurzó had been too savvy (and suspicious) to touch it. Thurzó confronted his cousin with the contents of Ponikenusz's whistle-blowing letter, but Erzsébet dismissed the allegations as "mad lies" and explained that the nine girls whose bodies they had found buried under the Csejthe church floor had expired from a contagious disease.

Thurzó wasn't buying any of her excuses, allegedly exclaiming, "Before God, you are responsible, and before the laws, which it's my duty to see are respected! If I weren't thinking of your family, I'd obey my conscience and imprison you on the spot, and then judge you." Thurzó convened a meeting of the Báthory family and ordered them to watch her like a hawk so that she would be unable to commit any further atrocities.

For three days the parliament, meeting at Hungary's capital, Pressburg, debated how to handle the matter. Finally, an emissary from King Matthias commanded Thurzó to conduct an inquiry at Csejthe. Thurzó accepted his commission, and on his arrival at the castle, discovered that his kinswoman's atrocities were even worse than he had imagined. As she'd been given little advance warning of his visit, Erzsébet hadn't been able to clean house and hide her crimes. The walls were caked with dried, splattered blood. As he nearly tripped over the corpse of a girl in the main hall, a groan grabbed his attention. It came from a dying girl whose body was so pierced with holes that she resembled a sieve. Broken sections of the defunct "iron virgin" led the investigators to the swift conclusion that the device had been an instrument of torture.

Dead and near-dead girls were found in a number of holding cells. In the basement several more victims were discovered hanging from the rafters, their bodies slit open and dripping blood into large vats placed on the floor below them that would be used for another of the countess's rejuvenating soaks.

After Thurzó ordered the excavation of the basement floor, another fifty corpses were uncovered. A maidservant named Zusanna directed him to Erzsébet's desk, where he found a ledger containing a tally, in the countess's handwriting, of her victims. Some 650 names were on the list, though her confederates would later dispute this number, placing the total body count at four to five dozen. However, between a hundred and two hundred bodies were removed from the castle by Thurzó's investigators. (It's worth noting here that according to a BBC biography of Erzsébet, the famous ledger was referred to in court, but never produced, which has recently raised suspicions about its existence; but at the time, and for centuries thereafter, the contents of the countess's alleged ledger were believed to be true.)

By the time Thurzó arrived at Castle Csejthe, the countess had already fled for a smaller castle farther down the hill, and her escape from this residence was already planned as well. Her coach awaited, packed with portable implements of torture.

Erzsébet's accomplices, Dorottya ("Dorka") Szentes; her children's former wet nurse Ilona Jó; and a washerwoman named Katarína Benická, were all arrested. Also apprehended was Erzsébet's dwarf, János Újváry, nicknamed both Ibis and Ficzko, and often described as "retarded." Erzsi Majorova, the woman who had urged the countess to import aristocratic virgins for her skin-care regimen, managed to escape, but was subsequently apprehended.

Erzsébet had maintained a diary in which she would comment on her victims and how they endured (or didn't) the various tortures she devised for them. After this journal was discovered, it was impossible to ignore her complicity.

Some historians claim that Erzsébet was arrested along with her servants; others state that because she was a noblewoman she could not be arrested. Because aristocrats were not permitted to be placed on trial, Erzsébet was never called upon to testify in her defense, although King Matthias's royal envoy wanted the countess to be tried like any other murderer and to be compelled to take the stand. "There are crimes to which no more than allusion has been made," the envoy insisted, and the crown wanted an airtight conviction.

Thurzó, however, was intent on shielding his kinswoman from the inevitable (and devastating) publicity. He maintained that putting Erzsébet herself on trial would permanently destroy the names of both the Báthory and Nádasdy families, damaging the reputations of her children, relations, and in-laws, all of whom had no connection to any of her crimes. "As long as I am the Lord Palatine of Hungary, this will not come to pass," Thurzó insisted. "The families which have won in the eyes of the nation such high honors on the battlefields shall not be disgraced by the murky shadow of this bestial female. . . . In the interest of future generations of Nádasdys everything is to be done in secret. For if a court were to try her, the whole of Hungary would learn of her murders. . . ."

Consequently, in the name of protecting their own reputations, the powerful Báthory and Nádasdy families were able to keep all mention of Erzsébet's heinous deeds—her mass murders, cannibalism, and vampirism—out of the official trial records.

From January 2 through 7, 1611, Erzsébet's accomplices were tried before a panel of twenty judges. In a highly unusual move for a trial involving charges of witchcraft and sorcery, the Church waived its right to try Erzsébet, or even to question her—an indication of the Báthorys' level of influence in the realm. Two hundred witnesses testified against the absent countess.

What they had to say undoubtedly shocked the court. When asked about the recruitment process Erzsébet's servants testified that they went from village to village seeking new blood, so to speak, and they named additional accomplices who performed the same duties.

Dorottya Szentes, known as "Dorka," testified that when her mistress was ailing and not feeling physically up to the task of inflicting major torture, "she would draw one of the serving maids suddenly to herself and bite a chunk of flesh from her cheeks and sink her teeth into her breast and shoulders. She would stick needles into a girl's fingers and say, 'If it hurts you, you famous whore, pull them out' but if the girl dared to draw the needles out her Ladyship ordered her to be beaten and her fingers slashed up."

And Ilona Jó, another accomplice (and the nanny for Erzsébet's children), told the judges that "Both her Ladyship and the women burned them [the servant girls] on their lips with the iron used to goffer [pleat] her ruffs," as well as in their "nose and the inside of their mouths."

The accomplices also testified that the girls, who were usually starved before they were tortured, were occasionally fed the roasted flesh of recent victims. Cannibalism was also inflicted upon the youths who dared to look lustfully upon young girls. Janós Ponikenusz, the priest from Csejthe who eventually blew the whistle on Erzsébet, reported that "We have heard here from the mouths of girls who had survived the ordeal that some of their fellow victims were forced to eat their own flesh roasted on fire. The flesh of other girls was chopped up fine like mushrooms, cooked and flavored, and given to young lads who did not know what they were eating."

Among the other revelations was the fate of a twelve-year-old girl named Pola who had managed to escape Erzsébet's clutches but was pursued by Dorka and Ilona and brought back to the castle. Pola was placed inside a spherical cage lined with dozens of spikes. As the cage was hauled up by a pulley, the unfortunate child was pierced all over and bled to death.

An aristocratic girl who tried to flee was also recaptured but committed suicide in her cell, preferring to die by her own hand than those of her tormentors. And one of Erzsébet's diary entries referred to a young maid who had died too quickly for her demise to provide much amusement; in her notations the countess deemed the girl "too small."

Matthias's representative also demanded that the countess's four accomplices be questioned about the torture and murder of the twenty-five young noblewomen, because the eleven identical questions posed to each of the defendants during the trial didn't even refer to the subject! But in the long run, the additional interrogation wouldn't have mattered, because the outcome of the trial offered few surprises.

Finally a verdict was rendered: The servant girl Zusanna was acquitted. Katarína was imprisoned for life. The dwarf Ficzko was beheaded and then burned. Erzsi, Dorka, and Ilona were all pronounced guilty of being witches; and because their fingers had been quite literally "dipped in the blood of Christians," these appendages were ripped from their hands with hot pincers, a weapon with which they were undoubtedly all too familiar.

But when it came to the countess's punishment, the Royal Magyar Chamber sent a petition to Matthias in March 1611, urging him to forgo the death penalty. "The choice is yours, O King, between the executioner's sword and perpetual imprisonment for Erzsébet Báthory. But we advise you not to execute her, because no one really stands to gain anything from the alternative." What the royal chamber was really saying was that treating a powerful member of the ruling class like a common criminal was bad for business. In the same blue-blooded vein, the High Court of Justice could not sentence Erzsébet to death because they had not found her personally complicit in the murder of the twenty-five noblewomen. Thurzó had done his best to suppress the information about the countess's literal bloodbaths. The High Court determined that the quintet of peasant accomplices was entirely responsible for the girls' deaths. King Matthias knew it was untrue and wrote a letter to that effect, but even a sovereign could not overturn a verdict rendered in a court of law. Although Matthias was confident of Erzsébet Báthory's complicity, he remained powerless to affect the wheels of justice, no matter how unevenly they turned.

Still, the countess did not get off entirely scot-free, and her sentence was rendered from a surprising source. Since Erzsébet's rank and influence had prevented her from being tried, her relatives took it upon themselves to exact punishment, an action that was hardly altruistic, because it conveniently kept her property within the family. (And because Erzsébet had cleverly, and legally, willed her property to her children, who were completely unconnected to her crimes, the crown could not have touched her estates even if she were to be executed.)

It was the ultimate house arrest. Erzsébet's family had her walled up within her bedchamber in Castle Csejthe, leaving only small slits in the thick walls and at the bottom of the heavy door that provided a bit of light and air and permitted food and water to be passed into the room. Immured in her cell, the "Blood Countess" was no longer considered a danger to anyone and she remained out of reach of King

Matthias. She was denied all human contact; unseen hands delivered her daily nutrition. The workmen who bricked up her chamber placed a quartet of scaffolds at each corner of the castle walls to indicate that a condemned person dwelled within.

Erzsébet's house arrest lasted a little more than three years. On August 21, 1614, the fifty-four-year-old countess was discovered lying facedown in her makeshift prison, having recently breathed her last. She was buried in the church at Csejthe, but after an outcry from the villagers, who refused to have a serial killer reposing among them, Erzsébet's body was moved to the Báthory family crypt located near her birthplace, at Ecsed.

In 1729, one hundred and eighteen years after her servants were tried and executed, the minutes of their trial were discovered by a Jesuit priest named Laszló Turáczi. The paper had substantially deteriorated, making some of the testimony illegible. Rats had chewed off part of the final page. In 1744, Turáczi published a treatise on Erzsébet Báthory, based on the documents he had found, as well as others relating to the trial that had been preserved in the Hapsburg archives in Vienna for years before being sent on to Budapest. Finally the gruesome story of Erzsébet Báthory was brought to light.

Although we may view Erzsébet's Transylvanian countryman Vlad Dracula (or even Ivan the Terrible, the other aristocratic, autocratic butcher in this volume) as a mass murderer, Vlad might have argued in his defense (if he didn't impale you first) that his brutality was a necessary evil in order to maintain law and order in a culture that lived and died by the sword, and to retain his occasionally tenuous possession of the Wallachian crown.

Erzsébet Báthory—the "Blood Countess," the "Beast," and the "Tigress of Csejthe"—was also a royal mass murderer; but there was no political rationale for her bloodlust. Her atrocities were committed for sport, though admittedly there came a time when they became a vital part of her skin-care regimen. Vanity never had a higher, or more gruesome, price.

PRINCE HENRY

Duke of Cumberland and Strathearn
1745–1790

URING THE MIDDLE AGES, AN ENGLISH MONARCH'S younger brothers all too often dedicated their lives to the pursuit of usurpation. By the eighteenth century, when Parliament wielded more political power than the sovereign, the siblings' primary activity became *dissipation*; conquests in the boudoir replaced those made on the field of battle. And the poster child for this brand of wildness was the randy and scandalous Prince Henry Frederick, Duke of Cumberland, a younger brother of King George III.

Actually, the rigidly moral George had *two* younger brothers whose amorous adventures embarrassed the crown and personally mortified the monarch. But the libidinous exploits of Prince Henry also had a lasting effect on British history.

The prince was seven years King George's junior, with the typical Hanoverian coloring—a fair complexion with rosy cheeks. An unusual facial feature, his nearly white eyebrows, made him easy to spot in a crowd. Henry suffered from another Hanoverian trait as well: an impediment that made his speech sound thick. Slight and slender, at least he had somehow avoided the royal family's gene for corpulence. And he was never regarded as the brightest of the brothers; their sister Augusta observed in 1764 that "dear Henry" would be much admired "if he can learn to think before he speaks."

In October 1766, when the prince reached his majority, King George created him Duke of Cumberland and Strathearn in the English peerage, and Baron of Dublin in the Irish peerage. Parliament granted him an annual income of £17,000 (almost $2.9 million today). At the age of twenty-one, Cumberland established his own household in the posh Pall Mall and set out to grab life with both hands—life consisting of a juicy female with a well-padded bumroll. Lady Sarah Lennox—who enjoyed the distinction of being George III's first crush—nicknamed Henry "the white pig" after he tried to seduce her, presumably without success.

In order to present a useful face to society so that Parliament could justify his income, in July of 1766 the young duke assumed the office of Ranger and Keeper of the Great Park at Windsor, a post previously held by his uncle, William Augustus, the former Duke of Cumberland. Henry immediately proceeded to install at Windsor Great Park his mistress of the moment, a petite, vivacious redheaded prostitute named Polly Jones. Her name suited her, as the duke developed a jones for this young lady after spotting her strolling in the Vauxhall pleasure gardens, a usual haunt for women of her ilk. He had purchased Polly's full-time favors from a madam named Mrs. Mitchell for the impressive sum of £70 (nearly $12,000 in today's economy).

Ann Sheldon, another woman of dubious repute, who was canny enough to pen her own memoirs, recalled Cumberland and Polly's antics at Windsor:

I now made frequent visits to Miss Jones, and used to accompany her and The Duke in their walks, which seemed chiefly to be taken in order to amuse His Royal Highness with her tumbling in the grass. . . . While she was tumbling heels over head, and throwing herself into indecent postures, he used to laugh with a degree of violence that I never beheld before or since.

But not too much later, according to Sheldon, Cumberland had confided that Polly's vulgarity "quite disgusted him"—at which point he promptly propositioned Miss Sheldon. Ann felt enough sororial affection for a fellow whore to tell Polly what her protector had done.

In solidarity, both women abandoned the duke. Polly, savvy girl, took her case to the press, claiming that Cumberland had stripped her of everything but the clothes on her back and that she merited restitution, telling anyone who would listen that her former royal lover had sent "the proper officers to dispossess me of my household furniture, which had been provided at his expense, and left me destitute, friendless and almost penniless after he had professed the greatest regard, esteem, and even love for me." Soon, everyone in London knew her sob story. And before we cue the violins, it should be mentioned that this cavalier behavior was par for the course among the Hanoverian males. Is it any wonder that the Duke of Cumberland would eventually be viewed as a mentor by his nephew, the Prince of Wales? The future George IV would treat the actress Mary Robinson, his first paramour and the toast of Drury Lane, with the same callous disregard when he tired of her charms.

Although Polly Jones swiftly found herself another noble protector whom she managed to fleece out of an annuity, through her tell-alls she was able to keep the Duke of Cumberland's name in the press (and in a decidely unflattering light) for more than a year.

In 1769, London could boast of having sixty newspapers. Several of them were the gossip blogs of their day, little more than sensationalist accounts of the scandalous shenanigans of society's upper crust. Because of England's rigid libel laws, the names of the parties in question were referred to by their initials, and often included a few of the letters in between, the intention being to "out" the participants in a scandal without running afoul of the law. To a public avid for salacious gossip, it became a grand guessing game, although the papers tended to print enough clues in a given article to allow little room for conjecture. Those in the know *knew*.

That year, *Town & Country* magazine's highly popular Tête à Tête feature exposed the Duke of Cumberland in yet another sex scandal, obliquely referring to Henry as "Nauticus" because of his brief career in the Royal Navy. After a year as a midshipman, in 1769 he was promoted to rear admiral; the following year he would receive another promotion, due more to rank than merit, becoming a vice admiral.

Admiral of vice was more like it.

The Tête à Tête in question revealed "Nauticus's" liaisons with various ladies, from Polly Jones to the more sophisticated, and celebrated, courtesan Grace Elliott, an Italian singer-dancer named Anna Zamperini, and Camilla D'Onhoff, a widow of dubious repute who claimed to be a Polish countess. More probably she was the castoff mistress of Poland's king.

George III feigned unconcern over the public airing of

his brother's soiled social linen. Rather than reprimand Cumberland for getting his sexual shenanigans splattered all over the press, the king seems to have kept his counsel. But there would come a time when it would be impossible for him to ignore Henry's escapades.

Richard, Baron Grosvenor, was one of London's wealthiest citizens, owning half the real estate in the posh neighborhood of Mayfair. On July 19, 1764, at the age of thirty-three, the tall, swarthy, rakish baron had married a pretty brunette named Henrietta Vernon, though like most men of his class, he didn't feel bound to give up his horses and his whores just because he needed to beget an heir. In fact he wasn't faithful for five seconds. Grosvenor was especially fond of blond street girls, procuring many of his conquests from the ubiquitous Ann Sheldon. Small wonder that he was riddled with venereal disease.

Still in her twenties at the time she met the Duke of Cumberland, Lady Grosvenor was beginning to regret her decision to marry the baron. Theirs had not been a lengthy courtship, as they'd gone to the altar only a month after they'd met during a chance rainstorm in Kensington Gardens.

About a year after their wedding, Henrietta told her brother that her husband had "used her extremely ill" and she was miserable. After she accomplished her dynastic duty by giving Grosvenor an heir in March 1767, she resumed her former social whirl, where she met the Duke of Cumberland. By the end of 1768 his attentions to her were becoming more persistent. The duke romantically flung himself at the unhappy baroness and she caught him with glee. During the early months of 1769, the lonely and neglected Lady Grosvenor and the young duke grew closer; by then, what had begun as a diverting flirtation had blossomed into a full-blown affair.

Lord Grosvenor was rich and powerful enough to have informants everywhere. It was easy to spot his wife because the baron's carriage was very recognizable and Henrietta tended to frequent popular public recreation destinations, like the opera and the pleasure gardens at Vauxhall and Ranelagh. Her twenty-three-year-old royal lover was also quite identifiable, with his odd white eyebrows, as well as his own familiar coach and liveries.

Nevertheless, the clandestine affair galloped apace, and naturally, Cumberland thought he was being discreet. Henrietta and the duke would tryst at the home of his former lover the countess-courtesan Lady D'Onhoff, who was mercenary enough to charge Henry for the privilege of using her apartments. To arrange their rendezvous, the illicit paramours corresponded through one of Lady D'Onhoff's servants, heedless of the dangers of committing their passion (and their eventual whereabouts) to paper. They were young and in lust; it was all too heady for either of them to stop and think about the consequences if their affair were to be discovered. After learning from the duke that he was ailing, Lady Grosvenor wrote to him:

> I thank you for your kind note, your tender manner of expressing yourself calling me your dear friend, and at this time that you should recollect me. I wish I dare be all the time by your bed and nurse you—for you will have nobody near you that love you as I do, thou dearest angel of my soul. O that I could but bear your pain for you I should be happy. What grieves me most is that they who *ought to feel* don't know the inestimable prize, the treasure they have in you.

It's quite a maudlin letter, but in her defense, not only was the baroness in love, but she was hormonal. Lady Grosvenor was seven months pregnant with her second child. Her behavior was doubly scandalous because well-born women of the era did not venture out during such an advanced stage of their condition.

The lovers' lack of caution came back to bite them. After Countess D'Onhoff proved just as willing as any chambermaid to sell her secrets about the couple's shenanigans, Cumberland dispatched his aide-de-camp Captain Foulkes on a reconnaissance mission for another love nest. Foulkes was commanded to visit a milliner's shop within spitting distance of Cumberland House for the purposes of inquiring of its forty-five-year-old widowed proprietress, Mary Reda Vemberght, whether she had a spare room or two that might be available.

Eighteenth-century milliners often had a less savory (but probably more lucrative) profession moonlighting as procuresses; and many courtesans began their horizontal careers as lowly milliners' assistants. Using two of Mrs. Vemberght's friends as go-betweens so that nothing could be traced directly back to the lovers, the duke and Lady Grosvenor rented the rooms above the millinery. Probably because her palm was crossed with silver, Mrs. Vemberght would later testify on Lord Grosvenor's behalf that she "supposed it was for something bad, that it was for girls" (referring to Captain Foulkes's inquiry about the availability of her rooms). However, she had cheerfully rented them at the time without bothering to ask any questions.

On June 7, 1769, Lady Grosvenor gave birth to another son. The randy duke was prevented from seeing his lover for a month owing to the customary postpartum lying-in.

During Henrietta's confinement Cumberland was sent to sea
for six weeks. From the captain's quarters of the aptly named
Venus he penned copious (and rather puerile) love letters to
his own Venus, Lady Grosvenor. When he'd first received his
orders, the duke confessed to Mrs. Vemberght that he had
no idea how he should survive at sea without his inamorata.
The milliner later testified that Henry "cried very much and
seemed almost distracted," and "said he should die" if she
didn't deliver his billets-doux to her ladyship.

During his month and a half aboard the *Venus*, the duke
sent more than thirty packets of correspondence through
his porters, and Mrs. Vemberght was compelled to devise
clever methods of sneaking them into Grosvenor House.
Letters were secreted inside of bandboxes; and Henrietta's
two sympathetic sisters, one of whom was a maid of honor
to Queen Charlotte, were pressed into service as couriers.

In a gross dereliction of duty, the duke, who by virtue
of his rank was in command, ordered Admiral Barrington
of the *Venus* not to sail because if they embarked on their
mission to perform the required naval maneuvers in the
English Channel, it would have kept him too far from
shore to maintain communication with his mistress. With
colossal smugness, Cumberland told Lady Grosvenor, "The
wind was not so contrary but we could have sailed,"
although he informed Barrington that he "had dispatches
of consequence to send to London," keeping the Royal
Navy waiting while he commandeered a fast-moving frigate to carry his love letters to her. Never much of an intel-
lect, he ungrammatically added:

> Indeed, my dear Angel, I need not tell you I know you read
> the reason too well that made me do it, it was to write to

you, for God knows I wrote to no-one else nor shall I at
any other time but to the King.

In one letter to Henrietta, the duke shared the denouement of a blue dream he'd had:

> I then lay down and dreamt of you . . . [I] had you on the
> dear little couch ten thousand times in my arms kissing you
> and telling you how much I adored you and you seemed
> pleased but alas when I awoke I found it all delusion,
> nobody but myself at sea. . . . I shan't forget you. God
> knows you have told me so before—I have your heart and
> it lies warm in my breast . . . thou joy of my life, adieu.

He also enclosed a love poem he had written to her.

This correspondence had been couriered to Lady Grosvenor by Caroline Vernon, her sixteen-year-old sister. Caroline was tremendously sympathetic toward an older sister
trapped in a miserable marriage to a whoring reprobate and
was vicariously giddy about the clandestine love affair and
the fairy-tale romance transpiring before her. But just as the
sisters were in the middle of reading the duke's letters, they
were surprised by Lord Grosvenor himself.

The baron demanded the paper his wife was holding. Naturally, she refused to relinquish it. A comical scene ensued
in which Caroline tried to pull his lordship away from her
sister, who was still holding the letter; Lord Grosvenor and
Caroline scuffled, and the baron eventually overpowered his
teenage sister-in-law and grabbed the love note from Henrietta. With a glance at his spouse that was so chilly it could
freeze beer he left the room without another word.

Grosvenor had a copy made of the duke's letter to his

wife, keeping the original as well. He began to intercept Cumberland's correspondence, sending it to be copied, as he calmly built a case against the duke and Lady Grosvenor. To make sure his legal complaint would be airtight he shunned both her presence and her bed. As he paid the servants' salaries, they were quite forthcoming with information regarding Henrietta's daily routines and had no qualms about spying on her. Eager to make a few extra bob off his lordship, even coachmen in the employ of others were quick to offer their services as anonymous informers.

As the days wore on, Henrietta's panic increased: How much did her husband know about her royal affair? The edgier she grew, the more placid he appeared. The baron lulled his wife into a false sense of security, deliberately leading her to conclude that he was ignorant of anything more than the contents of the letter he had so unceremoniously snatched from her hands. After the dustup in the drawing room she had even written to the duke to inform him that her husband was "rather in better temper today, so I'm in great hopes he did not get enough of the letter to make out much." However, Lord Grosvenor was making his plans to get rid of her. Witnesses were identified and their statements taken. The following year, their depositions were published in a pamphlet; chock-full of lurid details, it became an immediate bestseller.

With each additional letter, Lady Grosvenor further incriminated herself. On June 19, 1769, she wrote to her lover regarding her latest subterfuge to avoid accompanying her husband to the country:

I've already complained I've a pain in my side and I intend to say it's much worse at the end of the month and that I cannot bear the motion of a carriage. . . . At the end of five or six weeks I'll grow very ill and send for Fordyce the apothecary and make him send me a quantity of nasty draughts which I'll throw out the window. Only think how wicked I am, for in reality I'm already as strong and well as ever I was in my life.

But in order to have a valid cause of action for adultery, the baron had to catch the lovers literally in flagrante. Passionate correspondence alone would not be enough to convict them, nor would the hearsay of hirelings. The testimony given by people of the lower orders against their social betters, and particularly against a prince of the blood, would never be accepted in court over Cumberland's word.

During the last week in October 1769, Lord Grosvenor departed London for Newmarket, leaving his gullible wife with the impression that he was headed there to look at some new horses. Believing herself to be in the clear, the baroness clambered into the luxurious (and distinctive) family coach and set out via a circuitous route for Cheshire, a borough that her husband had represented as an MP, and where the Grosvenors always spent the two months before Christmas at the baron's estate, Eaton Hall.

Cumberland's carriage took the same roads, sometimes directly shadowing Henrietta's, sometimes deliberately falling behind in order to maintain a discreet distance, and at other times overtaking them and speeding on ahead to the agreed-upon rendezvous point.

Because he had become so recognizable thanks to the caricatures in print shops, the duke traveled incognito. But his attempts at disguise, straight out of a comedy by Goldsmith or Farquhar, were so outlandish that they would have been laughed off the most provincial stage in the kingdom. Depending on the coaching inn, Cumberland pretended to be either a farmer or a Welshman, although he hadn't the remotest bit of familiarity with either identity. At one inn, it perplexed the proprietor all the more that the purported Welshman spoke French to his dinner companions.

Henry and his entourage called even more attention to themselves in their endeavors to conceal their features. With their heads swathed in scarves, broad-brimmed hats shading their eyes, and sporting huge curly wigs and greatcoats—which were a favorite get-up of the duke's— they looked and behaved so suspiciously that at several of their layovers the innkeepers' staffs were certain they were cutpurses, cardsharps, or highwaymen.

Cumberland and Henrietta had made a plan: They would rendezvous at various locations along the way, and whoever was the first to arrive would mark their door with chalk so that the other lover could request an adjacent (and, if possible, adjoining) chamber. Lady Grosvenor was also traveling with her children (and, presumably, their nurse) and was careful to ensure that their rooms would in no way interfere with her plans for a nocturnal tryst.

Having arrived at Eaton Hall, the baron maintained his naive demeanor vis-à-vis his wife's extramarital affair. He put her off the scent by feigning an intense interest in the breeding lines of various horses. Lady Grosvenor was either too self-absorbed, too clueless, or too much in love to catch on. Her letters to the duke prove that she genuinely thought she'd duped her husband into thinking the liaison had been severed. However, Grosvenor knew otherwise, thanks to voluable, and bribable, servants, in addition to tips from a certain anonymous coachman who informed Lord Grosvenor that the duke had been seen in the area affecting various ludicrous disguises. The baron, however, was already aware that Cumberland had been meeting Henrietta in the nearby fields and country lanes.

In mid-November 1769, Lord Grosvenor ordered his butler, Matthew Stephens, to intercept Henrietta's letters and copy them. The baron made a big charade out of departing for his neighboring estate, leaving his wife with the impression that she would have Eaton Hall all to herself. On December 5, she hastily scribbled a note to her royal lover:

> The best thing we can do now is to make him believe it is all over between us, and we really have, I believe, blinded him for some time.

With supreme self-confidence, she added,

> At least he has no proof about us and I hope to God that by degrees his suspicions will be lulled and then we may form some plans for meeting happily. . . .

Because Henrietta's sister Caroline was a maid of honor to Queen Charlotte, she began to be of two minds regarding the whole affair. Aware of the baron's rampant debauchery and Henrietta's unhappiness over his flagrant infidelity, at first Caroline had been supportive of her sister's romantic royal escapade. However, if the baroness was caught in flagrante with Cumberland, Caroline would lose her position at court and with it the other perks she could ill afford to part with: a salary, her housing, and the opportunity to meet and marry a courtier. Consequently, her sympathy began to wane. She warned Henrietta that the queen and the dowager princess (mother to the king and Cumberland) were none too happy about her adulterous liaison with the duke. On the assumption that any royal anger directed at her older sister would jeopardize her own status, Caroline melodramatically urged Henrietta to end the affair.

> . . . could my simple advice be of any service to you I would implore you on my knees, nay serve you as a slave night and day, that you would for ever banish from your thoughts them whom you style your "Friend. . . ."

However, given the level of espionage going on at Eaton Hall at the time, it's possible that Henrietta never received Caroline's letter.

On December 14, 1769, Grosvenor made a point of ostentatiously announcing that he was going to stop at Newmarket before returning to London. His wife, predictably, fell for the ruse. So did her royal paramour. Cumberland sent Henrietta a letter under his new nom de plume, "R. Trusty"—a name that might as well have been lifted out of a popular sentimental comedy.

It appeared that they'd have a window of trysting time in London, owing to the baron's absence; so the illicit lovers decided to set out for the capital immediately, planning to rendezvous at the bustling White Hart inn in St. Albans. Repeating their modus operandi from their October meeting at the White Hart, they took connecting rooms on the first floor of the coaching inn. But while Lady Grosvenor was downstairs in the dining room, her husband's butler, Matthew Stephens, drilled a pair of peepholes in the door to her room.

Sometime after Henrietta returned to her chamber, Stephens brought her a warm drink. He wasn't being solicitous; he was verifying that she would be in the room when the time came to spring his employer's trap. In fact several of the baron's servants were on hand to witness the moment Lord Grosvenor had been anticipating for several months—catching his wife in a compromising sexual position with the Duke of Cumberland.

Just as the baron's hirelings had hoped, Henry made a guest appearance in Lady Grosvenor's room. But in true comedy-of-errors style, no one had checked ahead of time to ensure that the peepholes would afford the proper line of vision to the bed, or that the bed had been positioned to provide the requisite view. Consequently the passion posse overheard all the telltale signs of lovemaking, but couldn't see a thing! They would therefore be unable to give the baron the proof he required in order to secure his divorce. Stephens finally became so frustrated that he enlisted the aid of his fellow witnesses to batter down the door.

The ensuing scene owed more to French farce than British bedroom comedy. First, the lovers heard the lock give way, allowing them enough of a head start to hastily clothe themselves. As the door flew open, the countess was desperately endeavoring to button up her robe, a type of dressing gown known as a Jesuit dress. She tried to find a corner of the room in which to hide, but tripped over her own skirts. Meanwhile, Cumberland, fumbling with the buttons of his cream-colored waistcoat, bolted for the door to the adjoining room, but his path was blocked by Matthew Stephens and his brother, who were brandishing the hot pokers from the fireplace.

Subterfuge soon took a backseat to impertinence. "Do you know who I am?" the duke hotly demanded of the

witnesses. Despite his amorous exertions, he was still wearing the ridiculous curly black wig that would not have
looked out of place on Charles II. Nevertheless, the baron's
servants immediately replied to his question, stating that he
was "His Royal Highness, the Duke of Cumberland."

For some reason, it wasn't the answer Henry had been
expecting. In a moment worthy of a Monty Python sketch,
the duke hastily backpedaled, insisting that "he was not in
her ladyship's bedchamber, and that he would take his Bible
oath on it." Cumberland's equerry, a personal attendant
with clearly more brains than his employer, advised him to
just shut up and leave the room.

At this point Matthew Stephens ordered the inn's servants to examine the bed, which was described by Lord
Grosvenor's underbutler, Robert Betton, as "being much
tumbled from top to bottom, in a very extraordinary manner, all the bedclothes being much rumpled."

The duke returned to Cumberland House to await the
inevitable lawsuit for crim. con. (the abbreviation of "criminal conversation," which was the legalese euphemism for
adultery). Lady Grosvenor, her reputation in tatters, couldn't
possibly go home anymore, and so she rented anonymous
lodgings for herself and her children.

But shortly before Christmas, the newspapers printed
the allegation that "an assignation at the White Hart at
St. Albans between L____ G____, and a certain great
D____e, was disconcerted by my Lord's gentleman."

The "great D____e" was the Duke of Cumberland,
whose amorous plans were "disconcerted" or disrupted;
and of course L____ G____ was Lady Grosvenor. And on
March 1, 1770, three months after the duke and his inamorata were discovered in flagrante, Lord Grosvenor brought

a lawsuit against his wife in Doctors Commons, the consistory or ecclesiastical court. The Doctors Commons had the power to annul a religious marriage, if grounds for such annulment could be proved. However, they could not grant a civil divorce, which was usually what a petitioner with an adulterous spouse would have been seeking, in order to enable him to remarry. All that Lord Grosvenor could achieve through this lawsuit was a legal separation. But it was a carefully planned and calculated first step.

The libel against Lady Grosvenor that was filed by the baron's lawyers, Parthington and Garth, was a masterstroke of fiction in its depiction of her famously lecherous husband as "a man of sober, chaste, and virtuous life" who "always behaved towards his lady with true love and affection and did all in his power to render her completely happy." Her ladyship, on the other hand, was characterized as "unmindful of her conjugal vow, and not having the fear of God before her eyes. . . ." Further, that "moved and instigated by the devil [she] did contract and carry on a lewd and adulterous conversation with His Royal Highness [Prince Henry] Frederick. . . ." The baron therefore demanded a divorce "from the said Henrietta Lady Grosvenor his wife, because of adultery." It was an effort to publicly humiliate her, and if Grosvenor got his desired verdict it could be the first step toward a parliamentary divorce, enabling both parties to remarry. Divorces were exceptionally rare in eighteenth-century Britain. In general, only peers received them, and in almost every case it was the husband who petitioned to be rid of his wife.

One witness who offered damaging testimony against Cumberland during the libel trial in Doctors Commons was the ersatz Countess D'Onhoff. She told the consistory court of Doctors Commons that she had interrupted the illicit lovers in the act, right on her drawing room sofa, adding that the duke's breeches were down around his knees and that Lady Grosvenor had spread her petticoats in anticipation of his penetration.

Statements like that would certainly make Cumberland (and Henrietta, of course) seem deliciously guilty. That such embarrassingly graphic testimony might have unintended consequences never appeared to disconcert his lordship. The baron hadn't seemed concerned with the very tangible possibility that the angry and humiliated Lady Grosvenor had plenty of ammunition with which to countersue him for adultery. For some reason he surmised that she would never do so.

Cumberland assembled his own legal team, Buxton and Windus, as he waited for the proverbial other shoe—a crim. con. suit—to drop. The London miasma was made even thicker by the rumors that Lord Grosvenor's real goal in seeking an annulment was to blackmail the crown into awarding him a dukedom.

In the late spring of 1770 the baron filed his crim. con. suit, and in order to gin up sympathy, circulated copies of his wife's purloined love letters. Unfortunately, Grosvenor's own libertinism was so renowned, including his affinity for the most squalid whores he could procure, that it was a stretch for anyone to believe that he was the wronged party. Nonetheless, the content of the letters spoke for itself, duly compromising the authors' reputations. After the baron sent the lovers' correspondence to John Wheble, the publisher of the *Middlesex Journal* (which began to feature them in mid-June), John Bull had a field day over Cumberland's maudlin and ungrammatical billets-doux. The crown was emphatically embarrassed.

All of England was abuzz when the trial began in London during the first week of July. Sixty-five-year-old Lord Mansfield was charged with adjudicating the matter from the King's Bench. Everyone wondered whether the "Chesire Cornuto," as the cuckolded Grosvenor was dubbed, would receive his divorce. On July 5, the case of *Grosvenor v. Cumberland* commenced. The courtroom was packed to the rafters. However, the aggrieved parties were nowhere near the mob scene, because by law they were barred from being present at the trial. Instead, the lawyers for both sides did all the talking.

As if to convey that the whole three-ring circus was no concern of his, King George was several miles from the City; he took his younger brother riding in Richmond Park on the opening day of the trial.

Cumberland's attorneys presented fewer witnesses than the baron's representatives, but in the duke's case, quality (or the deliberate lack thereof) trumped quantity. Testifying on Cumberland's behalf (which really meant that they were trashing the baron's character, rather than defending the duke's) were the skankiest prostitutes in London, each of whom had a lurid anecdote to share with the court about procuring for, or directly pleasuring, Lord Grosvenor. It was all very entertaining, except that the baron's character (objectionable as it was) wasn't the focus of the trial.

It was the aim of Grosvenor's attorney, Lord Wedderburn, to embarrass the royal family by demanding an outrageous sum in damages. The usual figure awarded to a successful petitioner in a crim. con. suit was about £200. That figure in 1770 would be roughly equivalent to $36,500 today. On rare occasions British juries had awarded as much as £3,000 in damages (over $547,000 nowadays). Lord Wedderburn demanded £100,000—more than $18 million today.

To demonstrate his client's worthiness of such a magnanimous award, Wedderburn played to the gallery by reading aloud some of the lovers' torrid correspondence. The barrister's deadpan delivery illuminated His Royal Highness's inadequate education, particularly when he was unable to suppress a supercilious chuckle as he read the duke's mangled French.

> . . . *aimons toujours mon adorable petite amour je vous adore plusque la vie même.* [we (the "royal we") love always my adorable little lover; I adore you more than life itself.]

Cumberland's pathetic description of his frustrated erotic dream aboard the *Venus* also provoked gales of laughter. According to the *General Evening Post* the recitation of the love letters exchanged between Henrietta and the duke "occasioned much entertainment to the whole court, as they may truly be said to add to the novelty of epistolary writing." And this was an era when epistolary writing had been elevated to an art form!

In his summation on behalf of the complainant, Lord Wedderburn argued that the way a prince should behave was as much at issue as the crim. con. charges. By granting the exorbitant sum of damages to his client, the jury would be sending a clear message to the Duke of Cumberland, deterring him "from setting a bad example to the subordinate classes of society" and encouraging him to heed the example of his older brother, the king, "whose conjugal attachments, abstracted from his other virtues, not only ornamented the throne he filled, but shed a bright example to his subjects in general."

In his client's defense, Cumberland's barrister, the morbidly obese John Dunning, reminded the jury that the duke and Lady Grosvenor were never actually apprehended in the act of making love. Witnesses (albeit those in the duke's employ) had corroborated Dunning's assertion that the affair was unconsummated. One such witness was Robert Giddings, Cumberland's friend and gentleman porter. He testified to being in the lovers' presence when they met near Eaton, but that all the couple did was "sit upon the grass . . . and that His Royal Highness read a play or some book to the said Lady Grosvenor."

Dunning then summoned his parade of tawdry witnesses against Lord Grosvenor.

The judge, Lord Mansfield (who was known to generally rule for the crown), charged the jury to disregard the duke's rank, and, when they deliberated over the amount of damages, to consider the case merely as "a question between A and B." The jury entered a verdict of "guilty" but ignored Mansfield's instructions regarding the amount of damages. They socked it to the duke to the tune of £10,000, plus an additional £3,000 in legal fees. Thirteen thousand pounds in 1770 is worth more than $2.3 million today. Although some people thought that Cumberland should have been hit harder, they conceded that the duke lived on a fixed income and didn't have the money; consequently, any additional sums would have to come out of the royal treasury, punishing the taxpayer instead.

The royal family perennially lived beyond its means. Cumberland was so broke that he sought to borrow the

£13,000 in damages from his brother the king, further embarrassing the crown. Accompanied by Prince William Henry, Duke of Gloucester (George III's favorite brother until his own sexcapade cost him the monarch's goodwill), Cumberland approached George for the cash. But the king didn't have £13,000 in ready money either. Hat in hand, the monarch sheepishly applied to the prime minister, Lord North, to intercede for the royal family in Parliament and to authorize the expenditure from the Civil List. Even worse, time was of the essence. On November 5, the mortified king wrote to North:

> A subject of a most private and delicate kind obliges me to lose no time in acquainting you that my two brothers have this day applied to me on the difficulty that the folly of the youngest has drawn him into; the affair is too public for you to doubt but that it regards the lawsuit; the time will expire for this time seven night when he must pay the damages and the other expenses attending it. He has taken no step to raise the money, and he has now applied to me as the only means by which he can obtain it; I therefore promised to write to you, though I saw great difficulty in your finding so large a sum as thirteen thousand pounds in so short a time; but . . . [he pointed out to me] that the prosecutor would eventually force the House, which would at this licentious time occasion disagreeable reflections on the rest of his family as well as on him.

The king hastened to remind the PM, "Whatever can be done ought to be done," and it went without saying, though George did so anyway, that "I ought as little as possible to appear in so very improper a business." After Lord North managed to secure the funds through the treasurer, Le Grand, the sovereign assured Le Grand that he hadn't taken the whole sordid business sitting down, writing, "I flatter myself that the truths I have thought it incumbent to utter may be of some use in his future conduct."

King George was ever the responsible big brother. But their sister, Princess Amelia, cut off all communication with Cumberland following the verdict, although he'd been her favorite sibling. Amelia had agreed with the jury. According to Lady Coke, "the little remorse he seem'd to have for having ruin'd a whole family quite shocked her, and the little feeling he had for himself, though abus'd and ridiculed in every public paper, considering his rank, shocked her to the last degree."

Britons waited breathlessly for the next step. Would Lord Grosvenor (who claimed that he would donate the damages money to charity) move forward with an adultery trial and ask Parliament to grant him a divorce?

On July 28, 1770, the *Middlesex Journal* coyly reported that "a very Great Personage and his amiable Lady have expressed a wish to L[ord] G[rosvenor] that he not sue for divorce, fearing that an alliance by no means to be wished would be the consequence." That possible "consequence"— a marriage between Lady Grosvenor and her royal lover— would have been disastrous, creating even more humiliation for the crown. The former Henrietta Vernon would never have made an appropriate wife for a prince of the blood; and their marriage would have kept the House of Hanover from being able to cement another vital dynastic and political alliance by uniting Cumberland with some foreign princess.

The case of *Grosvenor v. Cumberland* continued to fuel the excitement of the press. One pamphleteer referred to the matter as "the most important and remarkable trial ever to come before a court of jurisdiction." And another anonymous author expressed the more or less middle-class opinion that royal princes should be held to the same moral standards as the king (and George III was nothing else if not a prig). A royal's conduct was "a matter of national as well as private concern, such a dangerous influence do they derive from their titular and elevated station." The consensus among members of the press was that Cumberland's behavior had disgraced the crown and, by extension, England herself.

A satirical ditty was published anonymously, unfavorably comparing the lecherous duke to his uncle—the previous Duke of Cumberland, who had routed Bonnie Prince Charlie at the Battle of Culloden.

The Adulterer, A Poem

See, how dishonouring his Noble Race
Thy nephew earns reproaches and disgrace
Whilst a vile deed of rapine and fraud
Shall spread his Name with Infamy abroad
And foreign nations shall this land abuse
—For who shall dare th'atrocious act excuse?

After the verdict was rendered Lord Grosvenor left for Newmarket, where he shamelessly appeared in public with his latest doxy on his arm. Suprisingly, Lady Grosvenor was the only party who more or less escaped whipping.

In fact, she was more pitied than censured. She swiftly became the heroine of a trio of sentimental novels, viewed as the victim of a loveless marriage, a situation that many eighteenth-century women could easily relate to. The titles, including *The Fair Adulteress* and *The Innocent Adulteress*, did not conceal Henrietta's guilt, but nonetheless found her blameless.

By the autumn of 1770 Lady Grosvenor had spent six months in rented lodgings and was running out of funds to sustain herself and her small household staff. The cruelest twist of all was that her handsome prince was not about to ride to her financial rescue. Cumberland soon revealed himself to be the slimiest of frogs. When the going got tough for his lover, and Henrietta wondered how she'd survive the coming winter, he dumped her. They never again crossed paths.

Come Christmas, Cumberland was dashing about town with his newest inamorata, a courtesan known as Mrs. Hailey. King George, who must have thought that things couldn't get worse after his brother had accepted treasury funds to pay Lord Grosvenor's legal damages, was utterly mortified by the duke's shameful conduct.

Nothing says revenge like a neglected wife and jilted lover. Once Henrietta realized that she would never wear the ermine mantle of a duchess, she decided to contest the lawsuit that her husband had filed in the consistory court in Doctors Commons—an action that Grosvenor had fully assumed she would not take—countersuing him for libel. Because her liaison with the duke was over, her ladyship didn't need a divorce anymore; she required *economic* freedom, which was exactly the sort of ruling the consistory court could give. If she won her countersuit, the

Grosvenors would be formally separated, though not legally divorced, and Henrietta hoped for a big payday.

Her case was an easy one to make, abetted by a sorority from a distant quarter; the creepiest prostitutes imaginable came crawling out of the woodwork to cheerfully testify that Grosvenor was a regular client. On April 22, 1771, Doctors Commons began deliberations, and soon reached its verdict: Although Lord Grosvenor had demonstrated proof of his wife's infidelity, he himself had been shown to have ". . . led, and doth continue to lead, a vicious, lewd, and debauched life and conversation, by visiting, corresponding with, and carnally knowing, diverse strange women of loose character."

The court vindicated Lady Grosvenor by awarding her £1,200 a year (more than $206,000 today), to be paid by her husband. It was a victory, but not a triumph. Henrietta remained ostracized from society and was compelled to watch her purse to make ends meet. But one presumes she eventually found at least a modicum of happiness when she hooked up with a younger man, Lt. Gen. George Porter, an MP for Stockbridge.

Lord Grosvenor was created 1st Earl Grosvenor in July 1784, and died on August 5, 1802, leaving Henrietta a widow. On September 1, she married Porter, who in 1819 inherited the Hungarian title of Baron de Hochepied. They both died in 1828, within three months of each other.

The Duke of Cumberland remained estranged from the king until November 3, 1771, when he arrived, uninvited, at Richmond Lodge. The thirty-three-year-old monarch undoubtedly wondered why his brother had suddenly reappeared. The men exchanged banal pleasantries, perhaps discussing the weather and everyone's general health.

And then the twenty-six-year-old duke took a letter from his pocket and wordlessly thrust it into the king's hands.

As he read it, King George grew more livid with every clause. A torrid affair that became the talk of the nation was nothing compared to what Cumberland had gone and done this time:

> Sir, [the note began] It is impossible for me to describe the emotions whilst I impart an event which I feel I never should have kept a moment secret from you if I had not found myself incapable of offering you the cruel alternative of either being involved in any inconvenience by giving your consent to it; or of pronouncing my future misery for life by your refusal. Sir, I am married to Mrs. Horton Lord Ihrnam's daughter and nothing now remains to make me one of the happiest of men but your approbation which I trust the sensibility of your heart and the amiable qualifications of the object of my choice will strongly plead for and fully justify.
>
> ~Your most
> anxious and
> dutiful brother

The statuesque and voluptuous Anne Horton, Cumberland's clandestine bride, had a slightly checkered past. Her father was a notorious rake, although that was often a badge of honor in the eighteenth century. She had been married previously, wedding Christopher Horton on August 4, 1765 (he died four years later), and was something of a flirt herself. Horace Walpole described her to Horace Mann as a "coquette beyond measure, artful as Cleopatra, and completely mistress of all her passions and projects." According to a contemporary, Anne had the most amorous eyes in the world, with long, luscious lashes.

Anne's brother was well-known—and not liked—in England, which made the duke's marriage an even stickier situation. He was Henry Lawes Luttrell, the candidate for Middlesex MP, shoehorned into Parliament against the wishes of the voters, who had preferred the firebrand John Wilkes. But Wilkes had been barred from taking his seat in the Commons because he was an outlaw, having been convicted of seditious libel.

Although it would have been proper for Cumberland to have asked the king's permission before he so rashly wed a commoner (and such a controversial one at that), there was at the time no law preventing the duke from doing so. And because he was twenty-six years old, Cumberland didn't require his mother's consent or that of the head of the family—King George. Henry had deliberately presented his older brother with a fait accompli because he knew full well that George would never have given the marriage his blessing. To have done so would have been tantamount to tossing away one of his international bargaining chips, and he had only a finite number of siblings to unite with members of the continental royal houses.

George keenly felt that Cumberland had shown zero sense of duty and had betrayed family, crown, and country by wedding Mrs. Horton. The king himself had once been madly in love with a commoner, Lady Sarah Lennox, but duty had compelled him to marry a German princess, the better to cement England's political alliances. If *he* had willingly sacrificed his happiness to the exigencies of obligation, so indeed should the rest of the royal family.

George III's specific reaction to the contents of Cumberland's letter has been preserved.

After walking some minutes in silence to smother my feelings, I without passion spoke to him to the following effect, that I could not believe he had taken the step declared in the paper, to which he answered that he would never tell me an untruth.

In a letter to their mother, the king confided,

The more I reflect on his conduct, the more I see it as his inevitable ruin and as a disgrace to the whole family.

And George expressed his private feelings in a letter to another of his younger brothers, Prince William, Duke of Gloucester—who was in Florence recuperating from an illness. Unbeknownst to King George, Gloucester had *also* contracted a clandestine marriage with a commoner, Maria Walpole, Countess Waldegrave.

It is grievous to me to be obliged to acquaint you with an event that as it disgraces the family must cause you pain. The D[uke] of C[umberland], not content with his unwarrantable conduct in the St. Albans business, his attendance on Mrs. Hailey, and his connection with Fetty Place and Newmarket grooms, has now stooped to marry Mrs. Horton, Lord Ihrnam's daughter. . . . In any country a Prince marrying a subject is looked upon as dishonourable, nay in Germany the children of such a marriage cannot succeed to any territories. But here where the crown is but too little respected it must be big with the greatest mischiefs. . . .

It is impossible I can ever receive her or ever look on him again unless he will promise not publicly to acknowledge [his marriage] . . . the story has been too industriously spread by her family for anyone to doubt the truth; but if he does not avow, her people will by degrees grow doubtful, and I can without disgrace see him. . . . His retiring out of the kingdom is the only decent thing he has done. I could not write but I have sent Deaken [Colonel Deaken was George's emissary] with my firm resolution of never seeing him again unless he consents to let this affair remain doubtful and that he never names the subject to his mother or me.

Cumberland and his wife had already sailed for the Continent. He assured the king that,

No person whatsoever knew of this transaction but one lady and the clergyman who married us on Weds 2nd of October 1771. . . . To avoid suspicion I have taken the name of Thomas Johnson Esq. [he was always one for disguises!] as I was obliged to have correspondence with a banker.

Writing to Colonel Deaken from Lille, Cumberland appeared flummoxed by George's demands.

The king does not desire that I disavow my marriage, but my wife is to be called Mrs. Horton and in the above condition alone I am to be admitted to His Majesty's presence—that is the King's commands. . . . I am not logician enough to be able to understand this paradox. She can only be my wife or not.

According to George III, his brother's lopsided marriage was "a stain the D of C has put on me." The duke would not publicly disavow his marriage to the former Anne Horton, although the couple was content to accept the king's refusal to permit Anne to use the title Duchess of Cumberland. Nevertheless, nearly everyone referred to her or addressed her as such, even if she was not so officially styled.

The king also made it clear that anyone visiting Cumberland House would not be permitted entrance to St. James's, meaning that if one were foolhardy enough to consider the duke his friend, he would no longer be welcome at court. George informed their mother (who evidently seemed inclined to support his view), "I now wash my hands of the whole affair and shall have no further intercourse with him."

After summoning his prime minister, Lord North, with an eerie prescience George expressed his concern to the PM that if he didn't do something to close the barn door (even after Cumberland had escaped through it), his other siblings, as well as his numerous progeny, might also be tempted to bolt and to make unsuitable marriages by following their hearts. Still unaware that the Duke of Gloucester had already done exactly that, the king confided to Gloucester, "I must . . . on the first occasion show my resentment," adding that Cumberland's children "must know what they have to expect if they could follow so infamous an example."

The eventual denouement of this determination was the Royal Marriages Act of 1772. The bill prohibited any descendants of George II from marrying without the consent of the king if they were under twenty-five years old. After they reached the age of twenty-five, they could wed whom they chose as long as they gave the privy council twelve months' notice—unless both houses of Parliament expressly declared their disapproval of the proposed match.

Perhaps because it was off-limits to anyone claiming to be a friend of the king, Cumberland House became a sort of rival court. It was as filled with gaiety, laughter, music, and amateur theatrics as St. James's was dull and fastidiously decorous. And King George had an even stronger reason to ostracize the duke when Cumberland took the young Prince of Wales under his wing. The future George IV found his uncle's entertainments, his friends, his politics, and his vacation destinations (such as the up-and-coming seaside town of Brighthelmstone, eventually shortened to Brighton) vastly preferable to his father's court. The Prince of Wales would also eventually (and secretly) wed a widowed commoner, and a Catholic one, at that. His marriage to Maria Fitzherbert violated numerous statutes, including the Royal Marriages Act of 1772.

The Cumberlands spent several years living on the Continent, chiefly because they could not afford to keep up appearances in England.

In 1775, the duke became the royal patron of a boat club, the Cumberland Fleet, which evolved into the Royal Thames Yacht Club. He was promoted to admiral of the Royal Navy, but was forbidden by the king to assume command— a lucky break for the seamen who would have served under him, because the duke's naval experience would have fit inside a barnacle.

Cumberland was diagnosed with ulcers on his lungs in 1779 and retired to Brighthelmstone for the healthful sea air. During the Gordon Riots that tore up London the following June, he and his other wayward brother, the Duke of Gloucester, were reconciled to the king (albeit not fully) when they offered their support to the crown. George still remained unprepared to forgive Cumberland for being a bad influence on the Prince of Wales. But at least both Cumberland and Gloucester were not hypocritical in supporting the prince's clandestine marriage to Mrs. Fitzherbert.

Between 1783 and 1786 the childless Cumberlands returned to the Continent. Aware of the king's continuing displeasure with him, the thirty-seven-year-old duke announced that he intended to become a "Citizen of the World," although it was really an effort to stave off his creditors that kept him on the opposite side of the Channel. But by 1787 he was back on English soil, acting as the emissary between the Prince of Wales and Prime Minister Pitt during the prince's first campaign to clear his debts.

On September 18, 1790, the Duke of Cumberland dropped dead in Pall Mall, outside Cumberland House. An autopsy of the forty-five-year-old royal found his right lung "universally diseased." He was buried ten days later in Westminster Abbey.

Anne, the unofficial duchess, was granted an annuity of £4,000 (over $641,000 today), a sum that she considered barely enough to keep herself in the manner to which she had become accustomed. To make ends meet she sold off her late husband's valuable collection of rare manuscripts and musical instruments. The Prince of Wales ended his friendship with her in 1794 after she dared to criticize Maria Fitzherbert.

Anne had been compelled to move out of Cumberland House in 1793, when her debts became too burdensome. Seven years later, she transferred the lease to her bankers and decamped to the Continent, where by law her creditors could not reach her. She died in the tiny town of Gorizia, near Trieste, on December 28, 1808.

The Duke of Cumberland's scandalous sexual escapades mortified both king and kingdom. And his marriage to Anne Horton left the British monarchy a permanent legacy. Had Cumberland not been such a royal pain, George III would never have felt the need for the creation of the Royal Marriages Act of 1772, the terms of which still bind England's ruling family.

Pauline Bonaparte

1780–1825

ONE OF THIS BOOK'S MORE ALLURING BRATS WAS THE bodacious and sexually rapacious Pauline Bonaparte, Napoleon's prettiest, and by far most promiscuous, sister. Her libidinous antics not only scandalized the emperor (quite a feat, as he was a pretty randy soul himself), but became the subject of international gossip. Wherever Pauline went, from Corsica to the Caribbean and numerous locations in between, she left a trail of illicit love affairs in her wake. These messes, which it too often fell to Napoleon to clean up, proved a tremendous distraction to a man who was busy trying to conquer the world. Despite the scoldings he gave her vis-à-vis her social and sexual shenanigans, Napoleon could never be angry with her for long. She was his favorite sibling, and the two of them shared a unique bond. Many were quick to believe it was something more.

Although Pauline eventually became a princess, a title she cheerfully flaunted in front of her other sisters (who were ennobled only through the good graces of their over-achieving brother), her life began with little promise of wealth and privilege. Maria Paola—twelve years younger than her famous brother, Napoleon—took her first breaths in a tenement house in Ajaccio, Corsica, the sixth of seven children born to Letizia and Charles Buonaparte.

Paoletta, as she was called, was only four when her father died, and although Napoleon was sent away to military school to make something of himself, she received little, if any, formal education. In the summer of 1793 her fate changed dramatically when the family was forced to flee Corsica, caught up in the island's war of independence from the French. The Buonapartes had sided with France. Napoleone (as he was then known), one of the army's rising stars, was compelled to rescue his family after their home had been torched by Corsican patriots. They were taken aboard a frigate to the south of France, where by degrees Paoletta became more Francofied, changing her name first to Paulette and eventually to Pauline. Napoleon was the one who modified the spelling of their surname to Bonaparte, dropping the "e" from the end of his Christian name in the process.

The teenage Pauline's fine features and chiseled beauty drew notice, but the attention was not necessarily favorable. Pauline believed her looks and vivacity afforded her a license to flirt outrageously and to blurt out whatever was on her mind at whatever moment she chose. As a result she developed the somewhat obnoxious habit of frequently interrupting dinner parties when some venerated adult was holding forth to make some inane exclamation or to laugh uproariously at her own joke.

At the age of fifteen she became engaged to a man twenty-six years older, Stanislaus Fréron, the pro-Consul in Marseille. In the summer of 1794 Robespierre had sent Fréron to the Midi to represent the face of the Terror in the region, and just weeks later, after Robespierre's execution and the Terror's subsequent collapse, Fréron had been placed in charge of establishing order. For a man who had energetically espoused the revolutionary beliefs and supported the execution of a king, and who had overseen the judicial murder of countless members of the titled nobility, Fréron lived like a pasha. His taste for extravagance was not, however, at odds with the Bonapartes. Although the family had come from modest circumstances and began their life in France as Corsican refugees, they had an innate sense of entitlement that was always antithetical to revolutionary ideals.

The Bonaparte family was divided as to whether Pauline was making a good match. The pair had been introduced by Napoleon's brother Lucien, who had been Fréron's aide-de-camp in Marseille. Napoleon himself initially supported the May-December marriage, but their mother, Letizia, was vehemently against it. Not only was Fréron more than old enough to be Pauline's father, but at the time the couple became engaged, he had been enjoying a five-year affair with an Italian actress, by whom he had 2.5 children (two, with one on the way, due sometime around his wedding day to Pauline).

Despite the vast difference in their ages, Pauline was very excited about her impending nuptials, insisting that she was passionately in love with her fiancé; and Letizia's antipathy only strengthened her belief that her relationship with Fréron was star-crossed.

On February 9, 1796, Pauline wrote to her intended:

> . . . I swear, dear Stanislaus, ever to love but you alone. My heart is not for sharing. It's given to you whole. Who could oppose the union of two souls who seek only happiness and who find it in loving each other? No, my love, not Maman, not anyone can refuse you my hand.

That spring, Napoleon, having just wed Josephine de Beau-harnais, was appointed Commander of the Interior and was given command of the French army in Italy. Although he had an older brother, Napoleon's position and potential for greatness made him the de facto head of the family. His siblings were to share his ambition in that he expected them to marry up. "No money, no match," was his philosophy.

By that reckoning, Stanislaus Fréron was about to self-eliminate from the list of eligible suitors for Pauline's hand. He was denounced for embezzlement on March 30, 1796. Mademoiselle Masson, his pregnant mistress, then stepped forward. After such a one-two punch, Napoleon swiftly changed his mind about his sister's impending marriage. He told their older brother, Joseph, "Please arrange the business of Paulette," then wrote to his colleague Paul Barras, who was also a friend of Fréron's, to persuade Stanilaus to gracefully back out of the engagement and not to insist on marrying "a child of sixteen of whom he is old enough to be the father. One does not try to marry when one has two children by a woman still living." Napoleon would always be extremely fastidious when it came to other people's morals, although his own were frequently questionable.

Despite her brother's efforts to end their engagement, Pauline still had her heart set on Fréron, even going so far as to write a letter to him commiserating with the condition of "that woman," saying, "I put myself in her place and feel for her."

And on July 2, after Pauline had fallen into a river and nearly drowned, she wrote to Fréron,

I don't talk more about your mistress. All that you say reassures me. I know your honest heart and approve the arrangements you are making in that respect. The water I drank in the river has not cooled the warmth of my heart for you. It was more likely nectar I swallowed.

That December, Napoleon gave orders for Pauline to quit Marseille and meet him at his army headquarters in Milan. Fréron was thus abandoned. He eventually wed his mistress and after a brief second act as commissioner in Saint-Domingue he slipped into poverty and obscurity, dying of yellow fever on the island in 1802.

Meanwhile, Pauline's star was on the ascent. In Milan she met one of her brother's officers, Adjutant General Victor Emmanuel Leclerc, in his mid-twenties, dashing, chiseled, and nicknamed "the blond Napoleon." Leclerc had adopted his mentor's manner of walking with his hands behind his back; and he also imitated a gesture Napoleon's older brother, Joseph, was fond of—that of crossing his right arm over his waist and tucking his hand inside his coat.

On April 20, 1797, Leclerc and Pauline announced their intention to wed.

However, there is a bit more to the story than a sudden *coup de foudre* of attraction. After Napoleon caught his sister with Leclerc in his study having ecstatic sex behind a screen, he determined that the sooner Pauline got married, the better.

Leclerc had evidently loved Pauline from afar for three years. But he was hardly marrying an heiress. Her dowry was an unimpressive forty thousand francs. They were also a pair of opposites: Leclerc was as serious as Pauline was vivacious, fondly referring to him as *mon joli petit gamin*—"my cute little imp."

At the time, the Milanese Republican army headquarters resembled a royal court, particularly after Josephine arrived with her daring, sophisticated coterie of friends. Pauline took advantage of the cultural and shopping opportunities to bedeck herself in gold, swanning into La Scala in all her gilded splendor. Wherever she went, Pauline made quite an impression, with her pale skin, sensuous mouth, dark eyes, and dark hair. She was particularly proud of her milky complexion and her dainty hands and feet. And at five-foot-six, she was more or less the same height as her ambitious brother.

The saucy Pauline was hardly a bashful, blushing bride-to-be. And modesty was never her strong suit. She knew full well that she was gorgeous and desirable, and played it to the hilt. According to the poet Antoine-Vincent Arnault, a friend of Leclerc's who had occasion to dine in Pauline's company, she was a "singular mix of all that was most complete in physical perfection and most bizarre in moral qualities." Arnault found Pauline "the prettiest and worst-behaved person imaginable" with "the deportment of a schoolgirl, chattering away without pause, laughing at nothing and everything, contradicting the most eminent personages, sticking out her tongue at her sister-in-law [Josephine] behind her back, nudging my knee when I wasn't paying sufficient attention, and drawing upon herself from time to time the most terrifying looks of reproof from her brother. . . . But this didn't work with her. A minute later she would start again. To have the authority of the general of the Army of Italy checked thus by the giddiness of a little girl!"

Arnault was far from the only one to recognize Pauline's combination of beauty and frivolity. The renowned Austrian statesman and diplomat Klemens Wenzel, Prince von Metternich, thought her "as pretty as it is possible to be," but "in love with herself and her only occupation was pleasure."

Pauline's animosity toward Josephine is intriguing because they shared many similarities. Each came from a modest background and had been given a minimal education. And both women had a certain magnetic appeal in addition to their beauty. Perhaps Pauline's jealousy stemmed from the fact that she herself was wildly in love with her brother.

On June 14, 1797, Pauline married Leclerc in a civil ceremony at Mombello, outside Milan, in which she formally renounced any claim to the Bonaparte family property. A religious ceremony was held that evening. Napoleon had requested a dispensation from the Milanese archbishop because the banns had been posted for only a civil marriage. Although the radical revolutionaries had secularized France, Leclerc was a religious man. Their church ceremony was a double wedding: Pauline's older sister Elisa wed a fellow Corsican, Felice Bacciochi.

The Leclercs honeymooned on Lake Como, and Pauline was soon pregnant. On April 20, 1798, she bore a son who was baptized Dermide Louis Napoleon Leclerc; the boy's first name was chosen by his godfather, Napoleon, after the hero of one of his favorite epic poems. It was a difficult birth that left Pauline with health problems for the rest of her life. Years later she would be diagnosed with salpingitis, an inflammation of the fallopian tubes, that might have stemmed from Dermide's birth, but might just as well have been the result of multiple sexual partners, or from gonorrhea. According to the late historian Christopher Hibbert, one symptom of salpingitis is nymphomania; and Pauline's recent biographer Flora

Fraser posits that the disease may have rendered Pauline nearly infertile, which gave her the freedom to indulge her promiscuity without fear of pregnancy. The symptoms of salpingitis include intense abdominal pain and difficulty walking—which might have accounted for Pauline's insistence over time that she be carried everywhere in a chair or on a litter. In the autumn of 1801, and again several years later, she required a purpose-built girdle to support her pelvis.

Ill health compelled Leclerc to resign his post as Commander in Chief of the Army of Italy. He received a transfer to Paris, which delighted his wife; naturally, she couldn't wait to shop. According to a contemporary, Madame Reinhardt, "The new vogues are of the utmost importance to her." Although Pauline was not an intellectual, she managed to hold her own at the most fashionable Parisian salons, basking in the reflected glory of her brother's Egyptian military victory.

She was eager to make her own mark in the capital, however, and quickly became known for her wardrobe— or lack thereof. At a ball given in her honor by an old family friend from Corsica, Madame Permon, Pauline arrived attired as a bacchante, with her hair dressed in a band of panther skin accentuated with a cluster of golden grapes. Gold bracelets and cameos jangled on her pale, bare arms. Unfortunately her evening was ruined when an envious guest called attention to Pauline's less than perfect ears, drawing all eyes to the physical flaw, and thereby eclipsing her exotic ensemble and fragile beauty. Pauline went home in tears.

But she soon learned to imitate the cruelty of her rivals, mastering the Parisian sophisticate's manner of flaying an adversary with cutting remarks. Female detractors aside, she began to attract, unsurprisingly, a cadre of male admirers.

Leclerc was soon posted abroad, and according to Madame Permon's daughter, Laure, Pauline began juggling three lovers. General Pierre de Ruel, later the Marquis de Beurnonville, was in his mid-forties when Pauline began having sex with him. Meanwhile she was just as enthusiastically entertaining General Moreau, the former leader of the French army in Germany, and General Etienne-Jacques Macdonald, governor of Versailles. Since her husband was also a military leader, she must have been one of those women who just couldn't resist a man in uniform. Long gone (if she ever really existed) was the girl who had promised Stanislaus Fréron her entire heart, because it was "not made for sharing."

All three generals were good friends, yet they allegedly knew nothing about the others' attachments to Pauline until, like the coquettish Célimène in Molière's *Le Misanthrope*, she indiscriminately disseminated nasty comments that one of her lovers had made about another. The generals compared notes and each in turn dumped her—another plot point straight out of *Le Misanthrope*.

Leclerc was the sort of man who was hard on himself, but indulgent to his young wife. According to Laure Permon, "Madame Leclerc treated her husband despotically, and yet she went in fear, not that her husband would rebuke her, but that the first consul would." In a bloodless coup on November 19, 1799, Napoleon had become the first consul in the new Directory government, making him the most powerful man in France.

Both Pauline and Leclerc were ambitious for his military career, but assignments in Dijon in 1800 and the following year as lieutenant general of the Army of the Observation of the Gironde, headed for Spain, resulted in little glory. Meanwhile, Pauline was envious of her younger sister Caroline. Two years Pauline's junior, the vivacious blonde Caroline had married another of Napoleon's aides, Joachim Murat, whose career was accelerating as Leclerc's was stalled in neutral.

In 1801 Napoleon recalled Leclerc from his Gironde position and placed him in command of a fleet whose mission was to retake the island of Saint-Domingue (present-day Haiti) from the rebel slaves who had seized control under the leadership of Toussaint L'Ouverture. Saint-Domingue was rich in sugar, indigo, coffee, and cotton, and once Leclerc had taken control of the island he was to remain there to govern it on behalf of France.

At the time, Paris was rife with gossip about Pauline's promiscuity, as well as her interest in the occult. She was fond of clairvoyants, tarot card readings, and divinations prophesied from reading the patterns of egg whites cracked into a glass of water, as well as the use of enemas concocted from the boiled intestines of farm animals. The capital also buzzed with rumors that she was riddled with venereal disease. One of her lovers, the Marquis de Sémonville, a former commissioner in Corsica, reminisced, "There were five of us sharing her favors in the same house before she left for Saint-Domingue . . . she was the greatest hussy you can imagine, but also the most tempting."

Pauline and Leclerc set sail for Saint-Domingue on December 14, 1801. The conflict was a bloody one, resulting in thousands of casualties and the torching of the island's capital city, Le Cap. But Leclerc managed to crush the rebellion in forty days, and ultimately enlisted L'Ouverture's men in his own army. He was also able to rebuild Le Cap in nine weeks.

While her husband was quashing the rebellion, Pauline was alleged to have alleviated her colonial boredom by indulging in numerous extramarital affairs, including ménages à trois with two other women, taking lovers of all colors and both genders. According to one rumor, among her many paramours were one of Leclerc's subordinates, General Jean-François Debelles, nicknamed the "Apollo of the French Army" for his golden good looks, and Jean Robert Humbert, a French bureaucrat renowned for his brutality. Although the rumors of Pauline's sexual insatiability were completely unsubstantiated, they were nonetheless both rampant and abundant. According to her detractors, none of whom were actually on Saint-Domingue at the time, "The tropical sun was, they say, astonished by the ardor of her passions."

Many of the allegations were part of a British smear campaign against Napoleon and his family, or were penned well over a decade later, after his ignominious fall from power. However, not all of them were written after the fact. Scurrilous remarks about his little sister's conduct reached Napoleon in France, because he warned Pauline to behave herself.

> . . . Remember that fatigue and suffering are nothing when one shares them with one's husband . . . make yourself beloved by . . . your affability, and behave prudently, never thoughtlessly. . . . Make sure all the world is pleased with you, and be worthy of your position.

Napoleon reminded Pauline to

> Take care of your husband . . . and don't give him any ground for jealousy. For a serious man, all flirtatious ways are insupportable. [Here, Napoleon was speaking of his

marriage to Josephine as much as Leclerc and Pauline's union.] A wife must be good and seek to pleasure, not demand. Your husband is now truly worthy of the title of my brother, given the glory he is amassing. . . . Unite with him in love and tender friendship.

Unfortunately, Leclerc's glory was short-lived. Responding to rumors that the French intended to reinstate slavery, the blacks rebelled again and the new governor was faced with another insurgency.

On October 22, 1802, Leclerc contracted yellow fever. Although he rallied temporarily, only ten days later—on November 1—Victor Emmanuel Leclerc died at the age of thirty, leaving behind a twenty-two-year-old widow and their four-year-old son. Pauline inherited only a modest seventy thousand francs from his will.

According to Napoleon's Civil Code, she was required to mourn her husband for ten months (the previous tradition had mandated a full year's mourning). Despite her widow's weeds, Pauline had no shortage of admirers and suitors for her hand. After all, she was young, gorgeous, and the sister of the first consul. She had also managed to connive three hundred thousand francs out of her illustrious brother in exchange for an elaborate carriage she had previously requested, in order to compete with their younger sister Caroline's equipage.

After the death of her *joli petit gamin*, Pauline chopped off her lustrous brown locks, fashioning the hair into tiny cushions that she placed beneath the bandages on Leclerc's lifeless face. In exchange, she demanded her husband's blond curls as a memento mori.

Still young, still restless, still vivacious, Pauline returned to Paris, chafing at the rules that governed her widowhood; she longed to be back in society and to once again reign as the capital's leading beauty.

In April 1803, Pope Pius III's legate, Cardinal Caprara, introduced Pauline to Prince Camillo Borghese. The darkly handsome, twenty-eight-year-old prince was of modest height, with similar angular features to Pauline's. According to Laure Junot, now the duchesse d'Abrantes, "This head with coal black eyes and mane of jet black hair, it seemed to me, must contain not only passionate, but great and noble ideas."

She could not have been more wrong. "He had nothing to say, although a lively manner of saying it," and, "No one was more capable of driving a four-in-hand, but no one was less capable of carrying on a conversation," were the sort of remarks Parisians made about him.

In historian Flora Fraser's words, "He was, to put it plainly, a booby, if a harmless one." Camillo's father, the illustrious Prince Marcantonio Borghese, had deliberately stinted on his son's education, and in that respect, at least, Camillo and the unschooled Pauline had something in common.

However, Prince Camillo Borghese was a very *wealthy* booby—from an ancient and prominent Roman family with significant real estate holdings in Tuscany (including Florence), and in Rome and its environs. And their vast art collections were already world-renowned. What made Camillo an even better catch was that he was genuine titled nobility.

Napoleon's older brother, Joseph Bonaparte, who had been his ambassador to Rome in 1798, was one of the men who contrived the grand plan to marry the doltish

Italian prince to Pauline. Most of the Bonapartes agreed to the scheme right away, and the proposed match was favored by the *famiglia* Borghese as well. Curiously, the only dissenting voice (or perhaps he was merely playing the devil's advocate) was Napoleon's.

And yet the plan proceeded apace. Team Bonaparte contrived to make the marriage seem like Camillo's idea—and when Pauline was responsive to it, the prince was so overwhelmed that he could scarcely believe his dream was about to come true.

Napoleon finally agreed to the match, but insisted that Pauline wait a full twelve months after Leclerc's death before heading to the altar again, violating his own Civil Code in favor of the old tradition.

On August 25, 1803, the couple signed a prenuptial agreement that contained the following assurances: Napoleon would provide Pauline with a five-hundred-thousand-franc dowry; Camillo bought her three hundred thousand francs' worth of diamonds and gave her access to the priceless Borghese family jewels. Pauline's inheritance from Leclerc would remain hers alone. If Camillo predeceased her, she would receive an annuity of fifty thousand francs a year, plus two luxurious carriages and the right to maintain apartments in two Borghese residences.

Although the civil marriage ceremony was not scheduled to take place until November, Pauline couldn't wait that long; always impetuous and impatient, she had consummated her relationship with Camillo in July. So on August 28, the twenty-two-year-old Pauline clandestinely wed her prince. Somehow they managed to keep the ceremony a secret from Napoleon's vast network of spies.

Pauline tingled with anticipation at the prospect of

making her Paris debut as a real princess. Dripping with her in-laws' diamonds, she attended a soiree hosted by Napoleon, palpably ecstatic when she was formally announced to the assemblage as "Princess Borghese." But she had not anticipated the dressing-down she received from her brother; after all, she was not supposed to be Princess Borghese for another quarter of a year. Napoleon was surprised, shocked, and humiliated to learn— in a public gathering, no less—that his favorite sister had flagrantly flouted his directive regarding her re-marriage, coldly informing Pauline, "Please understand, Madame, that there is no princess where I am. Have more modesty and do not take a title that your sisters do not possess."

Although he had succeeded in mortifying her, Napoleon did not remain angry with Pauline for long. He wrote to her in Rome, advising her to

Be sure to show sweetness and kindness to everyone, and great consideration for the ladies of your husband's family. . . . Never criticize anything or say "We do this or that better in Paris." . . . What I would most like to hear about you is that you are well behaved . . . love your hus-band, make your household happy, and above all do not be frivolous or capricious. You are twenty-four years old and ought to be mature and sensible by now. I love you.

The wish was not father to the deed, however. Pauline promptly violated her brother's precepts. She delayed a meeting in which she was to be presented to the pope because the dress she was planning to wear had not yet arrived from Paris. And she insulted her in-laws and most of Rome's high society by failing to attend a *cercle* given in her honor by her mother-in-law, pleading a violent headache, although she had appeared perfectly chipper and healthy at lunchtime.

Pauline had immediately regretted her second marriage. After their honeymoon, she took to calling Camillo a eunuch (one wonders what prevented him from performing with such a sexually charged wife, as allegations that he was homosexual have never been substantiated), and later maintained that but for her husband's riches, she wished she had remained a widow.

Nevertheless, Camillo, like his predecessor, remained in thrall to Pauline, instantly jealous of any man who paid attention to her. Given his wife's beauty and flirtatiousness, the prince must have been ready to tear half the men of Italy limb from limb.

Their union had been made in relative haste, and for the wrong reasons. In March 1804, within four months of the official "I do's" and "I will's," Camillo was confiding to one of the matchmakers, Chevalier Luigi Angiolini, that he was "almost continually discontented" with Pauline. And, unsurprisingly, Pauline had already taken a lover.

The object of Pauline's extramarital affections was the penniless hereditary prince of Mecklenburg-Strelitz. They enjoyed romantic picnics in the Roman countryside during the day; and in the evenings she would send her African page boy to escort the prince (who was affecting a disguise) to her apartments in the Palazzo Borghese via a secret staircase.

But all the disguises in the world couldn't mask Pauline's infidelity. Camillo caught her with a compromising letter he'd have "given the world not to have seen." And after their relative Cardinal Fesch was unable to persuade Pauline to behave herself, Napoleon himself dispatched a scathing rebuke.

> Madame and dear Sister: I learn to sorrow that you have not had the good sense to conform to the manners and customs of the city of Rome, that you have shown disdain for its people, and that your eyes are constantly turned toward Paris. . . . Do not count on me to help, if at your age you let yourself be governed by bad advice. As for Paris, be assured you will find no support here, for I shall never receive you without your husband. If you fall out with him, it will be entirely your own fault, and then France will be forbidden you. You will lose your happiness and my friendship.

It bears noting that Napoleon was an utter hypocrite regarding the sanctimony of matrimony. He was a prig when it came to the marriages of his promiscuous sister, and yet he enjoyed so many extramarital liaisons that he had a room adjacent to his office set aside for quickie trysts.

However, Pauline wasn't the powerful first consul of France, and her sexual indiscretions, while acceptable within her Paris coterie, were considered intolerable in Rome—not because she was cheating on her spouse, but because she paraded her infidelity. In contrast, Pauline's mother-in-law had discreetly enjoyed the favors of a lover for years, but successfully kept the affair quiet.

Pauline also flaunted her title, escalating the sibling rivalry among the Bonaparte sisters. Elisa and Caroline complained to Napoleon that Pauline was a princess while they lacked commensurate status. He tried to level the playing field by creating them imperial highnesses following the senate's May 1803 declaration that made him Emperor of the French, but Pauline became miffed because she wanted to claim the exalted rank for her own. She went so far as to remind Caroline of the good old revolutionary days, exclaiming that her late husband Victor Emmanuel Leclerc's Republican sensibilities would have rendered him "astonished" and "angry" at Napoleon's elevation to emperor. Had their brother remained first consul, Pauline would have been the only Bonaparte sister to enjoy a royal title by virtue of her marriage to Prince Camillo Borghese.

Camillo certainly didn't want to share his wife's body with other men, but it didn't stop him from being proud of it. In the summer of 1804, he commissioned the renowned sculptor Antonio Canova to immortalize Pauline as *Venus Victrix*—Venus Victorious. She posed nearly nude with an apple in her hand—the winner of Paris's famous judgment—temptation in marble. Only a flimsy bit of drapery below the waist concealed from public eyes the anatomy that was familiar enough to her husband and countless lovers. At the time, Pauline was unconcerned about any potential damage to her reputation: What stunning extrovert wouldn't want her fabulous looks preserved forever in the guise of the goddess of love and beauty? But Napoleon was predictably disgusted by her vulgarity. "Tell her from me she is no longer beautiful," he lied, "and she will be still less so in a few years, and it is more important to be good and esteemed." The full-size statue, known as "La Paolina" during its creation, was not completed until 1808.

In Italy Napoleon's flesh-and-blood sister was known as "*la diva* Paolina," captivating everyone who came within her orbit; she referred to her lithe, pale limbs, dainty hands and feet, slender hips, and perky breasts as "advantages of nature."

But Canova had to be cajoled into executing his commission. As a native Italian he deplored the ravaging of his homeland by Napoleon's Grande Armée. Yet even he was smitten by Pauline's allure, although he initially proposed that she should represent Diana, goddess of the hunt.

"But nobody would believe my chastity," Pauline replied candidly, insisting that she be immortalized as Venus instead. There was an additional historical allusion to the composition; the Borgheses claimed descent from the mythological founder of Rome, Romulus, son of the war god Mars, who had an astral love-hate relationship with Venus.

Pauline and Camillo's relationship was similarly fraught. Both were bons vivants, enjoying la dolce vita to the fullest; yet they would have separated had Napoleon not warned his sister that she would be unwelcome in France without her doltish husband, and if she didn't behave with at least a modicum of decorum.

But Pauline defended her conduct, writing to Napoleon that she had twisted herself in knots to achieve a felicitous marriage, and was merely the victim of envious gossip:

Despite the difficult and disputatious character of Prince Camillo, our household is the picture of happiness. For I have made sacrifices you would not have believed me capable of. . . . People jealous of advantages I have received by nature and fearing my return to Paris invent these black words to encourage you to abandon me. But write to Prince Camillo and his family, for their responses will convince you that my accusers play false.

In the summer of 1804, Pauline and Camillo went to Florence on holiday and from there traveled to the baths at Pisa. Pleading that the accommodations were too cramped, and that she had a large enough entourage already, the prince convinced Pauline to leave six-year-old Dermide, her son by Leclerc, in the care of Camillo's brother Don Cecco.

During the third week in August, while the royal couple vacationed in Tuscany (and Pauline herself was ill), Camillo received a devastating letter from his brother: Little Dermide had died of a fever. Pauline's lady-in-waiting Jenny Saint-Maur agreed to conceal the dreadful news from Pauline until her health improved, because the Borgheses believed the shock would be too great for her to bear. Ten tense days elapsed. Finally, Pauline divined the truth, after receiving a letter (also written postmortem) informing her of Dermide's illness. Jenny's gloominess and difficulty holding back tears in Pauline's presence confirmed her suspicions that the worst had already transpired.

Pauline immediately blamed Camillo for her son's death, exclaiming, "Without you I never would have been separated from him and he would still be alive. What will the Emperor have to say? And my family? Leave, monsieur, I cannot bear the sight of you. You, the butcher of my son!"

She now viewed Italy, and particularly Rome, as a cursed place and never wished to live there again. Dermide's death had conjured up nostalgically romantic memories of his handsome blond father. And just as she had done right after Leclerc's death, Pauline chopped off her hair, giving it to Jenny to place inside her son's little coffin. Although Napoleon wanted her to remain in Italy, Pauline insisted that her grief was so heavy that there was nowhere else to go but Montgobert, in France, where Leclerc was buried and where Dermide would join him.

Her son's death made Pauline even more self-centered. She initially refused to attend Napoleon's coronation in December 1804, primarily because she and her sisters were expected to act as train bearers for their detested sister-in-law Josephine as she was crowned empress. It was only after Dermide was laid to rest and one of Pauline's sisters sent her a sample of the latest fashion in court dresses (which was too delectably resplendent to resist for very long) that she decided to put in an appearance at the coronation after all. Pauline recast herself as Napoleon's greatest supporter, averring, "He is my protector, he will defend me against the evil designs of my husband."

Napoleon's sisters were expected to take turns hostessing his soirees. But Pauline was clearly more interested in showing off. She paid meticulous attention to her coiffure, and to her lavish wardrobe and lengthy toilette, but neglected to prepare as assiduously to receive their guests, happiest when she was the center of attention. Bawdy as well as irreligious, Pauline broke the decorous mood with a spontaneous peal of laughter one evening while dining with the imperial family; their uncle, Cardinal Fesch; and His Holiness the pope. In response to their shocked looks and sideways glances, she exclaimed, "I was just thinking how it would edify our contemporaries, and astonish posterity, had the Holy Father, who sits there so grave, been so fortunate as to convert me to Christianity, or if I possessed the wiles to pervert him into infidelity!"

With impeccable sangfroid the pope told Pauline that he was sure that "you, before your death, will become one of my flock."

"Then, Holy Father, you must live to a great age," the irreverent princess replied.

Napoleon was fully aware that his sister had no intentions of accompanying Camillo back to Rome. He was also cognizant of her numerous love affairs and didn't wish to leave her to her own devices in Paris. In order to satisfy this conundrum the emperor conferred upon Camillo an order he had established in 1802—the grand cordon of the Légion d'Honneur—which entitled Prince Borghese to immediate French citizenship.

But little could be done to ameliorate a bad marriage. The prince and princess were constantly at each other's throats. Pauline had begun referring to her husband as "His Serene Idiot." And even after Napoleon gave him a commission in his army, posting him to various distant fronts, things didn't get better; as far as Pauline was concerned, Camillo couldn't be sent far enough from her sight.

In order to maintain as much control as possible over his increasingly expanding empire, Napoleon appointed his relatives to rule as satraps—proxies or viceroys who would govern according to his wishes. Because he thought Camillo was a moron and knew how much Pauline disdained and derided court etiquette, the couple received no satrapy. Jealous of her siblings and brothers-in-law, Pauline balked. So Napoleon gave the Borgheses Guastalla. Pauline was delighted at becoming Duchess of Guastalla, fantasizing about presiding over a glittering court in her own little empire, until she thought to ask her brother where Guastalla was.

"A village, a borough—in the states of Parma and Piacenza," Napoleon informed her, admitting that the little duchy covered barely four square miles.

Pauline was incensed. "A village, a borough! What do you expect me to do with that?" she fumed.

"Whatever you like," the emperor coolly replied.

"What I like!" Pauline's vitriol increased; she referred to Guastalla as "a miserable village with a few beastly pigs," insisting that Napoleon treated their youngest sister, Caroline, better than he treated her. She tartly informed Napoleon that if he didn't give her "a proper state, a bit bigger than a pocket handkerchief, and with subjects who don't have four feet and wiggly tails," she'd scratch his eyes out. She then added, "And my poor Camillo, how can you do nothing for him?"

"He is an imbecile," Napoleon responded bluntly.

"True, but so what?"

Pauline ultimately *sold* the duchy of Guastalla to the kingdom of Italy (then a conglomerate of the northern city-states) for six million francs, pocketed the sum, as well as the revenue from Guastalla's feudal lands, and retained the title of duchess. She then invested the income in French government bonds that yielded an annual sum of four hundred thousand francs.

Pauline wanted everything both ways: She wished to take full advantage of her stature as the emperor's favorite sister, yet had little desire to assume most of the responsibilities commensurate with that status, expecting instead the deference owed to her as Principessa Borghese. A contemporaneous (and anonymously written) account of Napoleon's court published in England and titled *The Secret History of the Cabinet of Bonaparte* described Pauline as ". . . very

witty; and very frequently in her sallies, tells her imperial family some bold truths, and very often mocks them.
She thinks, I suppose, that, as she is married to a genuine
prince, such liberties are permitted."

The princess had no kind words at all for her husband,
going so far as to remark very publicly to Napoleon just
as Camillo was about to depart for the German front,
"After a useless life, a glorious death." Despite his personal opinion of the prince, the emperor bristled. "You
always go too far," he admonished Pauline.

Yes, she always did. According to a female court insider,
"She gave herself carte blanche with her favorites and took a
kind of pride in making her preferences public property," a
statement corroborated by a Polish countess, Anna Potocka.
"People talked of nothing but Pauline's intrigues, and they
certainly did provide material for lengthy discussion."

Sometime during the summer of 1806, Pauline told Laure
Junot, duchesse d'Abrantes, "To give oneself to Camillo
was to give oneself to no one." He was reputed to be impo-
tent, but when Pauline took a French count as her lover,
her husband tried to seduce one of her ladies-in-waiting.

That summer, plagued with gynecological concerns, lower
abdominal pain, and periodic pain in her lumbar spine
(her physician, Dr. Peyre, believed her ailments sprang from
an infection in her fallopian tubes), Pauline visited the spa
town of Plombières to take advantage of the hot springs.
There, she insisted on being carried everywhere (though
her pain, rather than divadom, may have been the real
reason for it), as well as bathing—and showering—in
milk. Aware that the dynamic between mistress and servant and the contrast of light and dark created additional
drama and scandal, Pauline would have her strapping black

servant Paul rinse the liquid from her body through a hole in the ceiling. And when people were scandalized that she permitted an African such intimacies, the princess blithely replied that a Negro was not a man.

As the houseguest of her former brother-in-law John Louis Leclerc, she requested one such milk shower. Her host apologized, saying he lacked the appropriate plumbing. No problem, Pauline replied dismissively. Jean Louis could just make a hole in the ceiling from which his servants might "pour the milk through when I am ready. It's a slight inconvenience to you, I know, but think of the consequences to my health."

Paul Barras, a former lover of the empress Josephine when she was between husbands, was certain he understood the genesis of Pauline's malady, after meeting her at another healing spa, Gréoux: "Excessive sexual activity, in consequence of *furor uterinus* [nymphomania] had given her an incurable ill. Too weak to walk, she was in such a state she had to be carried everywhere."

Josephine, too, considered her sister-in-law a nymphomaniac—among other things. She'd harbored her suspicions about the nature of Pauline's relationship with her husband for some time, but one evening at Malmaison during the winter of 1805–1806, after a dinner among family members and friends, the empress approached one of her usual confidants, the philosopher Constantin-François Chasseboeuf, comte de Volney, in tears, exclaiming that she was "wretched indeed. You don't know what I have just seen," Josephine told the count, who was accustomed to offering her a shoulder to cry on whenever she discovered Napoleon's latest marital infidelity. "The Emperor is a scoundrel," she continued. "I have just caught him in Pauline's arms. Do you hear! In his sister Pauline's arms!"

Josephine's outburst to the comte de Volney was not the first time she had expressed the view that her husband and his sister enjoyed an inappropriately intimate relationship. The American diplomat Gouverneur Morris had also heard the rumors, and characterized "the present Princess Borghese" as "a Messalina." Messalina, the wife of the emperor Claudius, reputedly competed with a renowned prostitute to see who could bed more lovers in a single night. When confronted with Josephine's suspicion via a third party, Pauline at first denied any such impropriety, insisting that ". . . the Empress was no better than she should be herself. At length she acknowledged it."

By that time many rumors had surfaced regarding the possibility of an illicit relationship between Pauline and Napoleon. The buzz had begun almost as soon as Napoleon had himself crowned emperor at the end of 1804. His opponents found in Pauline a perfect target for their character assassinations of both of them. Napoleon and his beautiful, promiscuous sister were accused of incest; and other tales circulated that at the age of fourteen Pauline had been a prostitute in a Corsican brothel run by their own mother, giving new meaning to the imperial title of "Madame Mère" that the emperor had bestowed on Letizia.

Further fueling the fires of speculation was the siblings' shared reputation for libidinousness and Napoleon's opinion that his exalted status afforded him license to satisfy "every fantasy." Pauline loved the limelight, and negative attention was still attention. Consequently, even in the absence of firm proof, it is certainly *plausible* that the siblings enjoyed an incestuous affair.

Pauline's recent biographer, historian Flora Fraser, has arrived at the same conclusion, stating that "The truth is, it seems, almost inevitable, given the strong sex drive for which Pauline and Napoleon were both renowned," and for "their mutual affection" and "clannish affinity," as well as their blasé attitude toward their sexual conquests. Not only that, but coming from Corsica, where intermarriage among relatives was a fairly common practice, the Bonapartes may have had a different cultural outlook on incest.

Whether or not it was true that they were lovers, Pauline flaunted her intimacy with the emperor and the odd sort of power that she alone of all her siblings wielded over the most powerful man on earth. She also loved to shock and titillate people.

And regardless of her special relationship with Napoleon, at Plombières in 1806 Pauline finally had a love affair that touched her heart. She began a torrid liaison with another spa visitor, the thirty-year-old Comte Auguste de Forbin, a mediocre painter who had studied in the atelier of the great revolutionary artist Jacques-Louis David. The comte, whose father had been guillotined, was an impoverished aristocrat who also fancied himself a poet. Keeping her affair a secret, Pauline begged Napoleon to employ Forbin as her chamberlain. That done, she paid Forbin's debts; and while Camillo was off fighting in central Europe with the imperial army, Pauline's emotional attachment to her new man did not go unremarked. She lavished him with perquisites, including an expensive carriage pulled by matching milk-white horses.

In 1807, Pauline became a fastidious hostess at her little satellite of the imperial court, her table as important as her toilette; and people clamored for an invitation to the Monday-evening soirees at her grand Parisian home, the Hôtel Charost.

But her physical condition had deteriorated. Pauline's doctors reported that her limbs were spasmodic. The imperial physician, Dr. Halle, confiding in the princess's personal medic, Dr. Peyres, was certain that her "over-stimulated uterus" was the origin of all her ailments. "The douche and the hose," he asserted, "cannot be held responsible for everything. One must suppose that there is a more substantial cause for the exhaustion this young and pretty woman [she was twenty-six years old] who is susceptible, so alone, displays."

Halle insisted that it was an immediate imperative to "save this woman from destruction. And if there is some-one who has preyed on her weakness and is complicit, this person, whoever he may be, could accuse not himself . . . but us—of having seen nothing, or having permitted every-thing." Who else but Napoleon would care enough about Pauline's health, or would be in the position, to accuse the doctors of malpractice? Camillo wasn't even in the coun-try; he was fighting on the fields of Poland at the time. And it isn't likely that Forbin, her erstwhile chamberlain, would have asserted himself so boldly in such an intimate discussion.

The doctors prescribed abstinence, coupled with medic-inal baths. Pauline wrote to Forbin to lament that they were being deliberately kept apart. Still, she managed to outwit her family and her physicians, sending for Forbin to meet up with her while she took her cure; she was even bold enough to visit Forbin's family's mansion in Aix-en-Provence without him. Pauline held out hope of enjoying their Provençal love nest indefinitely, assuring Forbin, "You are my real husband. Mine doesn't merit so sweet, so sacred a title." Referring to Forbin as her "dear idol," she wrote to say, "I send you flowers that have been at my breast, I have covered them with kisses. I love you, you alone."

Napoleon was displeased to hear from his spies that Pauline's erstwhile chamberlain was on his way to Aix-en-Provence to meet her. Camillo, now a general in the imperial army, was no less upset. He let it be known that if Pauline were not the emperor's sister, his revenge upon her would have been dire. Genuine royalty, Prince Borghese also resented playing second fiddle to his parvenue wife, who too often made him feel like he was *her* consort.

In 1807 on one lucky day for both prince and emperor, the lovers quarreled. Pauline hurled a book at Forbin's head and the love affair was over. Napoleon gave Forbin a commission in the Grande Armée and dispatched him to Portugal.

Without an illicit liaison for people to gossip about, they discussed Pauline's outré eccentricities, including her manner of using whoever was handy (servants, government officials, ladies-in-waiting) as human footstools, backrests, shelves, sedan chairs, and even as an arch support and massage roller—when she placed her feet on the throat of her supine waiting woman, Madame de Chambaudoin.

But Pauline soon had a new man in her life, an Italian musician named Felice Blangini, who was understandably terrified that their affair would become public knowledge, dreading most the inevitable wrath of the emperor. Blangini maintained that he "had no wish to go and sing my nocturnes in Spain to a chorus of cannonballs and gunfire."

Around the new year Napoleon named Camillo governor-general of the Transalpine Department of the French Empire, essentially the emperor's viceroy in the northern Italian states that had once comprised the kingdom of Savoy. Pauline was ordered to travel to Turin, the seat of government, and settle in as first lady of the realm. Although she resented being dispatched to a provincial backwater, she dropped Blangini like soiled linen and focused her energy on the new wardrobe that her status would require. She insisted that because she was French-born (which wasn't quite true, as Corsica was still endeavoring to assert its independence when she was a child), she took precedence over her Italian husband. Never mind that *Camillo* was the governor-general; Pauline wanted to be the one to meet with the dignitaries and to hear the common pleas of their new subjects. The couple quarreled vociferously over the issue and only the invocation of Napoleon's name and temper could muzzle Pauline. Once again, the emperor was compelled to advise her to "make yourself beloved, be affable to the world" and to treat her husband well.

Napoleon's admonishment was ignored. In Turin, according to historian Flora Fraser, Pauline may have embarked on yet another extramarital affair—this time a fling with the violinist Niccolò Paganini.

She returned to France when Napoleon began to seriously contemplate a divorce from Josephine, wholeheartedly in favor of her brother's scheme. There she played the role of court hostess to the hilt, determined to excel in her duties. But this docility did not come without a price; the responsibility was exchanged for an annuity: six hundred thousand francs to be paid to her annually by Napoleon and regarded as "separate property" from her marital funds, meaning that Camillo could never touch it.

Pauline was back in her element. According to the Austrian statesman Count Metternich, "She was in love with herself alone, and her sole occupation was pleasure," an account that was not only confirmed but enhanced by the princess's neighbor at Montgobert, Stanislas de Girardin. "Pauline Borghese was then in the full brilliance of her beauty. Men pressed about her to admire her, to pay court. And she enjoyed this homage as her due. In the glances she exchanged with some of them, indeed, there was a recognition of past favors granted or hints of romance to come. Few women have savored more the pleasure of being beautiful."

And few women have had a better knack for combining the dramatic and the exotic. Pauline would recline on a sofa while her black page boy brought her a basin of milk, which she would sip languidly, playing up her pale fragility as high society mingled about her. And when she decided to get up to waltz, "all the other dancers stop, so as not to hurt this delicate and gentle imperial highness. She is very pretty and says very amusing things," an unnamed Austrian observer noted.

Who knows what she was thinking as she sipped her milk. The Austrian diplomat Prince Clary noticed that Pauline "had a habit of falling into a reverie when contemplating an affair."

One of her conquests around this time was Conrad Friedrich, an impressionably young German-born lieutenant on a temporary mission to Paris to request reinforcements for Napoleon's occupying army in Italy. He visited Pauline in Neuilly in the hopes that she might influence her brother to secure the necessary troops. On their first meeting, Pauline and Friedrich enjoyed an idyllic walk in her gardens, and while she insisted to Friedrich that she had no special power over the emperor, she invited him to return the following day—for an assignation.

Her twenty-seven-year-old body thinly veiled and leaving little to the imagination, Pauline greeted the young lieutenant in a grand salon dominated by an enormous bathtub that Friedrich described in his memoirs as being "out of a novel, or even a fairy tale." He could hardly miss "the opulent and perfectly molded curves of her body. . . . She gave me her hand to kiss, wished me welcome and had me sit next to her on a yielding daybed. I was certainly not the seducer, but the one seduced, for in the cavernous twilight Pauline employed all her charms to bring my blood to boiling point and my senses to a point of frenzy. Soon the nameless emissions which marked our mutual passions were imprinted on the velvet cushions. In which Pauline revealed herself still more experienced a lover than I, having greater staying power." Later, "clothed in fine linen wrappers" they climbed into the bathtub. "We stayed nearly an hour in the azure waters, after which we ate in a neighboring room an exquisite meal, and there we stayed till dusk."

But their affair was a brief one, due to Friedrich's discomfort with not being special. "I had to promise to come back soon, and I spent more than one afternoon like that. All the same, I never felt very proud of my conquest, for Pauline had granted the last favors to more than one before me, and was later to grant them to many more. Moreover, she was almost too routine in seeking her own pleasure, and before long, it was more aversion than anticipation that I felt in going there, despite her beauty."

Ouch.

Friedrich was indeed one of numerous lovers Pauline took between 1808 and 1812. Many were foreign generals, and several of them were considerably older than she was. Napoleon divorced Josephine in January 1810 and married

Marie-Louise of Austria three months later. When Camillo, who had become a popular governor in Turin, came to Paris for the wedding, Pauline refused to see him or to speak with him further, after reading him a letter written by Napoleon setting up their "separate property." She declined to feed her husband's entourage, suggesting that they all dine at a restaurant instead. Because she had cut off all personal contact with him, Camillo tried to reach her by letter, but she would not open any of his correspondence.

When Pauline determined that she wasn't receiving enough attention, especially from her powerful brother, she would behave wildly and flaunt her latest extramarital fling. After Napoleon's only child, his son and heir Napoleon François Charles Joseph, was born on March 20, 1811, and the emperor began to lavish his affection on the infant (as well as on his nubile young wife), in retaliation Pauline took another paramour—one who would assuredly provoke her brother's attention.

"*Le beau* Montrond," as he was nicknamed, was a suave and rakish diplomat, a confidant of Napoleon's former foreign secretary Talleyrand. But the emperor had a dim view of Pauline's latest conquest, allegedly asserting, "There will never be morals in France as long as Montrond lives there." Even worse than Montrond's scruples was his politics. He had managed to get himself exiled from Paris for criticizing Napoleon's foreign policy strategy.

In 1812 the thirty-one-year-old Pauline embarked on an affair with the celebrated actor François-Joseph Talma, who was eighteen years her senior. Talma spent innumerable nights giving the equivalent of command performances for his audience of one as Pauline demanded that he read scene after scene of Molière every evening with her as his costar.

It no doubt delighted her to have an affinity with one of France's greatest talents, and perhaps the affair with Talma was somehow connected to Pauline's determination to be immortalized by the most celebrated artists of the day. Not only did Canova sculpt her as *Venus Victrix*, but he also did a cast of her hand. A commemorative medal was struck by Denon, featuring her noble profile on one side, and an image of the Three Graces on the reverse, with the inscription, *Beauty be our queen*. Jean François Bosio sculpted her bust; and her breast was used as the model for the one-of-a-kind golden goblet fashioned by the Paris goldsmith John-Baptiste Odiot.

On the outside Pauline's beauty may have appeared flawless, but her physical condition beneath the surface was entirely the opposite. In 1812, her chronic gynecological ailments were so painful that the doctors advised the application of leeches to her genitals, in addition to the usual purgatives, douches, and bleedings. At the time, leeches were commonly used to treat the effects of gonorrhea—and it's no surprise that Pauline might have contracted the disease, given her own Grande Armée of lovers. Naturally, she ignored all advice to practice abstinence in order to fully recuperate.

As Napoleon's star began to plummet, Pauline grew anxious. Following the 1812 defeat of his army in Russia, she downsized, converting some of her wealth into more portable assets. Defeat in Spain soon followed, and Pauline sold some of her important pieces of jewelry, offering the cash to Napoleon to help defray his astronomical military expenses. Her health continued to deteriorate as her brother's empire crumbled, bit by bit. Members of her entourage sought to keep her from hearing bad news.

On April 11, 1814, according to the terms of the treaty of Fontainebleau, Napoleon was forced to abdicate and instead accept the kingdom of Elba, a tiny island in the Tyrrhenian Sea, ironically not far from his native Corsica. Pauline insisted on joining him there, averring, "I have not always loved the Emperor as I should, but as my brother he has a claim on my allegiance . . . I must offer him my condolences, and if he wishes it, follow him to Elba."

Pauline packed her trunks and, in the company of a small entourage, set out for Elba, with a detour in southern Italy to avail herself of a spa cure. With characteristic entitlement, even after Napoleon's ignominious fate, she ordered some of the latest fashions sent to her in care of the Neapolitan minister at Paris.

Meanwhile, both Pauline and her estranged husband, Camillo, were in the pope's bad graces. During the Napoleonic wars His Holiness had been a prisoner at Savona, which was located within Camillo's governor-generalship. Because of Camillo's immoral lifestyle (he had been having an affair with one of his cousins, the Duchessa Lante della Rovere), the pope refused to allow him to move back to Rome.

Pauline was keen to deprive Camillo as well. When her Paris residence, the Hôtel Charost, was sold in 1814, she demanded that the finest paintings from the Borghese collection be removed from their frames and hidden so that the prince would not find them. Her intention was to use the treasures as bargaining chips, if necessary, presumably to protect her own interests, or Napoleon's. The Hôtel Charost was bought by the Duke of Wellington, Arthur

Wellesley, who would in due time defeat her brother at Waterloo.

On November 1, 1814, Pauline arrived in Elba and honored her promise to be Napoleon's "good angel . . . the treasure of the palace." She had recently celebrated her thirty-fourth birthday, although she still dressed like an ingenue of eighteen. On Elba she cultivated the image of the invalid, giving the stink eye to anyone who dared to remark upon her good health, even as she danced like a maniac at balls and soirees.

Napoleon made his daring escape from the island on February 26, 1815, sailing for the south of France aboard the *Inconstant*. Before his departure, in case he might be in need of funds, Pauline allegedly gave her brother the famous Borghese diamond necklace. It was purportedly hidden in a secret compartment in Napoleon's coach, which he abandoned on the battlefield at Waterloo. In any event, the diamond parure was never seen again.

A few days after her brother left for France, on March 4, 1815, Pauline departed as well, seeking sanctuary in Italy at their sister Elisa's residence at Compignano, near Lucca. Elisa, however, wasn't there; after the fall of Napoleon she had been placed under house arrest in Brünn (now Brno, in the Czech Republic). Once Pauline reached Elisa's villa, she was subject to the same form of internment, as Lucca was now under the control of an Austrian governor, Colonel Wercklein.

On March 20, 1815, Napoleon was carried like a hero into the Tuileries; but times had changed and he was faced with presenting himself to the French as a constitutional monarch rather than as an autocrat. Just three months later, on June 18, his army was routed at Waterloo, ending his hundred days of power. He was exiled by the allies to the remote island of St. Helena.

That October, Pauline went back to Rome, where the pope agreed to grant her refuge. Her movements, along with those of her other siblings, were carefully watched by Britain and Austria; but Pauline had never censored herself and was not about to begin to do so now.

She continued to wrangle with Camillo over her rights to apartments in the Palazzo Borghese. He now resided there with his mistress and wished to divorce Pauline so he could wed his paramour. Pauline wanted nothing more to do with him, but she did wish to retain the Borghese title and trappings and was holding on for dear life to her status as a bona fide Roman princess. A compromise was eventually reached. The couple received a judicial separation and Pauline was permitted to keep her apartments in the palazzo, along with two fine carriages and a cash settlement. She had reset the Borghese jewels so many times during the course of her marriage that she defied Camillo to identify which pieces had originally been among his family's treasures; consequently, she was able to keep the priceless jewelry.

Pauline still retained much of her beauty, and took a young lover. But when she began to appear somewhat haggard, primarily from fretting over Napoleon's health on St. Helena, she tried to prevent Camillo from exhibiting Canova's *Venus Victrix* to anyone, lest they make an unfavorable comparison between her former physical perfection and her present frailness. She declared the sculpture indecent and obscene, and even offered (unsuccessfully) to purchase it from Camillo, or to employ Canova to create another, more decorous likeness of her.

On May 5, 1821, the man who was perhaps her greatest

love died in his bed. But Napoleon's demise engendered no dramatic keening and hair chopping worthy of a Sophoclean heroine. Nevertheless, Pauline walked on emotional eggshells. "Anything that recalls my brother upsets me," she maintained. She grew obsessed with her own mortality, drawing up several wills, and frequently changing her mind regarding the beneficiaries. As she had no heirs, there was rampant speculation about how she might dispose of her property. Napoleon had once said, "My sister is the queen of trinkets." To whom would she leave them now?

In 1824 Pauline finally reached a rapprochement with Camillo after a papal tribunal upheld the 1816 decree regarding the distribution of their marital property, which meant that she could no longer get anything more out of him financially. She had been ill for several months, possibly suffering from liver cancer. The new pope, Leo X, urged the Borgheses to resume cohabitation, appealing to Camillo as a good Catholic and a Roman prince to take back his wayward wife. Camillo caved, relocating his mistress. But the prince and principessa were no longer one of Europe's most glamorous couples. Camillo was jowly and stout, and Pauline was very frail, her once milky complexion sallow. She was now suffering from pulmonary tuberculosis.

Her health further deteriorated the following May. On June 9, 1825, the forty-four-year-old Pauline agreed to receive last rites, then dictated her will. She bequeathed her house at Lucca to Camillo because "of the sincere care he has shown me in my last illness . . . and because he always behaved towards the Emperor, my brother, with the greatest loyalty." With her affairs punctiliously in order, she died at 1:00 p.m. that day from a tumor on the stomach, the same illness that had felled her father. Pauline was buried in the

Borghese family vault in the Basilica di Santa Maria Maggiore in Rome. Camillo outlived her by seven years, dying in Florence on May 9, 1832.

Although Pauline routinely disobeyed her famous brother, when push came to shove, she was the most loyal of his siblings, and the only one of them to voluntarily share his exile on Elba. During Napoleon's sojourn on St. Helena, he committed his reminiscences of Pauline to paper, and they make a fitting eulogy, warts and all.

> Pauline was probably the most beautiful woman of her time and . . . the best creature in the world. . . . But she was too prodigal, too wild. She could have been immensely rich considering the sums I gave her, but she gave it all away, though her mother often lectured her. She warned Pauline that she would die in the workhouse.

Letizia had once told their brother Joseph that Pauline "amuses herself with drawing up budgets but she never keeps to them for more than a month."

Yet Pauline proved her mother wrong. She departed this world with wealth, but moreover, left it with a lasting legacy of her beauty in the many surviving portraits and other artistic incarnations of her image. Regardless of her morals, in Canova's incomparably alluring masterpiece, the *Venus Victrix*, Pauline Bonaparte emerges permanently triumphant.

ARCHDUKE RUDOLF

Crown Prince of Austria, Hungary, and Bohemia
1858–1889

*H*E DOSED HIMSELF WITH LIQUOR AND MORPHINE AND ran around with a fast crowd. And he was at the epicenter of one of the nineteenth century's biggest royal scandals, in which sex and violence combustibly collided. How did the Hapsburgs' last crown prince become such a bad seed? Was it boredom, inbreeding, or both?

Royal marriages were made for nearly every reason but love—and most notably for political alliances and territorial gain. For centuries it was not unusual for first cousins from Europe's ruling houses to marry each other because they were appropriate social equals, a gene pool that became increasingly shallower as time wore on. Rarely was there an objection to such a union, other than the exceptionally close affinity or "consanguinity" as defined by the Catholic Church. But backs were mutually scratched, bargains made, favors returned, perhaps treasures exchanged hands; and somehow the petitioners always were forgiven by His Holiness. And in Protestant countries, papal approval of such kissing cousins was a nonissue.

Archduke Rudolf, the crown prince of Austria, Hungary, and Bohemia—great hope of the Hapsburg dynasty and heir to the vast Austro-Hungarian empire—was the progeny of two first cousins whose marriage was a rare royal love match. Sort of. Rudolf's drop-dead-gorgeous mother, who had been only fifteen on the day of her engagement, had allowed her girlish imagination to guide her to the altar. And his dashing father had taken one look at her and become the slave of his libido. Yet their marriage quickly became as miserable as any purely dynastic one.

However, the union between Emperor Franz Joseph II and his wife, the Empress Elisabeth, known as Sisi, a former duchess in Bavaria, was not disastrous merely because they were first cousins. Sisi's side of the family were Wittelsbachs, the dynasty that ruled Bavaria; and it was a Wittelsbach, Ludwig II of Bavaria, who was the nineteenth century's poster child for inbred, hereditary insanity. Nicknamed "Mad King Ludwig," he built Neuschwanstein (the "fairy-tale" castle that was Walt Disney's inspiration for Sleeping Beauty's abode). Ludwig was found drowned in Lake Starnberg on June 13, 1886, within hours of being officially declared insane and incarcerated at Berg Castle, ostensibly for his own good.

Despite the young emperor's infatuation with Sisi, she and Franz Joseph proved to be as ill suited as his mother, the formidable Dowager Empress Sophia (a Wittelsbach herself), had predicted. Sophia's biggest concern regarding her son's marital selection was not the threat of insanity, but the issue of compatibility. She had initially urged her son to wed Sisi's older sister Hélène, a girl who was closer to the young autocrat's age, and whose compliant personality better suited his rigid temperament.

Franz Josef followed the promptings of his heart (or a somewhat lower portion of his anatomy), but his marriage to the cousin of his dreams proved disastrous from the get-go. Sisi turned out to be both neurotic and frigid. She adored being admired, but hated sex. And she was so enamored of her own beauty that she was repulsed by pregnancy, especially because it ruined her figure. Sisi was devastated that her firstborn, Sophie, was a girl, because females could not inherit the imperial throne, and was doubly distraught that her second child, Gisela, was a daughter as well.

Rudolf was the third child and first son born to Franz Joseph and Sisi. As Rudolf grew older and Sisi saw his personality begin to take shape, she despaired of having passed him the "tainted" Wittelsbach blood. And the way the crown prince met his tragic and sordid demise—*if* in fact he had perished the way his mother suspected—gave her all the more reason to suspect that her son had indeed inherited "bad" blood.

For decades, people have accepted the fact that Rudolf's life ended in a brandy-infused double-suicide pact. But over the last few years, a raft of conspiracy theories that began at the time of the prince's death have resurfaced. What was the truth? What kind of royal pain did Rudolf become, as he matured from angsty adolescent to agitated adult? Was he unhappy—or unhinged?

Crown Prince Rudolf Francis Charles Joseph of Hapsburg-Lorraine was born on August 21, 1858, in the Hofburg Imperial Palace in Vienna. His twenty-eight-year-old father was thrilled to finally have an heir after three tries, although he described the baby as "not exactly beautiful, but well built and strong."

Twenty-year-old Sisi was probably even more relieved. She had little desire to be a mother, evincing a maternal interest only when it came to a power struggle with her mother-in-law over raising the children. Franz Joseph, who had become emperor at the age of eighteen, was accustomed to maintaining the same advisers his mother had favored. Sophia's managerial decisions extended to the nursery as well—with devastating consequences for Rudolf.

At the time of the crown prince's birth, economic conditions in the Austrian empire were dismal; Franz Joseph's foreign policy was disastrous, and Austria's international reputation was at an all-time low. The vast Hapsburg empire was a multilingual realm in which several religions and ethnicities—Jews, Italians, Slavs, Germans, Balkans, and Hungarians—were expected to peacefully coexist as cogs within the enormous imperial wheel; but Franz Joseph's expansionist agenda had cost him the loyalty and respect of the Hungarians and the Italians. He was not prepared to relinquish their territories without a fight. With the birth of an heir, his subjects hoped that the crown prince would eventually prove to be a healer.

As a boy Rudolf physically resembled his mother: beautiful, physically fragile, and emotionally high-strung. He was a sickly child who enjoyed watching Sisi dress for balls, but his father was adamant that Rudolf be prepared to inherit the imperial throne, force-feeding him the rigid education he'd never received himself. To begin with, the crown prince was expected to master all of the languages spoken in the Austrian Empire, plus English, French, and Latin, when he was barely out of leading strings. The Dowager Empress Sophia had selected Rudolf's nursemaid, as well as his first tutor, Count Gondrecourt, who was the worst possible choice for an overly sensitive child, and would have made a better boot-camp sergeant.

At the age of five, Rudolf contracted typhoid fever, and

the following year he received a concussion when he fell out of a tree, but Count Gondrecourt adamantly refused to coddle his delicate pupil. Awakened by noise in the pre-dawn hours one winter morning, Franz Joseph got out of bed and walked over to the window to look out over the snow-covered courtyard. There he saw Gondrecourt drilling Rudolf in military maneuvers by lantern light.

The count's idea of a field trip was to take his young charge to a nearby game park called the Lainzer Tiergarten, where he would shove the boy into one of the enclosures, alert him that a wild boar was coming—and then leave the crown prince alone to fend for himself! Gondrecourt was also fond of shooting off pistols in Rudolf's bedroom, presumably to toughen him up.

Finally, the empress, who had been attempting to take control of her son's schooling for years, had seen and heard enough of Gondrecourt's educational system. Sisi presented Franz Joseph with an ultimatum: Either Gondrecourt went or she did. Aware that her husband avoided anything that might upset his mother, she followed up her demand with a succinct letter.

> I wish to reserve for myself unlimited authority in every-thing concerning the children, the choice of their entou-rage, the place of their residence, the complete direction of their education, in one word, all this has to be decided by me alone until the children come of age.

The emperor gave the count his walking papers and seven-year-old Rudolf was assigned a new governor, the cultured, well-read Latour von Thurmberg. The crown prince instantly adored him, and Latour became his mentor for life, a confidant and correspondent long after Rudolf left the schoolroom. As governor, Latour supervised the youth's education, with nearly fifty different tutors under his aegis, each chosen for his erudition in his given field, even if the scholar's politics were not in concordance with the emperor's.

Unfortunately, too much focus was placed on rigorous academics, with scant attention paid to developing the prince's character. In not too many years, Rudolf's parents and their proxies would reap what they had sown. By the time the crown prince was ten, Latour noticed that the boy had the tendency to find the easiest way around a difficult hurdle. He also was exhibiting a penchant for insincerity, telling people (especially his paternal grandmother) what they wanted to hear, and covering his true opinions because they might be unpopular, or even scandalous.

Another watershed event at ten was Rudolf's first confession. At the time, he tended to view things quite literally, so he was understandably terrorized by the apocalyptic language of the prayer "O my God, I have provoked thy vengeance, I am not worthy of being called thy child any longer, I have deserved to be cast out forever."

Latour was reticent about offering too much comfort to the hysterical boy for fear that Rudolf would come to view religion too lightly if he pooh-poohed the drama of the liturgy. And when he observed that Rudolf tended to mumble his prayers before bedtime, the governor worried that "it seems that he wants to get it over with." Nonetheless, Latour decided not to make an issue of the matter, in case an admonishment would cause the crown prince to view prayer as something distasteful. But the damage had already been done. For the rest of his life, Rudolf would be emphatically anticlerical, writing lengthy screeds regarding the destructive influence of the Church on western European history.

Count Gondrecourt's malign influence had also left the prince with a morbid streak that he never overcame. Even as a little boy, Rudolf was fascinated by death, his interest in the subject far beyond the merely curious. When he learned that his father had a sister who had died quite young, Rudolf wanted to know all the sordid details. He liked to watch animals die, especially birds. Just six or seven years old when Franz Joseph took him on his first shooting venture, the child took to it like a duck to water. Rudolf would shoot little birds and have them cooked up for his lunch. Employing his artistic talents to draw pictures of himself with his quarry, he rendered the blood and gore as realistically as he could manage.

In twenty-first-century parlance, the adolescent Rudolf would qualify as an "emo boy," filling his journals with angsty poems and diatribes. During the summer of his fourteenth birthday, instead of viewing an afternoon's idyll in a rowboat on a pastoral lake as a pleasant diversion, he saw the scene as "gliding over death . . . How awe-inspiring that sounds. It makes one's blood run cold," the prince observed.

By the age of fourteen or fifteen, Rudolf was already pouring his political philosophies onto the page, writing in one of his journals in December 1872:

I am also convinced that mankind would have advanced much further without the terrible days of the Middle Ages . . . the clergy, always hand in glove with the proud aristocracy, used their influence over the people and did not permit the development of any free ideas; the Church chose ways dangerous for itself, for eventually the people would realize how they were treated and recognize the . . . means which the clergy had used to enrich themselves.

Rudolf's views could not have been farther from his father's. Although he came from the aristocracy, the crown prince viewed their caste as a "curse to humanity," writing, "The Nobility's selfishness brought about the incessant struggles in the Middle Ages, the poverty of the people, the obstruction of all development." His angry, progressive opinions undoubtedly annoyed the emperor no end. To Franz Joseph it must have felt as though his heir were biting the hand that fed him.

How much of Rudolf's adolescent outpourings were influenced by Latour and his tutors and how much reflected an expression of his own original views is open to conjecture. He certainly had a susceptible mind. But straight from the teen's tortured *soul* is a comment written during the Christmas holidays of 1873 in a notebook he called "Various Thoughts," which he dedicated to Latour.

> Thoughts of all kinds roam through my head; all seems confused, all day long my brain boils and toils . . . all thoughts contradicting, sometimes serene and merry, sometimes raven black, crowded with frenzy, they struggle with one another and slowly truth develops from them. I always ponder: What will be the end? . . . often I ask myself: Are you already a madman or will you become one? . . .

This little volume also contains strong views about the monarchy being a "mighty ruin" that would "ultimately tumble," because the people who had been blindly led by it for centuries would inevitably see the light.

They were prescient comments, as the assassination of his father's successor, Archduke Franz Ferdinand, would lead to the First World War, and the end of the Hapsburg Dynasty and the Austrian Empire. Romanov rule in Russia, and the Wittelsbach dynasty in Bavaria would crumble as well.

The Austria of Rudolf's teenage years offered little in the way of social freedoms, even to the wealthiest citizens. Civil marriages were recognized and the liberty to practice one's religion existed, but only the highest taxpayers qualified for these benefits, which was another way of soaking the Jews. There was industrialization without social legislation; the rise of the factory meant the demise of the small craftsman. The nouveau riche class of industrial capitalists suddenly vied with the aristocracy on an economic level.

During the 1870s, the Austrian nobility was fighting tooth and nail to preserve the status quo of the aristocracy and the Church. Rudolf's ideas, as well as his education, were viewed as dangerously progressive, if not downright radical.

One month before his nineteenth birthday, in July of 1877, Rudolf came of age, which meant that his education was formally over, and he was given his own court and a fixed allowance. Latour could be no more than a mentor now. Shortly after Christmas, the crown prince traveled to England with his mother, who had become a rabid Anglophile. There he toured factories, the Bank of England, the Coal Exchange, and the Smithfield and Billingsgate markets, and made an informal study of England's centuries-old parliamentary procedure. By the time he returned to Austria, Rudolf had formed the impression that his country's liberals should stop arguing with one another and organize themselves into a single political party.

He joined the army, not as a choice, but because it was an obligation. Franz Joseph sent his son to an ordinary regiment of the line, the 36th, stationed in Prague, the capital of what was then called Bohemia. The twenty-year-old crown prince, who disdained the nobility because he considered them clueless about life, was glad to get out among common men, who he believed were the *real* people. Rudolf took his military duties seriously, and his commanding officer praised his "warm heart and noble character."

The soldier-prince was often the target of rumors, particularly those that concerned love affairs. He went through puberty relatively late and wasn't taught the facts of life until he was in his midteens. Rudolf first evinced an interest in girls at the age of sixteen or seventeen, but after that, there was no stopping him, and it's possible that he became rather promiscuous in Prague. He had turned into a handsome and exceptionally charming, intelligent young man, with his mother's delicate features and an easy grace in company that would certainly have made him attractive to women. If those qualities didn't make him a chick magnet, his title surely would have done so.

Rudolf's taste in paramours was as iconoclastic as his politics. He fell madly in love with a girl from Prague's old Jewish ghetto. Recognizing that no good could possibly come of the affair, her parents sent her away, but she sneaked back into the city to see the crown prince, falling ill on the day of her arrival. She died without ever again laying eyes on her royal beloved and was buried in Prague's Jewish cemetery. Rudolf allegedly made regular visits to her grave, leaving a floral tribute on each occasion.

In the spring of 1879, the dashing twenty-year-old prince traveled to Spain. In the will he made before embarking, he signed off with bravado, leaving "a last farewell kiss in thought to all the beautiful women of Vienna whom I have loved so much."

Around the same time, Rudolf wrote to Latour:

> In later years, when I shall have obtained influence and experience, I shall dissuade the Emperor from the ways which are now used in military and political affairs, and which are wrong in my view, and I shall help to create a new system. To do so I would move to Vienna and gladly live there.

But Franz Joseph was a classic autocrat, not only uninterested and unwilling, but congenitally unable to cede his heir any political role or responsibility. Even if their opinions had been in accord, it is doubtful that the emperor would have permitted Rudolf to hold any meaningful governmental post.

His desire to micromanage every aspect of his son's life led to Franz Joseph's conclusion toward the end of 1879 that it was time for Rudolf to wed. The emperor settled on Princess Stephanie, the second daughter of King Leopold of the Belgians (Queen Victoria's uncle) and Marie Henriette, a Hapsburg princess from the Hungarian branch of the family. Although Franz Joseph had married for love, Rudolf would not be allowed the same luxury.

Rudolf arrived in Brussels on March 5, 1880. He proposed

to the fifteen-year-old Stephanie without fanfare and she promptly accepted him. On March 11, the prince wrote to Latour:

> I am intoxicated with happiness and contentment. . . . I think anxiously of the moment when I shall have to leave. I have learned to love my parents-in-law very much.

After telling Latour how impressed he was by Leopold's intelligence and political acumen, on March 13 the prince described his rather sheltered fiancée to his mentor:

> In Stephanie I have found a real angel, a faithful good being who loves me, a very clever, well educated and able companion for this life who will stand by my side well and successfully in all my difficult tasks. . . .

Although this sounds like an expression of euphoric ardor, readers should recall Latour's assessment of Rudolf's personality as a ten-year-old boy: He told people what he thought they wanted to hear. So, was the prince's effusion merely propaganda? Stephanie was by all other accounts dull and homely with zero spark and no critical faculties. The product of a strict Catholic education, she was also a bad dresser—heresy to her oh-so-chic mother-in-law, who had once been a provincial belle herself. Aware of her intellectual inferiority to Rudolf, Stephanie overcompensated by acting pushy and stubborn—a bad match indeed for the neurotic and sensitive crown prince. However, each of the young royals was starved for affection and should have had much in common. King Leopold was a serial philanderer and Stephanie's mother was a profoundly unhappy

268 ⚜ LESLIE CARROLL

woman. Rudolph and his fiancée could have been each other's life raft, but stories with princes and princesses in them don't always end with a happily-ever-after.

Although the royal wedding was planned for December 1880, the date was postponed because Stephanie hadn't matured enough physically. Perhaps she had not even gotten her first period at the time she became engaged.

Sisi was in England when she received the telegram announcing her son's betrothal. "Thank God it is not a calamity!" she exclaimed when she discovered that the delivery contained good news. But the empress presciently added, "Please, God, that it will not become one." Sisi's son had inherited her morbid personality, and even though she was not terribly maternal, her forebodings, especially those concerning her children, were invariably correct.

She worried because she knew that Rudolf, like her husband, regarded everything with the utmost seriousness. In his dreams, the crown prince hoped that his child bride would side with him politically while his father still reigned and become a full political partner when he eventually ascended the imperial throne. But Stephanie was way out of her depth, and Sisi never cautioned Rudolf not to push her, especially at the beginning of their relationship, or to expect too much from her too soon. Rudolf adored his mother and most likely would have heeded her warning, but one of Sisi's greatest failings was her inability to confront a situation after she acknowledged its existence. Instead, she routinely ran from anything unpleasant.

On May 22, 1881, the twenty-two-year-old Rudolf and Stephanie (eleven days shy of her seventeenth birthday) were wed in Vienna, exchanging the same rings that were worn by Marie Antoinette's parents, Francis of Lorraine and Maria Theresa, 150 years earlier. But just prior to the nuptials the groom experienced a fit of nerves; morose and tearful, he seemed to dread the impending ceremony.

During the honeymoon at Laxenburg Castle, the newly-weds had nothing to say to each other—literally as well as metaphorically. Having learned only schoolroom German, Stephanie didn't speak the Austrian dialect. The castle itself was unwelcoming: chilly, dreary, damp, and devoid of the slightest touches of warmth or hospitality—hardly a romantic venue for a bridal couple.

In her memoirs, penned decades after Rudolf's tragic demise, and published in 1935, Stephanie claimed to have been repelled by her husband's physical advances on their wedding night. We'll never know whether she was inexperienced, frightened, prudish, or whether Rudolf was not a tender or patient lover. Stephanie also claimed that she got to see him only when she accompanied him on his shooting expeditions, writing that "the Crown Prince cared little outside his own pleasure and sport."

The newlyweds settled in Prague, where Rudolf returned to his regiment. Two months into the marriage, Stephanie realized she was pregnant. With a child on the way, education reform was in the forefront of the prince's mind, although even before they'd met, Rudolph had voiced his radical political sentiments regarding the subject, writing in February 1881:

> I would much rather send my children to a school whose headmaster is a Jew than to one whose headmaster is a clergyman. . . . The State has to treat all denominations equally; a strengthening of the Catholic hierarchy has so far brought always evil consequences.

Obviously Rudolf had a lot more on his mind than "pleasure and sport." Either he never shared his passionate intellectual opinions with his wife, or else Stephanie had a reason to write a revisionist history of their relationship. She did remarry after Rudolf's demise and perhaps it was in her own interest to recast their life together in a decidedly unpleasant light.

Concerned about the sort of world their child would inherit, in November 1881 Rudolph drafted a twenty-page memorandum for his father, suggesting a number of well-considered progressive reforms.

The crown prince sent the draft to Latour for comment, confiding that, "Our emperor has no friend, his whole character and his disposition do not permit it. . . . Thus he knows little of the thoughts and feelings of the people, of their views and opinions. . . . He believes that we are living in one of the happiest periods of Austrian history, he is officially told so. In the newspapers he only reads the passages marked in red and so he is divorced from every human intercourse, from all impartial and really loyal advice."

And of his mother, Rudolf admitted, "There was a time when the Empress frequently concerned herself with politics, whether with luck or not I will not discuss now. . . . These times are past. The great lady no longer cares for anything but sport."

The crown prince and princess gave the outward impression, at least, of being very happily married. It was Stephanie, of all people, whom Rudolf pinned his hopes on, confessing to his mentor, "I am very much in love with her and she is the only one who would tempt me to do many things." Apparently Rudolf didn't see the woman his beloved mother referred to as "a moral heavyweight," an "ugly elephant," and *"das hässliche Trampeltier"*—the ugly, clumsy oaf.

Evidently Stephanie's 1881 pregnancy was a false alarm, or else she lost the baby, because there was no birth. In the beginning of 1883 she was enceinte again, and on September 2, the crown princess gave birth to a little girl they named Elisabeth.

As always with this couple, there were conflicting reports of their reactions. Regarding the birth of a daughter, Stephanie claimed in her memoirs that, "The Crown Prince was absolutely stricken, for he had set his heart upon an heir to the throne!" while Rudolf wrote of his delight to his friend the Jewish newspaper editor Moriz Szeps that when Stephanie had fretted over not having a boy, he had consoled her with the words, "Never mind, a girl is much sweeter."

Whom to believe when it comes to the events of Crown Prince Rudolf's life remains one of history's mysteries. Although Rudolf's biographer Fritz Judtmann insists that many documents survive regarding Rudolf's demise, an event known as the Mayerling tragedy, most of the correspondence between the crown prince and princess was burned or otherwise destroyed. Only one letter from his wife can be found among Rudolf's surviving papers. It was written in French and dates from 1887—the same year she traveled to a spa town in Bohemia in search of a cure for her infertility. Stephanie's letter to Rudolf is affectionate, but lacks the effusiveness of his known letters to her, in which he penned such phrases as, "I am longing terribly for you and count the days which still separate us. *Embracing you with all my heart.*"

Parenthetically, Rudolf's parents wrote adoring letters to each other when they were apart, but Sisi couldn't stand to be in the same room with Franz Joseph when they were together; therefore, even primary source material doesn't always tell the whole story. Some biographers have hinted (without providing details) that Rudolf gave his wife a venereal disease that necessitated an operation and made her unable to conceive again. They mention that the royal couple's sex life seems to have continued; yet in her memoirs Stephanie asserted that she was unable "to lead the affectionate existence of a young married couple."

The intense, über-angsty Rudolf could not have been easy to live with, although his brand of Mittel-European morbidity was in the air in fin-de-siècle Vienna. In 1882, when the crown prince was still a newlywed, his current mentor, Moriz Szeps, made note of a disturbing conversation in which Rudolf had confided, "From time to time I look for an opportunity to watch a dying person and to overhear his last breath. It is always for me a curious sight and of all the people whom I have seen dying, each has died in a different way. I observe with attention dying animals and try also to get my wife used to the sight."

Four years later, in 1886, Rudolf told the anatomist Professor Zuckerkandl (who had wed Szeps's daughter Bertha), "One should face the idea of death straightforwardly." The following year, Rudolf requested a skull from Zuckerkandl, which he awarded a place of honor on his desk.

Rudolf's friendship with Szeps was yet another problematic connection for the bureaucracy, because Szeps was a Jew as well as a journalist. And their relationship became increasingly suspicious as time wore on. The twenty-something crown prince was probably not being paranoid when at one point during the early 1880s he told his mentor, "I must draw your attention to a number of odd things. They are becoming very watchful and suspicious of me, and I see more clearly every day what a tight circle of espionage, denunciations, and supervision surrounds me. . . . I have good reason to believe that our relations are known in high quarters [likely by his own father]."

It would have been no surprise that Franz Joseph disapproved of his heir's personal, professional, and political associations. After all, the crown prince seemed to disdain or seek to contradict everything his father represented and believed. On July 26, 1882, Rudolf wrote to Szeps, "I consider the enmity of nations and races a decisive step backwards, and it is characteristic that just those elements hostile to progress in Europe indulge these principles and exploit them."

Rudolf was known to openly consort with what we might call "real people." Whether the gossip was accurate or part of a campaign to smear him, we may never know, but stories of his libertinism, rather than his liberalism, made the rounds of smoke-filled coffeehouses as well as elegant salons. He had become something of a darling among Vienna's emerging middle class, the progressive and enlightened segment of society that was at odds with the rest of Austria, just as New York City is anomalous to much of the balance of the rural and predominantly conservative New York State.

In May of 1883, Rudolf and Stephanie moved to Laxenburg Castle, just outside Vienna. That year, the crown prince was appointed commanding officer of the 25th infantry. Soon after the birth of their daughter, they moved into the Hofburg palace, although Rudolf maintained his bachelor quarters at the Hofburg as well. Stephanie hated the oppressive and backward atmosphere of the imposing palace, which still lacked bathrooms and running water and was illuminated with oil lamps, despite the recent introduction of electricity into bourgeois homes and the common use of gas lighting.

The move to Vienna was also part of the crown prince's overarching professional agenda. As he matured, Rudolf keenly acknowledged his duty as a royal. In January 1884, hyperaware of the tenor of the era, he wrote to Szeps:

> In a time like the present, members of dynasties must show themselves frequently and work hard to prove their right to exist. This is the reason why my wife and I intend this winter to visit many establishments. . . . It would be good if the people were to learn from your paper what we are doing so that we are not taken for useless parasites.

Yet Franz Joseph continued to keep Rudolf idle. As late as 1887, the crown prince remained deprived of any government post or responsibilities; nor did the emperor discuss with his heir the rationales behind his domestic and foreign policies in order to provide *his* perspective on the myriad issues plaguing the Austro-Hungarian empire.

As the 1880s rumbled on, Rudolf and Stephanie grew even farther apart. She was pretentious and pushy, ambitious for a lifestyle that Rudolf had disdained for years. Her lack of warmth may have chased him from the marital bed, although by then she may also have been tainted by venereal disease, the victim of his infidelities.

In the early months of 1886 Rudolf fell ill. Various diagnoses included an inflammation of the peritoneum and a catarrh of the bladder. A veneral infection was supposed but never conclusively confirmed.

Emil Franzel, a twentieth-century author who wrote a psychological study of the crown prince, observed that,

> . . . in his last years Rudolf not only drank a lot but also took drugs. It has been surmised that an abdominal complaint of his, as well as a complaint of his wife which prevented her from having any children after their only daughter, was probably of venereal origin, but this cannot now be proved. Certainly Rudolf's private life had been decidedly objectionable for years.

Other sources, including biographies of the Crown Princess Stephanie and the unpublished papers of one of Sisi's biographers, Egon Caesar Conte Corti, also refer to Stephanie's awareness that her inability to conceive any more children was because her husband had infected her with a venereal disease. And the Vienna court pharmacy's prescription book for 1886 refers to scrips filled in Stephanie's name for zinc sulfate and Copaiva balsam capsules, medications used to treat gonorrhea, in addition to huge doses of morphine, prescribed as a painkiller.

Whether the allegations are true or not, Rudolf lacked outlets for his sexual as well as his political passions. Stephanie lacked an amorous personality and her husband looked elsewhere for stimulus, as well as for the brand of sympathy that can be found only in a pair of soft and willing arms.

According to the memoirs of Count Monts, the legation counselor at the German Embassy in Vienna,

> Female hearts positively dropped into the lap of the Crown Prince. . . . Rudolf was too soft and too weak to tear

himself away . . . from this whirl. . . . Thus the young
Prince did too much in matters of Venus. . . . His body
was not up to the demands he made on it, and so the
Prince resorted to alcohol and the hypodermic. . . .

Rudolf began to spend hours every day engaged in shooting parties. As he began to lose hope and faith in a better
future, his world outlook grew bleak and his personality
became cynical and impatient. In 1886 or 1887 he commenced a love affair with Mizzi Kaspar, a demimondaine
who has euphemistically been described by some biographers as a dancer. Unfortunately for the crown prince,
who in some respects was still a naïf, Mizzi was a mini
Mata Hari. She was connected with a lawyer named
Florian Meissner, who was an informer for the German
embassy. Consequently, Rudolf's movements were known
by the German as well as the Austrian authorities. Rudolf
drank more during these years and indulged in outrageous behavior—such as sheltering another archduke who
had pulled a particularly disrespectful stunt by jumping
his horse over a coffin during a funeral procession and
days later horsewhipped a member of Austria's parliament. According to Rudolf's biographer Richard Barkeley,
the crown prince became an "imperial playboy," which
sapped him of his will to further his political interests,
but left him with enough energy to drink and whore with
impunity.

Although Rudolf was promoted to inspector general of
the infantry in 1888, conservative, anti-Semitic newspapers across Europe attacked him for leading a dissolute
life, partially to discredit him because of his friendship
with father figure Moriz Szeps.

In 1887 he began taking morphine to combat a chronic cough, and after suffering a fall from his horse on November 19, 1888, he ingested significant amounts of it to combat his pain. The hallucinogenic sedative, combined with Rudolf's alcohol consumption, was a disastrous combination. Stephanie noticed that, "He was frightfully changed; his skin was flaccid, his eyes were restless, his expression had completely changed."

Stephanie was so concerned about her husband's outlook and appearance that she asked Franz Joseph for his help, urging him to send his son on a long, recuperative holiday. But the emperor, who was raised never to admit impediments or weakness of any sort, dismissed Stephanie's fears by insisting that there was "nothing the matter with Rudolf . . . He is rather pale, gets about too much, expects too much of himself. He ought to stay at home with you more than he does."

In early October of 1888, during a visit by "Bertie," the Prince of Wales, Rudolf was introduced to a minor member of the nobility, Baroness Helene Vetsera and her daughter Mary—who at the time ostensibly had an "understanding" (a pseudoserious commitment to an engagement) with the much older Miguel, Duke of Braganza. According to Bertie (who had a notorious eye for feminine pulchritude), Mary "seemed a charming young lady and certainly one of the prettiest and most admired in Vienna."

Only seventeen years old, naive and romantic, Mary Vetsera had developed a raging crush on the crown prince the previous spring, when she saw him at the horse races, admitting that she would do anything to be with him. The girl visited the track so often she'd earned the nickname "turf angel." Although Helene found out about her daughter's infatuation and brought Mary to England for the summer in the hope that she would forget about Rudolf, absence only made the teen's untested heart grow fonder. She wrote him a letter expressing her attraction and Rudolf had replied, suggesting that they meet. Mary would later be tarred by the imperial family as nothing but a tawdry temptress who had led their precious heir astray.

Empress Sisi's cousin and lady-in-waiting, Countess Marie Larisch, became Rudolf's go-between with Mary, if not his outright procuress. Unlike Stephanie, Mary Vetsera was a very girly girl and as eager to please as a puppy.

Mary poured out her heart to Hermine, her former governess (who evidently did not condone the royal liaison), writing:

> I cannot live without having seen him or spoken to him. Dear Hermine, don't worry about me, I know that everything you say is true, but I cannot change the facts. I have two friends, you and Marie Larisch. *You* work for my soul's happiness and *Marie* works for my moral misfortune.

Mary and Rudolf enjoyed their first meeting in the Prater, the amusement park that at the time lay just outside Vienna, and on November 5, the countess conveyed Mary to the prince's bachelor rooms in the Hofburg. Marie Larisch lied to Baroness Helene Vetsera, telling her that she was chaperoning her teenage daughter on shopping expeditions. Days later Mary wrote to Hermine about her visit to Rudolf's rooms at the Hofburg:

> Today you will get a happy letter from me because I have been with him. Marie Larisch took me shopping with her

and then to be photographed—for him of course. Then we went . . . to the Burg. An old servant was waiting for us; he led us up several stairs and through several rooms until we reached one in which he left us. At our entrance a black bird—some kind of raven—flew at my head. A voice called from the next room "Please come in." Marie introduced me, then he said to me "Excuse me, but I would like to talk to the Countess privately for a few minutes." Then he went with Marie to another room. I looked around me. On his desk was a revolver and a skull. I picked up the skull, took it between my hands and looked at it from all sides. Suddenly Rudolf came in and took it from me with deep apprehension. When I said that I wasn't afraid, he smiled.

In the letter, Mary sought Hermine's promise not to tell a soul about the encounter and expressed her despair that any subsequent rendezvous with Rudolf would have to be postponed, owing to the Countess Larisch's departure for her home in Bohemia. Despondent without her pimping chaperone, Mary wrote to Hermine:

> . . . I wither with longing and cannot await the day of her return. . . . I count the hours, because since I have met him and talked to him my love has so much deepened. I ponder day and night how I could contrive to see him.

"He is my god, my everything!" she confessed to Hermine. In turn, Mary received from Rudolf an assurance of his love for her, accompanied by the revelation that he would go mad if he were deprived of ever seeing her again.

Although Rudolf never broke off his adulterous relationship with Mizzi Kaspar, he gave Mary Vetsera an iron wedding ring, which she wore suspended from a slender chain about her neck. It was inscribed with the initials ILVBIDT, an acronym for the words *In Liebe vereint bis in den Tod*—united in love till death.

The overly romantic Mary told her former governess:

If we could live together in a hut we would be so happy! We constantly talk of this, and love doing so; but alas, it cannot be! If I could give my life to see him happy, I would gladly do it, because I do not value my own life.

Mary also admitted to Hermine that she and Rudolf had made a suicide pact, in which—after spending a few happy hours together—they would kill themselves, although she had regrets about the prince taking his own life because "he must live for his nation. All that surrounds him must be splendor and glory."

Theirs was a very "goth" relationship. Mary, who at age seventeen was still young enough to view her former governess as her BFF, confided everything to Hermine about her affair with the thirty-year-old crown prince. Her parents tried to keep her away from Rudolf, but with limited success, as Countess Marie Larisch, who was pimping the girl, had access to the highest echelons of the imperial family.

Rudolf met Mary Vetsera at a particularly unhappy point in his life. Even Stephanie had noticed that her husband was looking tired, ill, and gaunt. In his last letter to Moriz Szeps, written during Christmas week of 1888 or around the start of the new year, the crown prince confessed that the political climate across the empire, and in most of continental Europe in general, gave him "the feeling of the calm before the storm."

In a professional capacity Szeps knew Rudolf perhaps better than anyone else. His reply to the crown prince went unanswered, although its contents have provided fodder for conspiracy theorists:

> You, Imperial Highness, have had to experience much malice and perfidy, but you have shaken it off with remarkable equanimity. It is well known that you desire great things, that you are capable of accomplishing them, and he who does not know feels it. This is why you are now being attacked by various means and your way into the future barred and you have already today many adversaries and enemies.

Although some like to point the finger directly at Franz Joseph, it was more than likely his prime minister, Count Eduard Taaffe (a boyhood friend of the emperor's and a vehement adversary of the crown prince), who was responsible for pouring the anti-Rudolf pestilence into Franz Joseph's ear.

As the new year of 1889 dawned, Rudolf was plagued by depression, apathy, and feelings of powerlessness. Stephanie had traveled to the south to avail herself of a warmer climate. On January 13, Mary Vetsera visited the Hofburg again. The next day she wrote to her governess Hermine:

> I was with him last night from seven till nine. We have both lost our heads. Now we belong to one another life and soul.

Had they confirmed their suicide pact that night, or consummated their affair? Since the summer of 1888, Rudolf had talked to his inamorata Mizzi Kaspar about killing himself, proposing a mutual suicide pact to be carried out in the Vienna Woods, but Mizzi had laughed in his face at the suggestion. And he had made the same proposition to his wife, who had clearly feared he would do himself some injury, despite her refusal to share his fate. During the final months of his life, the crown prince had become more obsessed than ever with the idea of death, remarking whenever he heard about someone's demise that they were "fortunate."

Stephanie returned to Vienna for the winter ball season, but didn't attend any of the festivities because the court was in official mourning for Sisi's father, who had died on November 15, 1888. Tensions were running high there. Rumors abounded regarding heated confrontations between Rudolf and his father during the month of January 1889. Although it has never been substantially proven, historians once believed that the crown prince sought to apply to Rome for the pope's permission to divorce Stephanie, and that the very devout emperor blew a gasket when he found out what his son had done, assuring Rudolf that he would never agree to let him have a divorce. This whole, probably invented contretemps stems from a chain of conversations much like a game of "Telephone" gone awry among various Russian diplomats. In an age before wiretapping, how the Russians would be privy to any *confidential*, closed-door exchanges among members of the Hapsburg imperial family (unless the subject of such discussions became common knowledge within the Hofburg) defies a good explanation. Certainly the rumors were spread, and reached as far as

London, but it is far more likely, given their lack of proof, that they were no more than Russian propaganda.

On Monday, January 28, 1889, Rudolf waited in the Hofburg for the delivery of a telegram before departing for Mayerling, his hunting lodge some seventeen miles southwest of Vienna. He had allegedly spent part of the previous night in Mizzi Kaspar's arms, and upon leaving her in the wee hours of the morning after enjoying copulation and copious quantities of champagne, he made the sign of the cross on her forehead—an unusual gesture, if true, for the anticlerical prince.

The telegram arrived at around eleven thirty that morning. As Rudolf perused it he was heard to exclaim, "It has to be!" and then he tossed the telegram on a table. His biographers have yet to clarify whether the missive was of a personal or a political nature; consequently, all sorts of theories have been propagated as to the telegram's author and its contents, allowing people to assert (with absolutely no proof) that the prince's exclamation cemented his plans for suicide, or that it referred to a political change in the winds in Hungary. The latter has since been conclusively disproved because the timing is off by days.

Rudolf drove his own coach to Mayerling, leaving word for Stephanie that he would return the following day by 5:00 p.m. According to Countess Larisch, Mary Vetsera had left a note at her mother's house announcing her intention to commit suicide. The countess insisted that she herself never took that threat seriously. Mary supposedly was brought to Mayerling via a charade worthy of a Bourne or Bond movie—creating subterfuges and distractions, and changing carriages and drivers at various locations.

On January 29, two of Rudolf's usual hunting buddies,

Count Hoyos and Stephanie's brother, Prince Coburg, arrived at Mayerling for the scheduled shooting party to find the blinds drawn—rather odd for a house expecting guests. Rudolf, who was wearing his coat indoors, told his friends he was warding off a chill and had determined that he'd better not go shooting that day after all. But his rationale struck his companions as bizarre: The prince had inexplicably insisted that the nearby hillsides (where he often roamed on such excursions) were too steep. He sent a telegram to Stephanie offering his excuses for not being able to return to Vienna that evening, apologizing for being obliged to miss the dinner honoring the engagement of his younger sister Valerie to Archduke Franz Salvator of Tuscany.

The crown princess purportedly had a premonition when she read the telegram, exclaiming to the messenger, Rudolph Puckerl, "O God, what shall I do! I feel so strange."

Months earlier, she had told Franz Joseph that her husband had proposed a suicide pact between the two of them, and the emperor had scoffed at her, scolding her for indulging in fantasies. Stephanie also knew about her husband's love affairs, but was powerless to convince him to break them off.

While Rudolf entertained his hunting companions at Mayerling, Mary Vetsera waited out of sight in his bedroom. That evening, the lovers were serenaded in the boudoir by the prince's coachman, Bratfisch, before the functionary was dismissed for the night. However, Bratfisch later claimed that he had figured out what was about to transpire.

Before the triggers were pulled (if indeed two different

guns were used, according to one of the many conspiracy theories), the couple composed farewell letters to their family members. To the older Baroness Vetsera, Mary had written:

Dear Mother,

Forgive me for what I have done. I could not resist my love. In an agreement with him I would like to be buried beside him at Alland. I am happier in death than in life.

Yours,
Mary

In her last letter to her sister, Mary wrote:

We are going blissfully into the uncertain beyond. Think of me now and then. Be happy and marry only for love. I could not do it, and since I could not resist love, I am going with him. . . . Do not weep for my sake. I am crossing the line merrily. . . .

Mary's intended husband, the Duke of Braganza, received only a glib note suggesting that he drape her fur boa on the wall above his bed as a memento.

Rudolf had written his farewells before he left Vienna. They were addressed individually to his sister Valerie, to Stephanie, and to his mother (in which he asked to be buried in the little cemetery at Heiligenkreuz, alongside "the pure angel who accompanied [him] into the other world"). No letter was written to his father. The prince's letter to his wife read:

You are relieved of my presence and vexation; be happy in your own way. Be kind to the poor little one [their daughter Elisabeth]; she is all that remains of me. . . . I approach death composedly; it alone can save my good name. I embrace you tenderly, your loving Rudolf.

Rudolf had discussed the method of suicide with Mary beforehand. She agreed that a revolver was a surer method than poison. "Rather a revolver, a revolver is safer," she'd had engraved inside an ashtray that she gave the prince as a gift. According to those who knew him well, Rudolf routinely slept with two revolvers under his pillow.

But when the moment of truth arrived, Mary Vetsera did not pull the trigger and take her own life. In the pre-dawn hours of January 30, 1889, Rudolf killed her with a single shot from one of his revolvers, placing a long-stemmed rose in her pale hands, which already clasped a white handkerchief. Her body would be found where she died, lying nude on Rudolf's bed. However, when it came to offing himself, the crown prince apparently hesitated, sitting for hours on the edge of the mattress, fortifying himself with brandy, and finally using a looking glass so that he could most accurately aim the deadly shot. Rudolf had been fascinated by the lurid details regarding the 1888 suicide of the renowned sportsman and big-game hunter Stefan Kégl. Kégl had used a hand mirror to make sure he would kill, rather than merely maim himself.

According to one version of events, at around 6:30 a.m. on January 30, Rudolf left his bedroom and told his valet and personal gun loader, Loschek, that he had decided to sleep in, asking Loschek to come and wake him at seven thirty. After Loschek later knocked, then pounded on the door, and still received no answer, he broke it down. He saw Rudolf, half lying on the edge of the bed in a pool of blood. In 1928, when Loschek wrote his memoirs, he claimed to have heard the gunshots, adding that he'd burst into the room to discover each of the victims, fully dressed, on separate beds—a description that contains two major lies. And yet in 1889, Loschek (who evidently hadn't spent too much time noticing the condition of the two corpses) made the strange determination that Rudolf had been killed with a heavy dose of the poison potassium cyanide, which had induced a hemorrhage.

Within hours, Count Hoyos left for Vienna to inform the royal family of the tragedy. Sisi was having her Greek lesson and insisted that she could be interrupted only if the news was dire. Hoyos broke it to her as gently as possible, sharing the poison theory. Sisi managed to dry her tears before sharing the news with her husband's erstwhile lover, the young actress Katarina Schratt, whom the imperial couple routinely insisted was merely a mutual close friend. The tenderhearted Frau Schratt, who had learned how to manage the emperor's moods, informed him of the crown prince's demise.

According to Stephanie's memoirs, the imperial couple had decided that the news was not important enough to interrupt her singing lesson. But as soon as she was summoned, Stephanie instinctively realized that Rudolf was gone.

Sisi informed Baroness Helene Vetsera that her daughter was dead, accusing Mary—according to the first disseminated version of events—of poisoning Rudolf before taking her own life with the potassium cyanide. The court physician, Dr. Widerhofer, who examined the corpses and must have realized that there had been no poison involved in the deaths, sent no telegram to the Hofburg contradicting that initial report. Stephanie confessed to Widerhofer that she felt guilty for not having been able to prevent the tragedy.

Once it became clear, however, that poison had not been a factor, the imperial family published the news that Rudolf had died of heart failure. The bulletin provided no explanation for Mary Vetsera's death—an aspect of the lurid story that Franz Joseph was eager to keep as hushed up as possible.

Of course the "official lie" was just that, and word soon spread that Rudolf and the young baroness had each died of a single shot to the head. But even then, the story was rewritten to imply that each of the deceased had committed suicide. There were several reasons for this. If the public were to learn that Mary had been murdered (and given the placement of her body and the items found in her cold, dead hands, it would have been nigh impossible for her to have shot herself), then the reputation of Rudolf and the imperial family would have been even more deeply tainted than it was by the presumption of suicide. To add the name of murderer was unthinkable. The supposition that Mary had taken her own life avoided the possibility of an embarrassing inquest. It also made it easier for the imperial flunkies to dispose of her corpse with neither fanfare nor delay.

The earlier reports from Mayerling mention that both bullets were found at the hunting lodge. But there are conflicting descriptions of the condition of Rudolf's face and head. Some people reported seeing his brains hanging out, or splattered on the floor, or that the top of the right side of his head was completely blown off. Rudolph's face was ultimately reconstructed using wax and paint, with his head discreetly bandaged, so that his body could lie in state attractively.

The autopsy conveniently concluded that the abnormalities found in his skull were consistent with mental derangement. Better for the imperial family that their heir should be a nut job than a depressive psychopath.

Additionally, Franz Joseph refused to issue a statement regarding the fact that the nude, dead body of a woman was lying on the bed beside his son. This little bit of information was released to the public as an afterthought. Perhaps it would have been wiser to allow people to assume that the crown prince was the victim of a doomed love affair.

Another rumor that immediately gained traction and had staying power well into the third quarter of the twentieth century (when the most recent biographies of Rudolf were published) was that Franz Joseph had to apply to the pope in order for his suicidal son to receive a Christian burial. Although there was copious correspondence between Rome and Vienna, in truth, the Austrian clerics had determined from the outset that the crown prince would receive all due honors, both state and religious. It is yet another conspiracy theory that the Vatican is concealing crucial documentation regarding high-level negotiations for a Catholic funeral. But the fact that the Austrian newspapers were prohibited from publishing any comment on the incident at Mayerling created a news blackout that only stoked the rumors.

Formal court mourning was ordered to be observed for several months. The crown prince's body lay in state for two days so that the public could pay their respects to his corpse. On the third day, February 5, 1889, Rudolph's modestly attended funeral was conducted. Franz Joseph had requested the crowned heads of Europe—especially

Stephanie's parents—to stay home. The Belgian king and queen came anyway. Rudolf's body was laid to rest in the imperial vault at the Kapuzinerkirche among generations of deceased Hapsburgs. Sisi descended into the crypt alone on February 9 and called out his name several times. She would later listen to spiritualists, occultists, and all manner of quacks in an effort to commune with the spirit of her dead son.

The Hapsburgs dragged Mary Vetsera's name through the mud, at first spreading the word that she had poisoned the crown prince; then the royal family refused Baroness Helene Vetsera any aid in burying her daughter. Mary's corpse—with a river of drying blood following the contours of her nude body, the wound in her left temple congealed, her unseeing eyes open, and still clutching the rose and handkerchief—was first dumped in an anteroom at Mayerling, unceremoniously covered in a heap of old clothes. Her body was then washed and dressed in her traveling ensemble, and bundled into a plain coach—propped up to give the impression that it was merely the slumping form of a sleeping traveler. Mary was not even allowed the dignity of a hearse. The unassuming carriage was then driven to the Cistercian monastery at the nearby village of Heiligenkreuz. On February 1, Mary's body was buried in the light of day (despite rumors to the contrary) in the monastery's cemetery. Although suicide had been (conveniently) listed as her cause of death, she received a Christian burial. The only mourners were a few policemen and Mary's two uncles, the Baltazzi brothers (Heinrich and Alexander)—who are often suspected of murdering the crown prince even though one of them, Alexander, was nowhere near Mayerling at the time.

The Austrian government was so keen to hush up Mary

Vetsera's involvement in the Mayerling tragedy that they disseminated the false story that Mary had still been alive at the end of January 1889, but that she'd caught a bad cold after accompanying her mother to Venice, and had expired there. Privately, Franz Joseph and Sisi gave Helene Vetsera permission to leave Austria with her daughter's coffin, which she could then reinter at a location of her choosing.

The baroness was insulted by the request and told the imperial family that under no circumstances would she disturb Mary's final resting place. In her anger, she had 250 copies of a pamphlet printed that claimed to tell the true story of Mary's death. The Austrian government attempted to round up and destroy as many of the pamphlets as they could, but some of them found their way into the newspaper offices of foreign countries, where they were eventually published, either in part or in their entirety. However, the first such instance of publication did not occur until 1891.

Most of Rudolf's personal papers were burned pursuant to a posthumous request found in a lockbox of his documents. The same request held true for the papers that remained in his writing desk. The official papers regarding the incident at Mayerling were given by Franz Joseph to Prime Minister Taaffe, who kept them in his possession rather than depositing them into the state archives. Over the ensuing decades various stories were disseminated regarding the whereabouts of these files. Taaffe lied when he insisted that the papers had been destroyed in a fire, because they had never been placed anywhere near the room that burned. His son and grandson took whatever secrets they may have had to their graves. The emperor's purported desire to release the contents of the files fifty years after his death (which would have been in 1966) turned out to be either a dilatory deception or merely wishful thinking.

A theory that Rudolf and Mary were murdered (and at the instigation of the imperial crown, no less) had gained little traction by the mid–twentieth century because there was scant documentation to support it. But by the last quarter of the century, the concept of a murder plot gained credence, and persists today, having found its way into Gabriel Ronay's 2008 article for *History Today* titled "Death in the Vienna Woods."

It was a cadre of Italian clerics who first propagated the idea of a double murder, although none of them had examined the bodies. Enhancing the credibility of their murder theory were the results of a forensic investigation conducted by Austrian authorities soon after the bodies were discovered, concluding that the revolver found at Rudolf's bedside did not belong to him. The report also asserted that all six shots of someone's revolver had been fired; that bullets were found embedded in the furniture; and that the victims had sustained "other wounds." No alternative theory was ever proposed regarding what the murder or assault weapon might have been, had it not been the revolver alone that caused the injuries. Further assertions were made that the wounds were not found in the victims' temples but on the tops of their skulls, with some theorists alleging that Rudolf's skull had been crushed, while others insisted that the top of his head had been so violently blown off that one could see his brain oozing out of his skull. Yet only one of the authors of these claims, the court secretary Dr. Heinrich Slatin, had closely inspected the corpses. It was Slatin who observed the prince's "face scarcely disfigured, but the top of his skull blown off, with blood and parts of the brain welling out, as it seems to me from a shot from closest range. . . ."

Clearly, there was a massive cover-up afoot. Reports were written and filed by people who never even witnessed the crime scene, or who had merely accorded it a cursory look, rather than a full investigation. Dr. Slatin, one of the few men who did see the victims, got the location of Mary Vetsera's body all wrong, an indication that his observations of Rudolf's corpse may have been invented as well, or that he chose to lie about the prince's naked lover for propriety's sake. Yet this is hardly the sort of notation one should expect from a medical man—a man of science who should have been fastidiously concerned with making an accurate report of the aftermath instead of putting a spin on it for some reason.

And in all the various conspiracy theories propounded since 1889, no one has ever questioned the legitimacy of Mary Vetsera's handwriting. Are we really expected to believe that a bunch of thugs held her at gunpoint, waiting for her to write her suicide notes—letters that echoed what she had personally been telling her confidantes for weeks? Found inside Mary's clothing was an unfinished letter to her sister regarding the reasons for her impending death.

> Today he finally confessed to me openly that I could never become his; he had given his father his word of honor that he will break with me. So everything is over! I go to my death serenely.

To Countess Marie Larisch Mary sent an odd sort of warning:

Dear Marie!

Forgive me all the sorrow that I have brought upon you. I thank you most warmly for all you did for me. If life should become difficult for you, and I fear it might after what we have done, follow us. It is the best you can do.

~Your Mary

Franz Joseph had never given credence to the idea that the crown prince had been murdered. This provided the conspiracy theorists with the argument that the emperor had tacitly accepted the double-suicide theory because it saved him from undertaking the unpleasant task of issuing a manhunt for the crown prince's alleged murderers—particularly if Rudolf's death was a politically motivated assassination carried out by men who might have been exceptionally close to the throne.

The only thing that doesn't quite tally with a double suicide, or even a murder-suicide scenario, is one report that the entire right temple of Rudolf's skull was smashed, which is seemingly inconsistent with a gunshot wound inflicted to the left temple. On the other hand, the report itself could be suspect.

Stephanie's impression of the events was written in her memoirs long after the tragedy. It is worth noting that she does not castigate Mary Vetsera as the rest of the imperial family had done.

As he found no-one else prepared for self-sacrifice, he used Mary Vetsera's passion to address his terrible request to her. She agreed blindly. . . . She really loved him. Let this observation, that Mary Vetsera's love for the Crown Prince was deep and genuine, be the flower which I, the deceived wife, place in forgiveness upon the resting place of the poor, misguided girl.

Additionally, there was one letter that Rudolf waited to write until he arrived at Mayerling. It may even have been penned after Mary Vetsera's death, because it contains the admission, "I have no right to go on living; I have killed."

And yet, if Rudolf and Mary had forged a premeditated *suicide* pact, what did he mean? Had the original intention of the plot been for Mary to kill herself and for Rudolf to follow suit—a double suicide after all? It was easy to scribble maudlin, moonstruck meditations on the subject of suicide, but as she held a gun to her temple, was she too terrified to do the deed; and had Rudolf then done the job for her—which had never been part of the plan? With a rose and handkerchief clasped poetically in her pale hands, had she in fact *begged* him to kill her because she didn't fear dying—but couldn't bring *herself* to pull the trigger? Was that what the imperial family was so eager to subvert: Their son's confession, written to his mother, that he had murdered Mary Vetsera? It was scandalous enough that the married crown prince had been found dead in the company of an equally dead (not to mention naked) girl. The only thing that could have been worse was that he had murdered the woman.

And yet, before long, Rudolf's image began to receive a radical makeover. In the years immediately following his death, the crown prince became the subject of a cultish fascination, and the tragedy at Mayerling was romanticized by the pop culture of the day, most notably in a stage play starring a cross-dressing Sarah Bernhardt.

The real players in the drama received their own

denouements. No longer a member of the imperial family, the widowed Stephanie moved on with her life. On March 22, 1900, she married a Hungarian count, Elemér Count Lónyay de Nagy-Lónyay es Vásárosnamény, moving to western Hungary, where they lived at Orosvár Castle. Stephanie died in 1945; her daughter by Rudolf, Archduchess Elisabeth, who was born on September 2, 1883, married Prince Otto of Windisch-Graetz on January 23, 1902. Elisabeth was divorced after World War I and married a member of Parliament, a Social Democrat named Leopold Petznek. She died in 1964 at her little villa located in Hütteldorf, a small town on the outskirts of Vienna.

The hunting lodge and its outbuildings at Mayerling became a Carmelite convent in 1889. After Franz Joseph oversaw its construction, he considered any self-imposed penance accomplished and refused any further association with the Carmelites.

As the Second World War raged on, in 1945, during a battle at Heiligenkreuz the Russians demolished part of the Carmelite convent and the adjacent cemetery. The bombing partially dislodged and disturbed several tombs, including that of Mary Vetsera. Many of the grave sites were looted; Mary's original copper coffin was among them.

Since her remains had been exposed already, what was left of Mary's body was examined, giving rise to additional conspiracy theories. One report claimed that there was no exit wound in her skull and that rather than her having been the victim of a bullet, her head had been crushed. Unfortunately, it's entirely possible that this accident occurred when the zealous Russians tore open her tomb with a garden hoe, searching for jewelry. The allegation in question is also contradicted by the 1889 medical report of Dr. Auchenthaler, which accords with the testimony of three eyewitnesses who saw Mary's dead body hours after her demise.

And yet—and yet—the funeral director's report raises the possibility that Mary was shot from above. This does not eliminate the contention that Rudolf murdered her, as no one has ever *genuinely* believed that Mary took her own life. It only contradicts the theory that the bullet entered her temple.

In 1992, Mary's remains were again disturbed and a forensics examination concluded that she died from several blows to the head. Gabriel Ronay in his 2008 article for *History Today* mentions that the document alleged to be the original 1889 police report finally came to light, and that it contains some startling revelations: namely that Rudolf had put up a fierce struggle before he died, suffering contusions to his knuckles and a broken jaw. But *when* did this report surface and why would it have been concealed or withheld for so long? It seems strange that at least two of Rudolf's more prominent biographers omit this information in their discussion of the police report.

Even in death, Rudolf was a royal pain—his bloody demise an embarrassment to the empire. But had his own family set him on the inevitable crash course with disaster? Should they share the blame for his becoming a bad seed?

Deprived well into adulthood, as were so many royal heirs, from exercising any role in his father's government and thereby denied any apprenticeship in how to rule, he had too much time on his hands, even as a military officer. The crown prince's progressive politics put him on the outs with his conservative imperial father, so despite his intellectual gifts, he became frustrated at being reduced to a political nonentity who was expected to fritter away his life at the racetrack and the opera while waiting for the emperor to die. Rudolf's acquaintance, the Prince of Wales, found himself in a similar situation, but Rudolf lacked the ebullient bonhomie that enabled Bertie to hang in there.

Consoling himself with liquor and lovers tarnished Rudolf's reputation and cast him as a pleasure-seeking waste of time and space, yet his dubious extracurricular pursuits didn't even begin to fill the aching void. Already a couple of knaves shy of a full deck, Rudolf became addicted to morphine in the final months of his life; and *that*, intensified by his alcohol consumption, was a recipe for disaster. His demons finally triumphed, and the tragedy at Mayerling permanently besmirched the Hapsburg family name and tarnished the imperial crown.

Although it remains speculative, only one conclusion makes any sense: Rudolf took his own life at Mayerling, and the great secret that no one wanted the world to discover was that he had murdered Mary Vetsera, whether the act was premeditated or a spontaneous change of plans. For the heir to the Austro-Hungarian empire to have done something so heinous, so criminal, would certainly appear worthy of being suppressed by the imperial bureaucrats and respun to cast anyone else as the perpetrator. Better for the reputation of the young baroness to be dragged through the mud. Failing that, it was preferable to allow rumors of conspiracy theories to run rampant and gain traction over the ensuing decades than to admit that the crown prince was a psychopath and a cold-blooded killer.

Some of these theories fingered the emperor himself. But any character study of Franz Joseph would illustrate that he could never have authorized the political assassination of his own son. True, Franz Joseph was an autocrat, but he never considered a single member of his family expendable, nor judicial murder a viable or expedient method of eliminating a political dissident. Sadly, rather than bringing the emperor closer to his beloved but peripatetic wife, Rudolf's death estranged his parents further, both geographically and emotionally.

Had Rudolf ascended the imperial throne upon the death of his father, perhaps there would have been no world wars; and if a European conflict had broken out nonetheless, it might have been over the new emperor's policies of religious and other forms of tolerance that would have been unacceptable to the anti-Semitic, anti-progressive Austrian aristocracy. We will never know.

PRINCE ALBERT VICTOR

Duke of Clarence and Avondale
1864–1892

$\mathscr{A}$LTHOUGH HIS OWN CONDUCT CERTAINLY CONTRIB-
uted in some way to his unfavorable reputation, Prince
Albert Victor, whose father, the Prince of Wales, was the
only one standing between him and the English throne, was
more or less an "accidental pain"—earning his stripes by
implication. Through a chain of circumstances the young
prince, known within the royal family as Eddy, became
embroiled in a series of scandals, one of which made
international headlines during his brief lifetime. Another
devastating contention—that he was the infamous serial
murderer Jack the Ripper—posthumously haunts Eddy and
continues to smear his reputation, because it remains one
of the first things that springs to mind when his name is
mentioned.

The allegations and assertions about Eddy's conduct and
character, several of which might just as easily have been
lifted from the plot of a tawdry Victorian melodrama, have
twisted his image into a "grotesque," someone his own relatives would not have recognized. Yet the prince's behavior
(and, just as often, his inactivity) did frustrate and sometimes mortify the royal family. His apparent lack of aca-
demic acumen made him the butt of journalists' jokes and

the subject of rampant speculation that when such a moron eventually ascended the throne it would spell the downfall of the English monarchy. Even worse than being a reigning dope or dullard was the possibility that Eddy might not be elegible to rule at all. Whispers of "gross indecency" grew to a roar. And practicing homosexuality, a felonious offense, was on the short list of items that could bar a prince from ever inheriting the throne.

Although his connection to a high-profile investigation into London's seedy gay underworld was never proved, Eddy *did* love, not wisely but too well, which created plenty of other scandals (including his potential ineligibility to become king) without the fictional addition of monstrous violence, secret babies, clandestine marriages, insanity, and "the love that dare not speak its name."

Prince Albert Victor, Duke of Clarence and Avondale, was the son of the Prince and Princess of Wales, "Bertie" and Alexandra of Denmark: He was born nearly two months premature in early January 1864, and two months later was christened Albert Victor Christian Edward—the name chosen by his royal grandmama Queen Victoria. During the Victorian era, plumpness connoted good health; consequently the queen found her infant grandson too frail. The queen, who never thought much of babies, with their "big body and little limbs and that terrible frog-like action" described Eddy's appearance when he was a year old as "a perfect bijou—very fairy-like, but quite healthy, very wise-looking and good. He lets all the family carry him and play with him—and Alix (Eddy's mother, Alexandra, Princess of Wales) likes him to be accustomed to it. He is very placid, almost melancholy-looking sometimes. What is not pretty is his very narrow chest (rather pigeon-chested) which is like

Alix's build and that of her family. . . . He is decisively like her; everyone is struck by it."

In truth, Eddy had his father's eyes—the heavy-lidded, protuberant Hanoverian orbs. When that particular genetic trait took on a certain vacuity of expression as he aged, it was small wonder he was often thought to be a dullard.

Princes have few friends, and Eddy's constant companion throughout his childhood and teenage years was his younger brother, George (the future George V). George was seventeen months Eddy's junior, and they also had three younger sisters (Louise, Victoria, and Maud, born in 1867, 1868, and 1869, respectively). The children traveled about with their parents, schlepped from one royal demesne to another as the family maintained its annual traditions, celebrating Christmas and the winter months at Sandringham in Norfolk; spring at the Waleses' London home, Marlborough House; and summers at Cowes for the regatta and at Balmoral in Scotland.

Neither of the Waleses was keen on forcing their sons to receive the sort of rigid upbringing that Bertie himself had endured, and the parents eventually reaped what they had sown. In fact, Bertie's chief aim, so he told his mother, was to keep the boys "simple, pure, and childlike for as long as possible." Unamused by their devil-may-care upbringing, Queen Victoria found her two grandsons "such ill-bred, ill-trained children." Additionally, neither of the young princes was remotely intellectual, and by the time their private tutelage ended, their education was so sorely inferior to that of their fellow students that they were always at the bottom of the class, although their exalted status excused them from having to take regular exams.

A number of elements contributed to Eddy's lackluster

aptitude for learning. He did not possess a terribly keen mind to begin with and neither of his parents were readers, so the concept of losing himself in a good book and catching a bit of knowledge on his own was an alien one. Reverend John Neale Dalton, the tutor engaged to educate both Eddy and George, who were schooled side by side, was evidently not only a dull lecturer but a terribly inept instructor. And Eddy seemed to tune out when a subject didn't interest him, which prompted many people, including Queen Victoria's private secretary, Sir Henry Ponsonby, to assume that the prince had inherited his mother's otosclerosis, a form of deafness that the Princess of Wales had inherited from her own mother, Queen Louise of Denmark.

Reverend Dalton condemned Eddy as a rather indifferent scholar, citing "the abnormally dormant condition of his mind," although the boy seemed to have energy to spare for the sportive pursuits in his curriculum—tennis, archery, gymnastics, fencing, and even croquet—and as he matured he would become a passionate hunter. It never occurred to Dalton that his pedagogy might be the reason for Eddy's lethargy.

Prince George was just as weak a student as his older brother, yet it was Eddy who seemed to be suffering from an inferiority complex. Dalton opined that "there was in him an apathy which his father tried—perhaps too roughly—to combat." Many years later, Sir Lionel Cust (who'd met Eddy when the prince was a student at Cambridge) wrote in his memoirs that he "told me of his devotion to his mother . . . from whom he inherited much which, had he lived, would have perhaps gone to a nation's heart and won it as Queen Alexandra (Eddy's mother) had done herself." However,

Eddy had also "confessed . . . to being rather afraid of his father, and aware that he was not quite up to what his father expected of him."

They are fascinating observations because Bertie was evidently re-creating the same overbearing-father/not-up-to-snuff-son relationship that he'd had with his own father, Prince Albert, and which he vowed never to foist upon his own children.

In 1876, when Eddy was twelve years old and George was ten and a half, the royal family debated whether to send the princes to a proper school. Queen Victoria was adamantly against enrolling the boys in one of the finer public schools like Eton or Harrow, owing to an ongoing scandal surrounding the seduction of some younger pupils by their tutors or by older boys. Mutual "unnatural" intimacies had formed, and consequently, public school was thought to be a thoroughly unsuitable milieu for the princes. The inherent irony in where they ended up instead must have been lost on the family.

Reverend Dalton advised against the princes' being separated from each other. George was already an arrogant brat, but Eddy's influence grounded him; while "Prince Albert Victor [Eddy] requires the stimulus of Prince George's company to induce him to work at all . . . the mutual influence of their characters on one another (totally different as they are in many ways) is very beneficial. Difficult as the education of Prince Albert Victor is now [because in Dalton's mind Eddy had no "motive power"], it would be doubly or trebly so if Prince George were to leave him."

The best way to keep the boys together was to sign them up for the Royal Navy. Dalton coached the princes so they could pass their entrance exams. In September

1877, they began their naval education as cadets aboard the HMS *Britannia*, the training ship for all officer candidates. Eddy was still only thirteen years old, with George not yet twelve. The Reverend Dalton accompanied them as a part-time tutor and ship's chaplain.

The princes graduated in July 1879, leaving *Britannia* for a three-year tour of duty aboard the *Bacchante*, traveling around the world until 1882, visiting exotic locales and sampling the native customs. They met the Mikado and got tattooed in Tokyo; Eddy was inked with red and blue dragons on his arms.

The youths' companions on the *Bacchante* had been handpicked to ensure that the princes would be surrounded by fine, upstanding boys. However, one of their mates was eventually deemed too feminine and was dismissed, according to George V's biographer Harold Nicolson, because he "induced them to take liberties with him which they should not."

At the end of their journeymanship aboard the *Bacchante*, the princes had to sit for another set of exams. Although Dalton was likely to blame for Eddy's ennui, he remained unimpressed by his elder pupil, griping that "he sits listless and vacant . . . and wastes as much time in doing nothing as he ever wasted . . . this weakness of brain, this feebleness and lack of power to grasp almost anything put before him, is manifested . . . also in his hours of recreation and social intercourse. It is a fault of nature. . . ."

An 1880 photo of Eddy in his cadet uniform taken at the age of sixteen bears out Dalton's "listless and vacant" portrayal of his pupil. Although the prince might have been just a typical sullen teen when it came to his studies or to the regimented schedule of royal duties, in the photograph,

Eddy does leave a rather dim-witted impression; absolutely nothing appears to be going on behind his heavy-lidded Hanoverian eyes.

In October 1883 Eddy entered Trinity College, Cambridge, while George continued in the navy. But the heir presumptive's university education was not quite the one shared by his fellow students. "He hardly knows the meaning of the words *to read*," complained J. K. Stephen, one of Eddy's tutors.

Lady Somerset, a lady-in-waiting to Queen Victoria's aunt, the Duchess of Cambridge, was appalled at the prince's ignorance. Although she found Eddy to be *"charmin*g, as nice a youth as could be, simple, unaffected, unspoiled, affectionate," she wanted to know, "What on earth stupid Dalton has been about all these years! He has taught him *nothing*!"

Eddy's university experience was fairly brief and none too illustrious. In July of 1885 he segued into the next phase of his life, a posting to his father's regiment, the 10th Hussars. The prince proved just as lackluster an army officer. According to his instructors at Aldershot, Eddy had problems retaining information and an embarrassingly dismal knowledge of military history. His inertia did not go unnoticed, as the Duke of Cambridge declared, "He is an inveterate and incurable dawdler, never *ready*, never *there*!"

But Eddy did at least evince an interest in *something*. The only quality he seemed to have inherited from his father was Bertie's sense of impeccable tailoring. The young prince had become a fashionable young man with a spiffy mustache, a natty dresser in the popular "masher" style, sporting high starched collars and oversize cuffs. It was a look that suited

Eddy, who had an unusually long neck and arms, prompting his father to nickname him "collar and cuffs."

The mashers were the dandies of their day, dull-witted but debonair, dressing to impress women. And Eddy had one particular female in mind. He had developed a crush on one of his first cousins, thirteen-year-old Alexandra of Hesse. By this time Eddy had twice seen "Alicky," as the family called her, at family weddings.

Nevertheless, the prince's attraction to Alicky didn't prevent him from indulging in the usual pursuits practiced by Victorian men of his class. Apart from Queen Victoria and the Prince of Wales, the members of the royal family would not have been recognized by the average Briton; and while their movements were often observed by plainclothesmen from Scotland Yard, Eddy did manage to enjoy the social life of a typical toff. He mingled with other lordlings at music halls, and perhaps crossed paths with them at brothels. Royal brothers Eddy and George even shared a "ripper" of a girl (an ironic choice of words, though it was popular slang for someone who was lots of fun) at a location in St. John's Wood. According to George's diary Eddy was also keeping a girl in Southsea.

In 1888, Bertie had to extricate his elder son from an unnamed, but clearly sordid situation. Perhaps it was an indiscretion regarding one of these working-class young ladies, although that would have been par for the course when it came to the extracurricular activities of the nobility. For this reason, some of Eddy's biographers have speculated that his transgression involved something significantly more scandalous. Precisely because the offense remained unspecified, these historians have taken the liberty of positing the theory that it had everything to do with "the love that dare not speak its name"—a homosexual encounter (or several). In any case, the matter, whatever it was, must have been surreptitiously cleared up, because there is no further mention of the event.

Instead, that autumn the headlines were filled with Jack the Ripper's string of hideous murders. For many readers it was their first encounter with London's destitute East End, a neighborhood so squalid that the police were finding it difficult to separate the Ripper's victims from the numerous other unfortunate souls who turned up dead.

As the madman's murder tally rose and no one had been apprehended, Queen Victoria expressed her disgust with the incompetence of Scotland Yard and the Metropolitan Police. She wanted results. Consequently, the coppers were eager to find a way to redeem their reputations.

Eddy undoubtedly read the papers, but Whitechapel was a world away from the Waleses' London residence, Marlborough House. His focus was not on the Ripper, but on romance.

In September 1888, when Jack the Ripper was slitting the throats of his first victims, the diffident, moonstruck Eddy was confessing his crush on Alexandra of Hesse to their cousin, Prince Louis of Battenberg, revealing his hopes of courting and marrying Alicky, despite the efforts of meddling relatives.

On September 6, Eddy wrote to Louis:

I thought you knew I was fond of Alicky. In fact I have been fond of her for years and have told no one with the exception of my parents, and that only a short time ago. . . . I fear that someone else must have told Alicky, which was I think a great mistake, and as you say relations can only spoil my chance by mixing themselves up in the affair. I guessed that myself last year, and therefore was very careful how I approached Alicky and did not give her the slightest sign that I loved her, although inwardly I was longing to tell her so, but thought I had better wait my time.

. . . I can only get her to give me some hope and encouragement if not more, that some day I may be her fortunate suitor. . . . I can't tell you what a happy creature I shall be if it only comes off right, for I do indeed know what a prize there is to be won.

Time had marched on. The new generation of royals remained mindful of their obligations to dynastic marital alliances, but now they wanted to wed for love as well. Once upon a time, it wouldn't have mattered a jot to the parents if there was no mutual attraction between the potential newlyweds, or even if an attraction was merely one-sided. Children weren't given the freedom to choose their spouses. Now, as the nineteenth century headed for the history books, the younger generation was putting a collective foot down and daring to refuse a prospective bride or groom as well as repudiating the notion of a love-less marriage.

In the absence of any romantic encouragement from Alicky, Eddy might have found another outlet for his manly urges. Or not. Nevertheless, his name was about to be coupled with one of the greatest scandals of the century. To set the stage, in 1885 an amendment was passed to the Criminal Law Act, enacting penalties of up to two years' imprisonment, with or without hard labor, if a man was convicted of "gross indecency"—attempting to commit, committing, or procuring sex acts from other men. It was known as the Labouchère Amendment (for Henry Labouchère, the MP who introduced it into Parliament), but was nicknamed the "Blackmailer's Charter." The amendment wended its way through Parliament with little scrutiny because homosexuality was considered an indecent topic for discussion by such an august body as the House of Commons.

Four years later, in July of 1889, a male brothel located at 19 Cleveland Street and run by Charles Hammond was raided by the Metropolitan Police. The brothel was empty at the time, Hammond and his young male companion having managed to flee to the Continent.

The incident mushroomed into a national scandal after it was revealed that telegraph boys in the employ of the General Post Office had been receiving money for performing certain sexual favors for gentlemen at the Cleveland Street brothel. Several of the youths had been recruited by George Veck, one of Hammond's pals, who routinely posed as a parson in order to gain the boys' trust. Veck had been sacked from his employment at the post office for "improper conduct" with telegraph boys and in 1889 was living with his boyfriend, a youth of seventeen.

Inspector Abberline of Scotland Yard was pulled off the Ripper case and assigned to handle the Cleveland Street Affair. He took his assignment very seriously, determined to quash criticism of the Yard's unsatisfactory detective work on the Whitechapel serial murders. But because many of the adolescent rent boys were telegraph couriers, the post office was equally determined to keep the matter as quiet as possible.

The frightened teens began to name names; their targets

included a bevy of rich and titled gentlemen and decorated military officers. According to a fifteen-year-old telegraph-cum-rent boy with the improbably ironic name of Henry Newlove, one of the biggest fish in the Cleveland Street pond was Lord Arthur Somerset (nicknamed "Podge"), extra equerry to the Prince of Wales and master of the stables. A dapper thirty-eight-year-old living well above his means, the tall, blond Somerset (known to the rent boys as "Mr. Brown") was a younger son of the Duke of Beaufort. Terrified that he would be ruined if his boss were to get wind of his predilections, Somerset hired Arthur Newton, a thoroughly unscrupulous young solicitor who was making a name for himself defending some of London's seamier residents. Newton was already representing the proprietor of 19 Cleveland Street, Charles Hammond, and the faux vicar George Veck, as well as the young boys who were implicated in the scandal.

Maintaining a discreet silence about the whole affair, Somerset took a leave of absence from his job and hightailed it to the Continent. However, some members of the government were keen on covering up Somerset's involvement, insisting to Scotland Yard that there was insufficient evidence (merely the word of teenage telegraph boys who sold their services) to extradite a duke's son.

However, Hamilton Cuffe, the deputy to the treasury solicitor, *was* interested in justice being served. In Cuffe's view, if there was enough evidence to prosecute the boys, Hammond, and Veck, then surely Somerset was just as culpable and should be made to appear before the bar.

Somerset was desperate to keep his name out of the press and his body out of the courts. And his solicitor,

Arthur Newton, was equally determined to help him. It was most likely Newton who floated the rumor that there was a powerful reason for Somerset's silence on the whole affair: He was protecting the name of a very important personage in the kingdom whose name and association with the Cleveland Street brothel—were the information to be revealed—would send shock waves through England and change the face of the monarchy forever.

On September 16, 1889, Hamilton Cuffe wrote to Sir Augustus Stephenson, the treasury solicitor, "I'm told that Newton has boasted that if we go on, a very distinguished person (PAV) will be involved. I don't mean to say that [I] for one instant credit it—but in such a case as this one never knows what may be said, concocted or true."

Stephenson replied to Cuffe the following day, characterizing Newton as "a dangerous man, and he may—or his clients may—make utterly false accusations against others—with respect to whom so far as our information goes—or the descriptions given by the boys—there is no shadow of grounds for imputation. Still such imputation may be made." Stephenson thought Newton was bluffing. No one else at any time had mentioned Eddy's name, whether in earnest or as a way to deflect attention from his own participation in the scandal. Not one police officer stationed near the brothel to observe the comings and goings of its clients saw Eddy. Even during the prince's years as a naval cadet, and his stint at Trinity College, Cambridge, where he hobnobbed with a clique of young men, some of whom were rumored to be homosexual, there was never so much as a hint or a whisper that Eddy might be gay.

While the civil servants were fairly certain that Newton was lying, the politicians and cabinet ministers weren't about to take any chances by calling the lawyer's bluff. They were willing enough to credit Newton's allegations, which was all the more reason to keep Eddy's name out of the scandal and to come up with any number of reasons to avoid issuing a warrant for Somerset's arrest. If Somerset's sexuality was outed in a court of law, he would have nothing left to lose, and would surely implicate the prince as another of the Cleveland Street clients.

Somerset was traveling in Constantinople when his sister Blanche, Marchioness of Waterford, took it upon herself to defend the reputation of both men.

> Please correct any impression that Arthur [Somerset] and *the boy* ever went out together. . . . Arthur knows nothing of his movements and was horrified to think he might be supposed to take the Father's money and lead the son into mischief of ANY kind. I am sure the boy is as straight as a line.

Dighton Probyn, private secretary to the Princess of Wales, wrote to Somerset's mother, the Duchess of Beaufort, advising her that "Nobody accused your son of having mentioned PAV's name, but his excuse to everybody for having to leave England is that he has been forced to do so to screen another and that his lips are closed. The only conclusion therefore people can draw from this is that he is sacrificing himself to save the young Prince. Who else is there for whom he could make such a sacrifice?"

Oliver Montagu, an extra equerry to the Prince and Princess of Wales, wrote to Somerset rhetorically inquiring whether his lordship was "aware of the irreparable harm he was doing by still persisting in his silence as to the real cause of his leaving the country and insinuating that it was for the sakes of others that he had done so. . . ."

Somerset addressed both queries in a reply to the (also homosexual) Reginald Brett, Lord Esher, insisting in a very couched manner that the "real cause" *was* because he was protecting the prince.

Theo Aronson, one of Eddy's biographers, is far more willing than other historians to conclude that the prince was concealing a homosexual lifestyle. Aronson maintains that the reason the Prince of Wales was so eager to silence the rumors and innuendo surrounding Eddy's connection to the Cleveland Street brothel was not because it was an outrageous lie, but because it was *true*. Many of the private papers of Queen Victoria and of the Prince and Princess of Wales (later Edward VII and Queen Alexandra) were burned after their deaths, destroyed on their instructions. And according to Aronson, the Royal Archives has insisted that Prince Eddy's file "has not survived."

Nevertheless, these allegations of homosexual conduct with young boys that mortified the royal family by dragging the prince's reputation through the mud remain far-fetched. Lord Somerset and Eddy barely knew each other. The Prince of Wales's extra equerry would have had little reason to come into contact with His Royal Highness's son.

Yet the tacit assertions about Eddy's predilection for teenage rent boys sent the crown into a tizzy because it didn't take long for Somerset to begin to *believe* his solicitor's lie. Sir Arthur's new line of reasoning went something like this: Although he had never crossed paths with Eddy at the brothel, nor had ever accompanied him there, that in itself was no proof that Eddy was *not* a client!

On December 10, 1889, Somerset wrote:

I can quite understand the Prince of Wales being much annoyed at his son's name being coupled with the thing but that was the case before I left—in fact in June or July. . . . It had no more to do with me than the fact that we (that is Prince and I) must both perform bodily functions which we cannot do for each other. In the same way we were both accused of going to this place but not together; and different people were supposed to have gone there to meet us. . . . Nothing will ever make me divulge anything I know even if I were arrested. . . . It has very often, I may say constantly occurred to me that it rests with me to clear up this business, but what can I do? A great many people would never speak to me again as it is; but if I went into Court, and told all I knew, no one who called himself a man would ever speak to me again.

Eddy, meanwhile, was touring India and the East on an official series of visits that had been several months in the planning; it was not, as some asserted, a hastily organized excursion to get the heir presumptive conveniently out of town.

While British journalists kept the extent of the scandal somewhat under wraps, the foreign press was eager to report all the news that was fit—or not—to print.

The London correspondent for the *New York Times* had a field day speculating about Eddy's involvement in the Cleveland Street Affair, insisting that it was "obvious to everybody that there has come to be within the last few days a general conviction that this long-necked, narrow-headed young dullard was mixed up in the scandal, and out of this had sprung a half-whimsical, half-serious notion which one hears propounded now about clubland, that matters will be arranged that he will never return from India. The most popular idea is that he will be killed in a tiger hunt, but runaway horses or a fractious elephant might serve as well. What this really mirrors is a public awakening to the fact that this stupid, perverse boy has become a man and has only two precious lives [Victoria's and Bertie's] between him and the English throne and is an utter blackguard and ruffian.

"Something besides a harmless simpleton has created a very painful feeling everywhere. Although he looks so strikingly like his mother, it turns out that he gets only his face from the Danish race and that morally and mentally he combines the worst attributes of those sons of George III, at whose mention history still holds her nose. It is not too early to predict that such a fellow will never be allowed to ascend the British throne; that is as clear as anything can be."

And on November 10, the *New York Times* crowed, "Current rumor says that Prince Albert Victor will not return from India until the matter is completely over and forgotten, but there are certain stubborn moralists at work on the case who profess determination that it shall not be judicially burked, and the prospects are that the whole terrible affair will be dragged out into light."

Somerset corroborated this when he wrote that Newton was not to be trifled with.

I don't think they should have tackled a strong and dangerous man in N. If they put him in a corner he will very likely give them a nasty one. . . . I feel sure that with all this virulent prosecution of everybody they will end by having out in open court exactly what they are all trying to keep quiet. I wonder if it is really a fact or only an invention of that arch ruffian H[ammond].

Had Charles Hammond been the one to tell Newton that Prince Eddy was one of his clients, or had Newton planted that seed as part of a deal to get Hammond off the hook? Either way, the damage to Eddy's reputation had been done.

It's hard to imagine that the prince had a secret life diddling telegraph boys when his thoughts were so clearly focused on how he might win the heart of his first cousin Alexandra of Hesse. On October 7, 1889, the twenty-five-year-old prince wrote to Prince Louis of Battenburg, his confidant in the matter, reiterating his despair over Alicky's coolness to his suit, and his intentions of convincing her of his love. Eddy played the queen card, insisting that his grandmother was overwhelmingly in favor of the match. After all, he would one day be king of England—the most prestigious and glamorous job in the world! What wasn't to like?

Anxious for answers, Eddy asked Louis to intercede for him and to find out whether Alicky believed that he had in some way wronged or offended her, as perhaps that was the reason for her indifference.

The prince got his jollies with "fancy women" from time to time, but with girls of his own class, he was painfully shy. Where Alicky was concerned, Eddy was terrified of getting his heart broken by his beautiful cousin. As much of a sophisticated man-about-town as Bertie was, and a master seducer of the ladies, his son was something of a social naïf, in many ways ignorant of the world. Victorians were keen on infantilizing their offspring for as long as possible, and the queen herself was the greatest one of all for wishing to keep her children and grandchildren in a state of perpetual innocence.

Around the same time that Eddy was writing to Louis of Battenberg as though he were Dear Abby, the Prince of Wales learned that his extra equerry Sir Arthur Somerset had been implicated in the Cleveland Street Affair. At first, he was unwilling to believe that this manly, mustachioed former soldier was really involved in the scandal.

Eddy was still touring the Middle East with his father, while back in London rumors abounded regarding Somerset's connection with the brothel, and by extension, Eddy's. Many people were all too willing to believe that Somerset was not only guilty of gross indecency, but that he was the conduit by which the prince got his illicit kicks. However, Somerset would never actually be apprehended or tried, though a warrant was issued for his arrest. He was permitted to remain in self-imposed exile on the Continent. Hammond and his boy toy were also permitted to slip away from Antwerp on a boat bound for America. Only Veck, the faux parson, and Henry Newlove, one of the telegraph boys who had prostituted himself, were convicted and sentenced to hard labor. As is so often the case in royal scandals (see Erzsébet Báthory), the nobility's involvement is downplayed, whitewashed, or ignored, while their hirelings and those from the lower social orders receive the full brunt of the punishment.

As 1890 dawned, and journalists refused to shake the Cleveland Street scandal from their teeth, Eddy's parents became even more determined to find their elder son a bride. He would turn twenty-six in early January. The Waleses were adamant that their son marry a royal, but the pickings were slim; many of the single princesses were too young, too old, or too ugly.

Princess May of Teck had been scratched from the running years before, because, according to Queen Victoria's private secretary, Sir Henry Ponsonby, "The Prince and Princess of Wales have no love for the parents, and the boy does not care for the girl." Kaiser Wilhelm's sister Margaret, known as "Mossy," had also been eliminated for being both homely and German.

Alicky had written Eddy a "Dear John" letter, rejecting his suit. Although she liked him as a cousin, she didn't love him. She would eventually make a love match, wedding another cousin, Nicholas, the czarevitch of Russia. Their marriage was one of the great royal love stories of the century, though it would end in tragedy in 1918 when their entire family was assassinated by the Bolsheviks.

As further proof that Eddy probably didn't have a secret life engaging in hole-in-the-wall trysts with underage boys, he developed a new passion for another gorgeous royal. With Alicky out of the picture, the prince had already begun to focus his sights elsewhere, falling just as madly in love with Hélène d'Orléans, the daughter of the comte de Paris, the pretender to the French throne. He had been delighted to learn that she reciprocated his ardor.

But just as a homosexual couldn't become king (because "gross indecency" was a felonious offense), the 1707 Act of Union barred Catholics, or anyone married to a Catholic, from inheriting the throne. Accordingly, although the chestnut-haired Hélène was lovely, accomplished, and vivacious, her religion made her eminently ineligible to be the future queen of England. Were Eddy to wed her, he would have to forfeit his rights to the crown.

Queen Victoria was not amused, writing to her grandson:

I wish to say a few words about the subject of your future marriage. I quite agree with you that you should not be hurried [yet the prince was twenty-six; what was he waiting for?] and I feel sure that you will resist all the wiles and attempts of intriguers and bad women to catch you. But I wish to say that I have heard it rumoured that *you* had been thinking and talking of Princesse Hélène of Orleans! I can't believe this for you know that I told you (as did your parents who agreed with me) that such a marriage is utterly *impossible*. None of our family can marry a Catholic without losing all their rights and I am sure that she would never change her religion and to change her religion merely to marry is a thing much to be deprecated, and which would have the very worst effect possible and be most unpopular, besides which *you* could not marry the daughter of the Pretender to the French throne. Politically in this way it would also be impossible.

Victoria's letter had no effect. Eddy's clandestine flirtation with the nineteen-year-old Hélène continued throughout the summer. That June he received a title so that he could take his place in the House of Lords, becoming Duke of Clarence and Avondale and Earl of Athlone. The queen of micromanagement, Her Majesty herself, had chosen her grandson's title, although she considered it a demotion from prince. Eddy would still be a prince, of course, but from then on he was styled as a duke.

As some politicians and sports stars will insist, the romantic love one has for one's wife has nothing to do with a man's need to satisfy his lust with other women.

And as Eddy's prospective brides were expected to remain virginal until their wedding night, the prince needed to take care of business from time to time. But actions have consequences. In mid-July 1890, Eddy was hospitalized with a fever, although his symptoms were suspiciously venereal. His chain-smoking didn't ameliorate matters, despite the efforts of his treating physician, a young doctor named Alfred Fripp, to get him to reduce his tobacco consumption.

Fripp chronicled his sessions with his royal patient, but betrayed Eddy's trust by sharing the details with his father, writing to the elder Fripp, "HRH pours out all his little woes [including the details of "his love affair" with Princesse Hélène] and always makes me smoke in his room. He smokes himself until he is stupid. I have knocked him down to three cigarettes and one cigar a day." However, Dr. Fripp cautioned his father, "don't mention HRH's illness outside our house as the Prince of Wales particularly wants it not to get into the papers. He is afraid the public will get the impression that his son is a chronic invalid."

Eddy's biographer Theo Aronson suggests that there was another reason Bertie wanted the prince's ailment to remain a secret. Although the palace's official lie was that Eddy was convalescing after a nasty fall from a horse, Aronson believes that Dr. Fripp was treating the young prince for symptoms of gonorrhea.

The Prince of Wales had given Fripp an ultimatum: It was imperative to cure Eddy before any thoughts of a royal engagement could take place. Dr. Fripp must have been successful, because the prince was prepared to press his suit for Hélène's hand with the highest authority, bringing her to Balmoral to meet his grandmother.

Queen Victoria advised her prime minister, Lord Salisbury:

> . . . a message came that "Prince Albert Victor" wished to speak to me. . . . He came in and said "I have brought Hélène with me" taking her by the hand and bringing her up to where I sat, saying they were devoted to each other and hoped I would help them. I answered they knew it was impossible, on which he said she was prepared to change her religion for his sake. I said to her would it not be very difficult to do this and she answered in a most pathetic way with tears in her eyes "For him, only for him. Oh! Help pray do" and he said the same and that "She has been attached to me for years and I never knew it," that he was sure I would try and help them. I assured them, I would do what I could to help them but it might be difficult. He told me she had not told her parents of it—she had done it all of her own free will. "I thought I would come straight to you. I have not told Mama even," he said.

The queen quizzed Hélène about her parents' reaction to her willingness to become a Protestant if it meant that she could wed Eddy, and the young girl admitted that while "her mother winked at it," her father would be livid.

Miraculously, Victoria came around and was willing to support the match, on the condition that Hélène abjure her Catholicism. The French princess was clever, strong, and healthy and would make a good mate for the lethargic Eddy.

A. J. Balfour, the Secretary for Ireland and a Conservative MP, was gravely concerned that the young couple had managed to win over the queen. "The political objections a little frighten her, but she is in process of persuading herself that they may be ignored," he wrote to his uncle, Prime Minister Robert Cecil, 3rd Marquess of Salisbury.

Salisbury's reply was blunt. "Prevent any Royal consent being given."

The marital pickings were slim, which was one reason Victoria had caved so readily. Laying out the situation in detail, Balfour reminded Lord Salisbury,

> According to her [Victoria] there are but three marriageable Protestant princesses at this moment in Europe, besides the Teck girl and the Hesse girl [Alicky]. The Teck girl they won't have because they hate Teck and because the vision of [May Teck's prodigiously fat mother] haunting Marlborough House makes the Prince of Wales ill. . . . The Hesse girl won't have him. There remain a Mecklenburg and two Anhalt Princesses (I am not sure that I have the names right). According to her Majesty they are all three ugly, unhealthy, and idiotic; and if that be not enough, they are also penniless and narrow-minded—or as she put it—German of the Germans! They might do perhaps (as she said) for a younger son, but . . . here we have (she went on) a charming and clever young lady—against whom no legal objection can be urged, who has loved Prince Eddy for three years (NB she is only 19 now) to whom he is devoted, and who will fill her position splendidly—how can it be stopped? The Prince will never marry anyone else—his health will break down—and so on.

It was a genuine scandal; behind the scenes, in what they viewed as the interest of the realm, government officials at the highest levels were endeavoring to manipulate the personal lives of the royal family, including the queen.

Stalling for time, hoping the whole unpleasant business would blow over, Balfour felt the mixed marriage *might* be pulled off "by patiently carrying out a well considered policy for some years . . . If *he* [Eddy] showed for a sufficient length of time that he would look at no one else, and *she* [Hélène] began to advertise her conversion by attending the parish church . . ."

Eddy was politely exasperated, under the impression that all that was required for the match was Victoria's consent, as the monarch, and that her ministers were bound to abide by her decision.

However, there was another good reason to delay any engagement. Bertie knew the clap when he saw it, although he tried to keep the details of Eddy's illness from his prudish grandmother. However, the Prince of Wales did encourage Dr. Fripp to inform Eddy's mother that their son's condition was "far more serious than she has any idea of."

Alix's private secretary, Sir Dighton Probyn, wrote to Fripp, couching his instructions in euphemism: "The gout *and every other ailment must be completely eradicated* from the system. . . ."

Sir Henry Thompson, a specialist in urinary tract infections, was quietly brought on board to consult. Thompson's other specialty was venereal disease.

By this time the Waleses thought it best that Eddy have a minder at all times, to keep him from getting into further trouble. More often than not, the task fell to Dr. Fripp, who was a year and a half younger than his royal patient.

Both Eddy and Victoria continued to review all avenues by which a marriage with Hélène might be feasible. The queen's secretary, Sir Henry Ponsonby, wrote to Balfour on September 10, 1890:

The queen asks for your opinion as to whom the succession would go if the Duke of Clarence [Eddy] married a Papist but had children who were Protestants. His Royal Highness saw the Queen yesterday and was depressed at the aspect of affairs. He told the Queen that if consent to the marriage was refused he would marry PH [Princesse Hélène] and lose his rights to the throne. But that his children would be Protestants and he imagined would therefore [be eligible to] succeed.

Like it or not, the constitution was on Eddy's side and he was correct about the rules of succession. That autumn he remained as passionate about Hélène as ever, writing to his younger brother, "You have no idea how I love this sweet girl now, and I feel I could never be happy without her."

And yet, as besotted as he may have been with the French princess, Eddy's indiscretions with other women had already cost him his health. Now he was about to be hit in the wallet. The prince had become involved with *two* disreputable ladies and had foolishly written to at least one of the girls, a Miss Richardson—who had already extracted £200 (over $27,000 today) for the return of a number of compromising letters Eddy had written to her. She then demanded an additional £100 for her silence.

No wonder the prince's family had determined that he needed a babysitter!

Meanwhile, the prime minister was brushing up on his continental history. Because she was still under twenty-one, Hélène would need her father's consent to wed. And even if she were to receive it, her marriage would not be considered valid in France until she turned twenty-five, unless she received a special dispensation from the pope. Additionally, a religious conversion from Catholicism would still be in contravention of England's Act of Succession, which barred a Catholic (or someone married to one) from ascending the throne. Once a Papist, always a Papist, evidently.

There would be social ramifications as well. The English Catholics would fume over Hélène's rejection of her religion for the sake of a crown. And the Anglicans would still view her as Catholic, no matter what religion she adopted.

But all concerns regarding the problematic royal marriage were laid to rest when Hélène's father, the comte de Paris, refused his consent. Hélène went above his head and appealed to the pope, but His Holiness was equally disinclined to support the match. In the spring of 1891 Hélène wrote to Eddy to release him from his prenuptial promise. The prince was distraught, but his mother, who had pinned all her hopes on the Bourbon alliance, was even more devastated.

However, a young man's heart is a resilient organ, and before long Eddy was head over heels in love with someone else. The young woman in question, Lady Sybil St. Clair-Erskine, was the beautiful and vivacious sister of the profligate 5th Earl of Rosslyn and the stepsister of Daisy Brooke, the Countess of Warwick. Daisy was the Prince of Wales's current mistress; therefore, a marriage between Eddy and Lady Sybil would create a scandal of a most embarrassing magnitude. It would make Daisy one of the (albeit extended) family, thereby placing Alix, the Princess of Wales, in the awkward position of countenancing her husband's paramour as an in-law.

Adding spice to the mix was the fact that even as Eddy continued to explore every avenue by which he might marry Princesse Hélène d'Orléans, he was pouring out his heart to Lady Sybil. In June 1891, months before Hélène was compelled to formally reject him, the two-timing prince wrote to Sybil:

> I thought it was impossible a short time ago, to love more than one person at the same time. . . . I can explain it easier to you when next we meet, than by writing. I only hope that this charming creature [he addressed Sybil in the third person] which has so fascinated me is not merely playing with my feelings. . . . I can't believe she would after all she has already said, and asked me to say . . . I am writing in an odd way and have no doubt you will think so but I do it for a particular reason. . . .

A week later, he wrote to Sybil:

> I wonder if you really love me a little? I ought not to ask such a silly question I suppose but still I should be very pleased if you did just a little bit. . . . You may trust me not to show your letters to anyone. . . . You can't be too careful what you do in these days, when hardly anybody is to be trusted.

Eddy had learned something (sort of) from his little bribery-and-blackmail episode with the tarty Miss Richardson. What he'd gleaned from the experience, however, was *not* to avoid writing compromising love letters, but to eliminate all traces that he was the sender. The prince begged Sybil to excise his signature and the royal crest from the stationery.

There is nothing new under the sun. Gold diggers are found in every generation and walk of life. Needless to say, Lady Sybil did not snip the crest and signature from

Eddy's billets-doux. She was also two-timing him with the son of the Duke of Westmorland.

Eddy's life seemed to be stalled in neutral. At the age of twenty-seven he remained unwed, and consequently without his own establishment, in adolescent stasis until he married. His army career was also going nowhere fast. To his father's vast disappointment Eddy was still a major in the 10th Hussars when other men who had come up at the same time were lieutenant colonels. The heir presumptive was proving himself to be demonstrably unsuited for a military career—yet was he suited for *anything*?

Field Marshal Garnet Joseph Wolseley, the highly decorated commander, observed that "HRH [His Royal Highness] has far more in him than he is often given credit for, but I should describe his brain and thinking powers as maturing slowly. Personally I think he is very much to be liked, thoughtful for others, and always anxious to do the right thing. He is, however, young for his age and requires to be brought out."

To "bring [Eddy] out," the queen and his parents determined that he should travel, the better to broaden his exceptionally limited knowledge of the world. But where? They despaired of his getting into further sexual scrapes, and designing women could be found on every continent.

Unable to agree on an appropriate itinerary for Eddy, the royal family determined to find him a bride. But of all the eligible prospects, the best choice was one who had been eliminated from consideration years earlier—the impoverished Princess May of Teck. Bertie would have to overcome his distaste for May's morbidly obese mother, Princess Mary Adelaide of Cambridge. At least Mary Adelaide had a proper pedigree. Like Queen Victoria, she was a granddaughter of George III.

Victoria approved of May. She was pretty, but not gorgeous; and intelligent, but not clever (clever, witty people made Her Majesty feel inadequate). By the end of October 1891 Bertie had given his formal consent, and Eddy prepared to accept his marital destiny. The only person who had no idea what was going on was the prospective bride.

There was just one more T to be crossed before the prince was fully ready to commit to May. On November 29, Eddy wrote to Lady Sybil St. Clair-Erskine asking whether there was any truth to the rumor that she had become engaged to Lord Burghersh, the Duke of Westmorland's son. Stung by her affirmative reply, the prince responded, "Don't be surprised if you hear before long that I am engaged also, for I expect it will come off soon."

Eddy proposed to May on December 3, 1891. Twenty-four years old, she had been certain she'd die a spinster. At the prospect of becoming a married woman, and a future queen of England, she became so excited that she literally twirled about the room, displaying what she knew were her best features—her ankles and calves.

It seemed like a solid match. Eddy was sweet and kind, even vulnerable. May was pragmatic and steady. They both enjoyed many of the same interests, including genealogy and the theater. And each was anxious to be loved. They didn't, however, love each other, although they may have felt mutual affection and esteem.

Britain's royal family has never believed in long engagements. The wedding date was set for February 27, 1892, and the young couple began to shop for furnishings for the apartment they would occupy in St. James's Palace. Eddy wrote to his aunt Louise and her husband, the Marquess of Lorne (who was known to dash out for nocturnal homosexual trysts in Hyde Park):

I wonder if you were surprised when you saw that I was engaged? . . . for I must say I made up my mind rather suddenly . . . and it is really time that I thought of getting married, if ever I am to be. . . . I think I have done well in my choice, for I feel certain that May will make an excellent wife, and you may be certain that I shall do my best to make her a good husband.

On January 4 the Waleses and the Tecks traveled from London to Sandringham, where they planned to spend the next several weeks. Everyone, including Eddy, seemed to have a cold, but his symptoms worsened after he insisted on going hunting for his twenty-eighth birthday, January 8. Dr. Laking, physician-in-ordinary to the Prince of Wales, diagnosed Eddy's illness as influenza and incipient pneumonia. The influenza epidemic had everyone nervous, and the disease was about to claim yet another victim. Over the next few days Eddy's fever spiked to 103 degrees and, after a brief rally, soared to 107. His family and the doctors could only ease his discomfort. Alix didn't leave her son's side. Outside, below the prince's window, Eddy's younger brother Prince George strolled along the frozen ground hand in hand with May. Was something going on between them? Or were they comforting each other as the person they had in common slipped away? The gesture was remarkable enough at the time for Laking to remember it years later.

Eddy's final words, repeated several consecutive times in the throes of delirium, were, "Who is it?" He died on the morning of January 14, 1892, just six days after his twenty-eighth birthday.

Although Eddy had been completely indifferent to the army, his robust father insisted that he be accorded a full military funeral at which no women (including Eddy's mother, May, or his aunts) were permitted to be present. Eddy would have hated it. The women sneaked in anyway, much to Bertie's consternation. Eddy was interred at St. George's Chapel, Windsor Park, in an Art Nouveau tomb far more glorious than the prince's life had ever been. His parents kept his room at Sandringham as if it were a shrine, with a Union Jack draped over the bed, and Eddy's shooting hat on the hook where he had last placed it; even his toothpaste and soap dish were displayed as relics.

The Prince of Wales was immeasurably distraught, writing to his mother, "Gladly would I have given my life for his, as I put no value on mine . . . it is hard that poor little May should virtually become a widow before she is a wife."

Prince George was now the heir presumptive. And after a suitable period of mourning, *he* wed Princess May of Teck on July 6, 1893. It was not a love match, despite the incident of hand-holding at Sandringham. Their children would eventually characterize their gruff father as verbally abusive to their mother.

Princesse Hélène d'Orléans, the one that got away, married the Duke of Aosta in 1895. Lady Sybil St. Clair-Erskine wed the Duke of Westmorland's son, who eventually inherited his father's title. She died in 1910.

In the summer of 1911, solicitor Arthur Newton, who had represented Lord Arthur Somerset and the other participants involved in the Cleveland Street brothel scandal, had his law license suspended for fraud. Two years later he was accused of conspiring to swindle a wealthy Hungarian, was disbarred, and sentenced to three years in prison.

Bertie finally ascended the throne on the death of his mother, Queen Victoria, in 1901. His nine-year reign, the Edwardian era, was known for its gilded splendor, an age of fast cars, fast horses, and fast women. Eddy's younger brother George succeeded their father in 1910, reigning as George V until his demise in 1936.

Perhaps those who still remembered Eddy's lackluster and somewhat dim persona believed that with his death the British Empire had dodged a metaphorical bullet, allowing his somewhat brighter brother to eventually ascend the throne. But no one could have predicted that more than three-quarters of a century after Eddy's demise, he would be posthumously cast as the ultimate sort of royal pain: a brutish murderer.

Between September and November 1888, five prostitutes were gruesomely slain, eviscerated, and mutilated in London's seedy East End neighborhood of Whitechapel. The press dubbed the killer "Jack the Ripper." Although the body of one suspect was found in the Thames, weighed down by four stones, the Ripper was never apprehended or conclusively identified. During the succeeding decades, the names of more than a hundred suspects have been floated.

And then, in the 1970s, two different authors published startling revelations, naming Eddy—the heir presumptive to Britain's throne—as the notorious Ripper. Not only did they assert that the prince was a violent serial killer, but they revived the specter of the Cleveland Street brothel scandal, also pegging Eddy as a closet queen, an allegation that further tarnished the image of the royal family, who were now confronted with some nasty allegations regarding one of their ancestors.

In 1970 the eighty-five-year-old T. E. A. Stowell published an article in the *Criminologist*, stating unequivocally that Eddy was Jack the Ripper, a contention he had first asserted a decade earlier. Stowell maintained that the prince was insane at the time of each attack, in the grip of the symptoms of syphilis. Buckingham Palace dismissed Stowell's claims as a "mischievous calumny . . . too ridiculous for comment." Their avowal was not spin-doctoring. Every movement of the royal family was minutely chronicled and Eddy was nowhere near East London each time the Ripper struck. He was attending public functions in the performance of his royal obligations, with plenty of witnesses to corroborate his whereabouts.

In the face of such nasty little things as facts, Stowell began to backtrack. But he died on November 8, 1970, before he could expound further on the elements of the story that he insisted were genuine. Stowell's son immediately burned his manuscripts, stating, "I read just enough to make certain that there was nothing of importance. My family decided that this was the right thing to do. I am not prepared to discuss our grounds for doing so."

It didn't matter whether T. E. A. Stowell had crafted a ripping yarn out of thin air. By the time he died, approximately three thousand publications had disseminated his allegations. The posthumous damage to Prince Albert Victor's reputation was done. In the minds of late-twentieth-century historians and their readers, "Eddy" was a syphilitic serial killer.

But Stowell wasn't the only self-aggrandizing nutcase to hitch his wagon to the dead and defenseless Eddy's star in the hopes of either a big payday or at least international notoriety. Another story emerged, bolstering the belief of the current generation of scholars and royal watchers that Eddy was a royal pain of the most sinister kind.

In 1973 a man calling himself Joseph Sickert approached a producer for the BBC claiming to be Eddy's grandson. Sickert asserted that his mother was the prince's illegitimate daughter, born to a part-time artist's model and Cleveland Street shopgirl, Annie Crook. According to Sickert, Annie, who just happened to be working-class, illiterate, and Catholic, had met the prince after the minor Victorian painter Walter Sickert was asked by Eddy's mother, the Princess of Wales, to take the lad around and show him the seamier side of London. Joseph Sickert's story gained traction, despite the fact that during the time he claimed that Eddy was trysting with Annie Crook, the prince was busy with his studies at Cambridge or was visiting Heidelberg.

Sickert asserted that after Annie bore Eddy a love child (a baby that was allegedly raised in a workhouse), she was purportedly taken to a hospital and declared insane. There, an operation was performed on her brain to genuinely render her a mental incompetent. According to Sickert, Annie died in an asylum in 1920.

To spice up this drama even more, Sickert introduced a Masonic conspiracy headed by the Prince of Wales to murder all of Annie's friends who knew anything about the secret baby and the couple's subsequent clandestine marriage.

This was Sickert's explanation for the grisly deaths of the five East End prostitutes. If these were Annie's purported confidantes, she didn't travel in very good company.

As time passed and Sickert acquired coauthors for his published versions of these sordid events, the story grew more fanciful with the retelling. In *The Ripper and the Royals*, written with Melvyn Fairclough, Sickert alleged that Eddy did not die in 1892 (as the world heretofore believed), but had been locked away in Glamis Castle in Scotland (where he was said to have perished in 1933), to prevent him from ever ascending the throne—his punishment for wedding a Catholic.

However, none of Sickert's story is true. It was all an elaborate hoax. Sickert wasn't even the charlatan's surname. He was born Joseph Gorman in 1925. Yet, even after Gorman admitted that he had invented each of his contentions, for some reason (perhaps he was desperate to convince people that he wasn't a *complete* pathological liar) he continued to stubbornly maintain that he *was* Eddy's descendant.

In any event, Stowell and Sickert's damaging and completely fictitious stories cast a wide shadow over Eddy's reputation, irreparably tarring him as a syphilitic serial killer.

Add another, genuine historian to the stew and make that a *homosexual* syphilitic serial killer. Even the well-respected and prolific royal biographer Theo Aronson concluded in the 1980s that because there was such a conspiracy to keep Eddy's name out of the courts (and the press) after the July 1889 raid of a male brothel in London's Cleveland Street, the twenty-five-year-old prince must have been a client. In the absence of any unequivocal verification that Eddy *never* visited 19 Cleveland Street, Aronson posited that this dearth of evidence is proof itself that the prince frequented this notorious homosexual haunt.

With such dodgy claims still reposing in library stacks, Eddy's name remains marked with a metaphorical asterisk in the English monarchy's hall of fame—or shame, as the case may be. It is precisely his enduring *infamy* that classifies the hapless Prince Albert Victor, Duke of Clarence and Avondale, as a royal pain.

PRINCESS MARGARET

Countess of Snowdon
1930–2002

ONE EVENING DURING THE 1940S, THE QUEEN OF ENGLAND scolded her younger daughter as the teen was preparing to leave for a costume party, dressed as an angel. "You don't look very angelic, Margaret," her mother, Elizabeth, said disapprovingly. Without missing a beat the princess replied, "That's all right. I'll be a Holy Terror."

Most families have their share of sibling rivalries, and the royal houses of England are no exception. For centuries, younger brothers and sisters have envied the heirs, and when they made a bid for attention, some of them did so in a big way. Prince John crept onto his older brother Richard I's throne while the Lionheart was in the Holy Land slashing at Saracens. George, Duke of Clarence, participated in four revolts against Edward IV, reasoning that if his big brother had usurped the crown by force, the same method might work for him as well.

But younger sisters don't operate in the same way. And in a constitutional monarchy where the sovereign's role is largely ceremonial and she can't nab the crown, there's only one sphere left in which she can compete with her older sibling: by grabbing the spotlight. After all, as the saying goes, "All publicity is good publicity."

Except when it's not.

Nicknamed the "palace brat," Princess Margaret became a royal pain by acting up and acting out. Her sexy good looks and vibrant personality eclipsed those of her staid older sister, who acceded to the throne in 1952 as Elizabeth II. Margaret's expensive, jet-setting lifestyle at the expense of the British taxpayers and her clear preference for posh nightclubs over charity balls earned her the enmity of both Parliament and the press. And the subject of her youthful grand passion, which readers of a certain generation may remember as if it were yesterday, generated such a scandal for the monarchy that the biggest players from both Church and state were harnessed in an endeavor to resolve it. If *The Sound of Music* had been written about an English princess instead of an Austrian nun, the House of Windsor would have chorused, "How do you solve a problem like Margaret?"

Ever since she could pronounce it, Her Royal Highness Princess Margaret Rose hated her name. For one thing, she had only two first names, while her older sister Elizabeth Alexandra Mary had three. It only increased Margaret's dislike of her name when young Elizabeth, whom the family called Lilibet, insisted on referring to her baby sister as "Bud."

"She's not a real rose yet, is she? She's only a bud," Elizabeth, who was four years Margaret's senior, pertly told Lady Cynthia Asquith.

Born into the royal House of Windsor, the girls were the daughters of the Duke and Duchess of York, the painfully shy and stammering second son of King George V, Prince Albert Frederick Arthur George (like his grandfather, known as "Bertie"), and Lady Elizabeth Bowes-Lyon, a petite and vivacious Scottish commoner.

The sisters were brought up by a nanny, Mrs. Clara Knight, whom the girls nicknamed "Allah," and a governess, a young Scotswoman named Marion Crawford. The Yorks were careful to raise their daughters in a nurturing environment, but the duchess saw no reason to inundate them with too much book learning. Good deportment, manners, the typical ladylike pursuits that were popular during Queen Victoria's day, such as drawing and musicality, as well as plenty of fresh country air was all they needed in order to end up successfully married. After all, this system had worked splendidly for the duchess herself, as she was quick to tell any detractors.

Marion Crawford, or "Crawfie," as the girls called her, entered the Yorks' household in 1932, when Margaret was all of two years old and Elizabeth was six. Crawfie was not short of opinions, although she was likely paid well not to have any. Her initial reaction to Margaret was that she "was an enchanting, doll-like child, even in the nursery . . . the baby everyone loves at sight. . . ."

Crawfie's first impressions of the York girls were later recorded for posterity in a scandalous tell-all published in 1950 titled *The Little Princesses*. She had not received permission from the queen—in fact Her Majesty had pointedly refused it; but Crawfie had gone behind her back and signed a deal with an American publisher. Her betrayal of the royal family became eponymous. From then on "doing a Crawfie" was the catchphrase for an act of perfidy or disloyalty. Several passages from Crawfie's book were excised from the English edition, but it was too little and far too late. The former governess was evicted from her grace-and-favor cottage, her entry in *Who's Who* was deleted, and when she died in 1987 no member of the royal family attended her funeral.

However, it's worth noting that none of Crawfie's assertions regarding the princesses' childhood has ever been refuted by the Windsors, even though they took umbrage at what she had written.

Crawfie's assessment of her charges was correct. While Elizabeth was diligent and steady, with a rock-solid conscientiousness when it came to duty, even as a toddler Margaret distinguished herself as the vivacious one. She was spoiled, undisciplined, and overindulged, especially by her father, who doted on her. Margaret loved to mock and mimic others; but because she had such a talent for it, she was never chastised for her unkind impressions, however amusing they might have been. Looking back on her childhood, with classic British understatement Margaret described herself as "rather chatty." She was also skilled at deflecting attention from anything she deemed unpleasant, delaying her lessons by telling Crawfie about her "appalling dreams," which she would then dramatically reenact for the governess.

According to Crawfie, "Margaret was often naughty, but she had a gay bouncing way with her, which was hard to deal with." Crawfie's verbal portrait of Margaret paints her as talented, adorable, and winsome, but untidy, impetuous, and willful. In short, she was everything her older sister was not. The governess admitted that she had a difficult time schooling two girls with such different temperaments.

Occasionally the sibling rivalry between the royal sisters would escalate into violence. The sainted Elizabeth would slap and the scrappy Margaret would bite. "Margaret always wants what I want," Elizabeth would complain.

Adolescence was even harder for Margaret than her childhood had been, because what was adorable, or excusable, from a pudgy little girl was far less charming in a coltish teen. Crawfie wrote, "It was to be her misfortune that the ordinary exploits of adolescence, the natural life of a healthy and vivacious girl, in her case made newspaper paragraphs, instead of being dismissed with a laugh."

The York family made a quaint and cozy foursome until the December 1936 abdication of Bertie's older brother, Edward VIII, to wed his lover, the American divorcée Wallis Warfield Simpson. On December 10, the king signed the instrument of abdication, and with the stroke of a pen the girls' forty-one-year-old father was no longer the Duke of York. He was now George VI of England. "Does that mean that you will be the next queen?" the four-year-old Margaret Rose asked her sister.

"Yes, someday," Elizabeth replied.

"Poor you," responded Margaret.

Yet at their father's coronation on May 12, 1937, little Margaret was envious of her older sister's trappings. The girls were garbed identically in white lace dresses trimmed with silver bows, accessorized with silver slippers and white schoolgirl socks. Small, lightweight tiaras were perched on their blond heads. But Margaret was jealous that Elizabeth's ermine-trimmed purple mantle was longer than hers. It took a good deal of convincing for her to accept that the reason was because Margaret, being four years younger, was so much smaller than Lilibet.

After it became apparent that the girls would never have a brother and that Elizabeth would indeed inherit her father's throne, the sisters began to be treated differently from each other. While the precocious and overindulged Margaret continued to enjoy a social life that few children her age ever would have had, increased emphasis was being placed on preparing Elizabeth for her future responsibilities.

By the summer of 1939 grim reality was intruding on the

Windsors' fairy tale. Hitler was on the brink of invading Poland; war was inevitable because France and England were bound by an international treaty to defend Poland against foreign aggression.

Nazi Germany and Soviet Russia signed a mutual non-aggression pact on August 21. Two days later, Princesses Margaret and Elizabeth were taken to Birkhall on the royal estate of Balmoral in Scotland. And on September 1, Hitler invaded Poland.

At Birkhall, the princesses' guardians tried to maintain a semblance of normality. The girls' lessons continued, although Elizabeth's constitutional history lessons with Sir Henry Marten, vice provost of Eton, were maintained through the mail. To do their part for the war effort, the young royals handed out tea and cakes to the volunteers.

In the spring of 1940, after Hitler invaded Denmark, Norway, and the Netherlands, the queen instructed Crawfie to move the princesses to Windsor Castle. The girls remained there for the next five years, until the Second World War was over. Marten came up to Windsor to personally tutor Elizabeth. Naturally, Margaret wanted what her older sister had, but was curtly informed that it was "not necessary," just another reminder that the differences between herself and Lilibet were vaster than the span of four calendar years. Margaret Rose (it was assumed) would never sit on the throne.

Safely ensconced at Windsor for the duration of the war, the princesses rolled bandages and knitted socks for the troops. And to demonstrate that the royal family understood the necessity of doing their part, the princesses were given the same rationing coupons as all Britons, and Elizabeth wore her mother's hand-me-down clothes, while Margaret ended up with her older sister's castoffs.

In 1940, the princesses performed in the annual Christmas panto, traditionally a charity event for the Queen's Wool Fund. Elizabeth was skeptical about charging the suggested admission price of seven and sixpence (37½P or about fifty cents nowadays), not only because of the deprivations of wartime, but because the princesses were hardly professional-caliber performers. It was ten-year-old Margaret who understood the public-relations allure of being a royal. "Nonsense, they'll pay anything to see us!" she insisted.

The monarchs' efforts to protect their daughters from the horrors of war resulted in the continued overindulgence of the already precocious Margaret. A visiting entertainer to Windsor Castle noticed that at the age of thirteen or fourteen the princess was already wearing high-heeled shoes with pointed toes. And a courtier's daughter observed, "The King spoiled Princess Margaret dreadfully. She was his pet . . . she was always allowed to stay up to dinner at the age of thirteen and to grow up too quickly. The courtiers didn't like her much—they found her amusing but . . . she used to keep her parents and everyone waiting for dinner because she wanted to listen to the end of a programme on the radio."

Already quite the entitled young lady, Margaret was also becoming aware of her own sexuality and its effect on members of the opposite sex. Even as a burgeoning adolescent she had a charming way of putting shy visiting servicemen at ease by "slipping her small hand into a large one," and inviting the young men to "come and look at the gardens," or asking, "Have you seen the horses?" according to one officer who witnessed her poise and self-assurance during those years.

In the spring of 1944, Rebecca West, who was writing an article for the *New York Times* on Princess Elizabeth's eighteenth birthday, interviewed both princesses. West found the heir apparent "too good, too sexless," but she noticed fourteen-year-old Margaret's "shrewd egotism" and observed, "When she grows up, people will fall in love with her as if she were not royal. . . ."

The girls were at an age when every parent begins to worry; beaux were on the horizon. Elizabeth met her handsome cousin Prince Philip of Greece in 1939, when he was just an eighteen-year-old cadet. They kept in touch during the war years and Elizabeth maintained that she had fallen in love with him at first sight. Of course, she had been all of thirteen at the time, but even when she reached the age of eighteen in 1944 and was eager to wed the dashing Philip, the king and queen deemed her too young to marry.

Another captivating war hero would enter the Windsors' lives in 1944. But instead of leading to a royal wedding, his relationship with one of the princesses would foment a scandal of national proportions.

Group Captain Peter Townsend, slender and sensitive, was a decorated RAF pilot for his bravery in the Battle of Britain. He'd had a wartime wedding in 1941 to a girl he barely knew, Rosemary Pawle. In 1944 at the age of twenty-nine he was made a temporary equerry in the service of George VI. His royal appointment came with a grace-and-favor cottage at Windsor, and he and Rosemary moved in with their two young sons.

But Townsend's job required him to travel with the king, leaving Rosemary stuck at Windsor with their children—and Townsend with plenty of time to become acquainted with the princesses. His first impression of the

fourteen-year-old Margaret was that she was "unremark-
able," though he did notice that the color of her dark blue
eyes was "like those of a tropical sea." He gets points
for poetry but none for grammar and syntax. Townsend
was also impressed with the way the adolescent princess
would make "some shattering wisecrack," after which, "to
her unconcealed delight, all eyes were upon her." During
family gatherings, although Margaret was not the most
important person in the room, she was well aware of how
to become the center of attention.

Margaret turned fifteen in August 1945 and remained
as keen as ever to distinguish herself from the rest of her
immediate family. To begin with, she disdained her sister's beloved Welsh Corgis; Margaret's dog of choice was
a Cavalier King Charles Spaniel named Rowley (an inside
joke, as it was one of Charles II's nicknames, as well as
that of the "Merry Monarch's" favorite stud horse). And
Margaret never shared her family's passion for the rustic-
ity of Balmoral and the sportsmanlike pursuits of hunting
and fishing that went with the territory. "She didn't care
for sporting women and thought shooting unwomanly,"
Crawfie wrote in *The Little Princesses*. So while her older
sister was out stalking, Margaret was smoking—through
a soigné ivory cigarette holder that would become one of
her trademarks. Her interests tallied with those of her fey
and flamboyant uncle the Duke of Kent, with his penchant for theaters, ballet, jazz, and nightclubs.

In February 1947, "the Firm," as the royal family referred
to themselves, was to have a final excursion as a tight-knit
foursome: a three-month state visit to South Africa. Prince
Philip had proposed to Elizabeth the previous autumn and
she had joyfully accepted, but their engagement, at least
for the time being, remained a secret.

Despite Margaret's enduring reputation as the "palace brat," the sixteen-year-old princess turned out to be the acknowledged belle of the South African trip. Margaret looked older than her years, a sex kitten in bright red lipstick. Her appearance was a marked visual contrast to that of her reserved older sister, and her vibrant smile made everyone fall in love with her. But she couldn't keep a lid on her urge to mimic others, particularly the portly wives of the African dignitaries, and no matter how mature she looked, she still giggled at them like a schoolgirl. Nevertheless, the experience whetted Margaret's appetite for exotic, sun-drenched locales. That attraction, too, would set her apart from her sister and their parents.

Elizabeth's engagement to Prince Philip was officially announced on July 10, 1947, a few months after the royal family returned from South Africa. Since Margaret was generally acknowledged to be the more scintillating sister, Philip was teased by a friend for having "chosen the wrong girl. Margaret is much better looking."

Philip evidently retorted, "You wouldn't say that if you knew them. Elizabeth is sweet and kind, just like her mother." The obvious implication was chivalrously left hanging in the air.

Margaret was a bridesmaid at the November 20 royal wedding, although she walked three paces ahead of the other seven attendants, to emphasize her rank. For the next several years, she would be regarded as one of the world's most glamorous and eligible bachelorettes. The American press dubbed her "Britain's No. One item for public scrutiny," opining that "People are more interested in her than in the House of Commons or the dollar crisis."

And who can wonder why? Physically, she was the perfect package, a pocket Venus dressed in Christian Dior's radical and exceptionally feminine "New Look," accessorized with peep-toe platform heels. And when *she* wore Dior, ten million Englishwomen followed suit. At a whisper over five feet tall, Princess Margaret (she dropped the "Rose" in 1947 as well) was "perfectly made," with a waspish twenty-three-inch waist and thirty-four-inch bustline. Young adulthood had mellowed the golden hair of her childhood to a rich shade of brown. Her mouth was a sensuous red pout; her eyes, as Group Captain Peter Townsend so rhapsodically observed, were deep pools of dark blue, and her kilowatt smile and vivacity made her the life of every party. Where the other females in her family were dowdy, Margaret was the epitome of chic.

She was now mature enough to make official visits on her own. In February 1948, she toured Amsterdam, accompanied by equerry Peter Townsend. Tongues wagged as she danced every number with him at the ball hosted in her honor by the International Culture Center. Townsend would later write in his memoirs, "Without realizing it, I was being carried a little further from home, a little nearer the Princess."

Elizabeth's younger sister was gaining a reputation as a party girl. Her coterie of friends, known as the "Margaret set," consisted of the age's society belles and young lordlings. Naturally, there was rampant speculation as to which of these "chinless wonders" she would marry. Shocking polite society at the age of nineteen, Margaret was caught smoking in a West End restaurant. Not only did her behavior cause a national commotion, but, predictably, it sparked a trend. Margaret's cigarette habit, which she'd flaunted in a photograph taken at Balmoral when she was fifteen, would catch up with her in time, snuffing out her life when she was in her early seventies, although she came from a family of long-lived women.

But heart and lung problems would arrive decades in the future, and might just as well have been light-years away for a teenage princess who was hell-bent on being the center of attention wherever she went. And Margaret was fully aware of her allure. She once dared a dance partner to "look into my eyes. Do you realize that you are looking into the most beautiful eyes in the world?" With a bit of self-mockery the princess admitted that she was parroting a newspaper quote about her, but in many ways she believed her own press.

The good-time royal enjoyed being shocking. Employing her more than modest musical talents, she once decided to entertain a dour Presbyterian minister with her rendition of one of the hit numbers from the 1943 Rodgers and Hammerstein musical *Oklahoma!* Brightly accompanying herself at the keyboard she belted out the innuendo-laden, sexually charged "I Cain't Say No."

Margaret often stayed out late, returning to Buckingham Palace at four a.m. Her antics were gently indulged by the queen, who with perfect equanimity reminded Crawfie, "We are only young once . . . we want her to have a good time. With Lilibet gone, it is lonely for her here." The only time Her Majesty was less inclined to leniency was on an occasion when Margaret planned to swan about in an evening gown with a deep décolletage. Displaying the royal cleavage just wouldn't do, so the queen insisted that the dress be altered with the addition of a pair of straps.

In 1950 Crawfie's book *The Little Princesses* was published, and its text reinforced the public's impression that Margaret was a mischievous and spoiled little hoyden as a child, and had become an inconsiderate, exacting, and untidy young lady. But there was another side to Margaret that the public seldom, if ever, saw: the nonbratty aspect of her personality. Like all members of the royal family, she was patron of a number of charities, philanthropic trusts, and good-works societies. And, surprisingly for a young woman intent on breaking as many rules as possible, the princess was also devoutly religious and keenly interested in theology. Consequently, she became well versed in Church doctrine and took it very seriously, never traveling without her Bible bound in white leather and blocked in gold.

Group Captain Peter Townsend saw his own version of Margaret, asserting, "Behind the dazzling façade, the apparent self-assurance, you would find, if you looked for it, a rare softness and sincerity. She could make you bend double with laughing; she could also touch you deeply." If those sound like the sentiments of a man in love, they were. The very married equerry had fallen hard for the boss's daughter, describing her as "a girl of unusual, intense beauty, confined as it was in her short, slender figure and centered about large purple-blue eyes, gener-ous, sensitive lips and a complexion as smooth as a peach. She was capable, in her face and her whole being, of an astonishing power of expression. It could change in an instant from saintly, almost melancholic, composure to hilarious, uncontrollable joy. She was by nature, generous, volatile. . . ."

In August 1950 Townsend was promoted to Master of the Household, a permanent position requiring a one hun-dred percent commitment to King George. By then his marriage to Rosemary Pawle was headed for rocky shoals. The infatuation between courtier and princess was mutual. In his memoirs Townsend recalled falling asleep in the heather one afternoon after a picnic and being gently awakened by someone protectively covering him with a coat. It was Margaret, her face almost close enough for a kiss. Townsend whispered to her, "You know your father is watching us." Margaret laughed, and left to rejoin the king, who had been leaning on his walking stick, observing the socially mismatched couple from a distance. "Then she took his arm and walked away, leaving me to my dreams," the equerry wrote.

Margaret was a real daddy's girl. Perhaps unsurprisingly, her great loves—Peter Townsend; the man she would eventually wed, Antony Armstrong-Jones; and her future lover Roddy Llewellyn—bore more than a passing resemblance to George VI: handsome, slight, sensitive.

She was devastated by her father's death on February 6, 1952. The ascension of Elizabeth to the throne also heralded Margaret's eviction from Buckingham Palace, where the new sovereign would reside with her young family. Margaret and Queen Elizabeth The Queen Mother, as George VI's widow would now be styled, moved into Clarence House, adjacent to St. James's Palace.

Peter Townsend was on hand to console Margaret during the mandated period of court mourning for the late king, claiming in his memoirs that "the King's death had left a greater void than ever in Princess Margaret's life." The death of George VI also meant that Townsend was out of a job. Luckily, the queen mum liked him, and appointed him Comptroller of her Household.

But he had something to cry about as well. ". . . my own [life] was clouded by the failure of my marriage." A couple of years earlier, his lonely wife, Rosemary, had taken a lover, John de László, the son of a prominent society portraitist. Rosemary's infidelity may have triggered a switch in Townsend's subconscious: the freedom to fantasize about a deeper relationship with Margaret.

On December 20, 1950, the thirty-eight-year-old Townsend was granted a divorce on the grounds of Rosemary's "misconduct" with de László, making the courtier the "innocent party" in the proceedings. Two months after the decree was issued Rosemary and de László married.

In *Time and Chance*, Townsend's memoirs, which were published in 1978, he wrote about the moment his relationship with Margaret changed forever. "It was then [February, 1953] that we made the mutual discovery [in an empty drawing room at Sandringham] of how much we meant to each other. She listened, without uttering a word, as I told her, very quietly, of my feelings. Then she simply said 'That is how I feel, too.' It was, to us, an immensely gladdening disclosure, but one which sorely troubled us."

Interestingly, Margaret's official biography places this "discovery" even later, in April 1953, and cites the location as the red drawing room in Windsor Castle.

Another of Margaret's biographers, Theo Aronson, is fairly sure that Townsend was shading the truth about the event and that the pair had expressed their desire for each other long before then—likely when the courtier was still married. Aronson refers to the cairn (a heap of stones to mark a memorial of sorts) that the couple built together on a hilltop at Balmoral. Each excursion to the summit warranted the placing of a stone, until the cairn stood three feet high.

Peter Townsend's memoir described their mutual passion in terms that might be familiar to romance readers: "Our love, for such it was, took no heed of wealth and rank and all the other worldly conventional barriers which separated us. We hardly noticed them; all we saw was one another, man and woman, and what we saw pleased us."

According to the lovestruck equerry, "Marriage . . . seemed the least likely solution; and anyway, at the prospect of my becoming a member of the Royal Family, the imagination boggled, most of all my own. Neither the Princess nor I had the faintest idea how it might be possible to share our lives."

And yet, Townsend insisted that they intended to become united in every way: "God alone knew how—and never be parted." Queen Elizabeth was said to be sympathetic to their wishes; but the queen mother, despite liking Townsend personally, was very upset by the news. For her it was an echo of the 1936 trauma regarding Edward VIII's insistence on wedding the American divorcée Wallis Simpson and the ensuing political mess it made for England and the entire Windsor family.

No one was particularly enthusiastic about Townsend as a viable beau for Margaret. The queen's private secretary, Sir Alan ("Tommy") Lascelles, exclaimed that Townsend "must be either mad or bad!" Corroborating this shocked reaction, Townsend characterized Lascelles as "visibly shaken" when he "very quietly" disclosed the facts of the relationship.

For one thing, the courtier's romantic aspirations were far above his station; for another, his divorce, despite the fact that he had been the injured party, was a permanent blot on his social status. Although adulterers were welcomed, divorced persons were still not permitted to be presented at court or to enter the royal enclosure at Ascot! And a divorced person such as Peter Townsend (or as Wallis Simpson had been), whose former spouse(s) still lived, was marked as a religious pariah because at the time, the Church of England did not recognize divorce.

Although Margaret blamed Tommy Lascelles for not directly telling the couple that they couldn't wed, as an amateur theologian she would have already known the arguments presented by the Church as impediments to a marriage with Peter Townsend. The stickiest wicket was that because Margaret was under twenty-five years old, she was still subject to George III's Royal Marriages Act of 1772, which meant that she required the sovereign's permission to wed. But the monarch is also the Supreme Governor of the Church of England, and as much as the queen might have wished her sister to be happy, Elizabeth could not therefore condone or sanction her marriage to Townsend.

Yet the queen didn't quash her younger sister's expectations entirely. Instead, she advised Margaret to wait until she was twenty-five, when she could apply directly to Parliament for permission to wed Townsend and the decision would be in their hands. The princess wasn't happy about it, but being told to sit tight and bide her time was preferable to an outright denial. There was still hope.

However, Margaret's little romantic secret would reveal itself after Elizabeth's coronation ceremony on June 2, 1953. As the royal family was processing out of Westminster Abbey, the Fleet Street press discovered that the princess had a *tendre* for Peter Townsend. She approached him outside the abbey, and in an affectionate, intimate gesture, delicately plucked a bit of fluff from his RAF tunic (in which she thought he looked especially sexy). Unlike today, where the news would be tweeted across the Internet within milliseconds, the British press maintained a discreet code of silence about the event—for a while, anyway. Twelve days after the coronation, on Sunday, June 14, *The People* broke the news by insisting that there was no truth at all to the "scandalous rumors" being spread about the affinity between Margaret and the queen mother's Comptroller of her Household, asserting, "It is quite unthinkable that a Royal Princess, third in line of succession to the throne, should even contemplate a marriage with a man who has been through the divorce courts."

It was time for the palace to step in and perform some damage control. After the queen's private secretary, Tommy Lascelles, informed Prime Minister Winston Churchill's private secretary, Jock Colville, about Margaret's desire to marry Townsend, Colville hustled down to Chequers, Churchill's country estate, to have a word with the PM.

But on hearing the news, Churchill dramatically exclaimed, "What a delightful match! A lovely young royal lady married to a gallant young airman, safe from the perils and horrors of war!" Colville had to point out to the PM that he wasn't there to seek approval for the marriage, but to request that he find a way to refuse it.

Churchill's patient wife, Clementine, set the old boy straight. For Clemmie, Margaret's romance was an unpleasant déjà vu. Issuing her husband an ultimatum, Clementine declared, "Winston, if you are going to begin the Abdication all over again, I'm going to leave. I shall take a flat and go and live in Brighton."

Churchill ultimately agreed that a scandal had to be avoided. He ordered the attorney general to review the government's constitutional position on such a matter and to poll the various prime ministers of the dominions within the British Commonwealth for their opinions on a potential marriage between Margaret and Townsend.

Queen Elizabeth was pressured to send Townsend away on some distant diplomatic posting but was hesitant to do so, unwilling to destroy her sister's happiness. Only after Her Majesty was assured that the commonwealth ministers as well as the British cabinet ministers opposed such a match did she banish Margaret's beau. Given a choice of locales, Townsend chose Brussels, the geographically closest of his options, not merely because he might be able to visit the princess from time to time, but because it put him in proximity to his young sons. His Belgian assignment would keep him on the Continent for two years.

To slightly assuage Margaret's inevitable grief, Elizabeth decided to delay Townsend's departure until after the princess returned from a state visit to Rhodesia. But the Firm pulled a fast one on its thorniest member, moving the courtier's exit to the day *before* Margaret was scheduled to return. After her mother broke the news to her, the princess disappeared for four days; the official version of events was that Margaret had become ill.

But the couple's enforced separation didn't make the thwarted royal love affair fade from the headlines. Journalists were quick to deride the palace's outmoded mores and the cabinet's cowardly and hypocritical stand, given that some of the ministers were themselves divorced. Their unanimity in favor of Margaret's right to choose her own marital destiny was overwhelming.

Michael Foot, a future Labour Party leader, wrote in the *Tribune,* "This intolerable piece of interference with a girl's private life is all part of the absurd myth about the Royal

Family which has been so sedulously built up by interested parties in recent years. . . . The laws of England say that a man, whether he has divorced his wife or been divorced himself, is fully entitled to marry again. In some respects, those divorce laws are still too harsh. But no self-appointed busybody has the right to make them still harsher. If these laws are good, they are good enough for the Royal Family."

In the annals of royal history, prudery was a relatively recent invention. Post-Albert Victorian priggishness was a temporary hiccup. Even Victoria's son, Edward VII, had been a rake; his mistress was at his bedside until just before he breathed his last. Over ninety-five percent of Britons polled by the *Daily Mirror* were in favor of the Margaret/Townsend match as well. But the issue wasn't up for a democratic vote.

Queen Elizabeth's heir, Prince Charles, was just a toddler in 1953. If she were to die while he was still underage, a regent would have to be appointed. A proposed amendment to the Regency Council Act of 1937 would drop Margaret (who was named regent in the 1937 act) in favor of Prince Philip, the Duke of Edinburgh. It made sense because Philip was Charles's father—but many people saw this potential "demotion" of Princess Margaret as the palace's step toward sanctioning an eventual marriage with Peter Townsend. However, it was merely wishful thinking, because Margaret could never sit on the throne under any circumstances, even as a regent, if she were wed to a divorcé. The new regency bill (intended to be pro-daddy, as opposed to anti-aunt) passed both houses of Parliament and became law on November 19, 1953.

In Townsend's absence, Margaret kept up her usual schedule of appearances, duties, and obligations; but the couple communicated almost daily by letter or phone. Their close friends were certain that the pair were true soul mates and were deeply in love.

They arranged a secret rendezvous in July 1954, meeting at Clarence House for all of two delirious hours; but while there was a changing of the political guard at Number 10 Downing Street, most members of Parliament remained staunchly against the idea of Princess Margaret marrying a divorced commoner. Even Margaret's family no longer had any sympathy for their lovestruck relative; her mismatched romance had become a major, and highly inconvenient, headache.

Margaret turned twenty-five on August 21, 1955, and reunited once again with her beau at Clarence House on October 13. As the queen's permission was no longer a factor in their ability to wed, the kingdom held its collective breath to see what would happen. For the next nineteen days the couple endeavored to escape prying eyes and the pop of paparazzi flashbulbs, while behind closed doors the subject of their marriage was discussed by representatives of both Church and state. Clerics argued that it would be an affront to the Anglican religion, and the couple's lay supporters insisted that the church doctrine was both outmoded and hypocritical. Why, even the current prime minister, Anthony Eden, had been divorced!

When Margaret had turned twenty-one in 1951 she became eligible for an allowance from the Civil List. The amount of the annuity would be increased with time as her responsibilities grew, but the starting figure was £600 (more than $23,000 today). The Civil List income is intended to reimburse a member of the royal family for expenses incurred in the performing of their official duties.

In the best of scenarios, a bill could be introduced into Parliament that would permit Margaret to marry Group Captain Townsend and permit her to retain her title and rank; additionally, her Civil List income would increase upon her marriage, as no doubt her husband would be expected to accompany her to state-related appearances. But Margaret would have to wed Townsend in a civil ceremony (as the Church would not recognize the divorced groom) and agree to a two-year banishment from the United Kingdom. She'd also have to renounce all rights to the throne, even though she was dropping farther and farther down the line of succession with each new niece or nephew. Townsend, who was a nice enough bloke, but had a tendency to waffle when the going got rough, wasn't sure he wanted such a weighty responsibility; perhaps he was asking the princess to sacrifice too much. The lovers were being placed unceremoniously over a barrel.

For someone as literally entitled as Margaret, the dilemma was huge. And her own deeply held religious convictions were most likely a factor as well—or would be, in the long run. *And*—in the long run—once the first flush of newlywed-dom paled, would she regret her decision? She was a vivacious party girl of twenty-five; Townsend was a stay-at-home type of forty-one. What would happen if that sixteen-year age gap began to feel even wider as the years progressed and the still-vital Margaret felt yoked to a paunchy, balding couch potato?

Michael De-la-Noy, who wrote the chapter on Princess Margaret for the esteemed *Oxford Dictionary of National Biography*, disputes a claim asserted by other biographers of the princess: that if she were to wed Townsend she would be stripped of her rank and title, as well as her

Civil List income, asserting that certain documents prove those allegations to be incorrect. De-la-Noy contends that Margaret's religious convictions became the deciding factor, that ultimately she was unable to accept the idea of not being married in the eyes of the Church. Margaret's friend Lady Glenconner arrived at the same conclusion, as did Kenneth Rose, royal biographer and founder of the *Sunday Telegraph*, citing the princess's "faith . . . built on granite, but ringed by qualifications."

Yet, as an avid theologian, Margaret would have been perfectly aware of the teachings of the Anglican Church and would have known all along that she and Townsend would be denied a church wedding—unless she expected that being a princess entitled her to an exemption from the canon law of her religion.

Her reasons may never fully be revealed or understood, but the result remains the same. Margaret issued a tidy statement of renunciation that reads like it came from the pen of a palace flack:

I would like it to be known that I have decided not to marry Group Captain Peter Townsend. I have been aware that, subject to renouncing my rights of succession, it might have been possible for me to contract a civil marriage. But mindful of the Church's teachings that Christian marriage is indissoluble, and conscious of my duty to the Commonwealth, I have resolved to put these considerations before others. I have reached this decision entirely alone and in doing so have been strengthened by the unfailing support and devotion of Group Captain Townsend. I am deeply grateful for the concern of all those who have constantly prayed for my happiness.

Resigned to the inevitable, on October 31, 1955, Townsend declared, "Without dishonour, we have played out our destiny." Yet his memoirs contain the assertion that the Church of England had frequently married the innocent or wronged party in a divorce, quoting the Archbishop of Canterbury's statement, "I do not feel able to forbid good people who come to me for advice to embark on a second marriage."

Reaction to the renunciation was mixed. The inimitable wit Noël Coward, who must have numbered himself among those who "constantly prayed for [Margaret's] happiness," quipped, "I hope that they had the sense to hop into bed a couple of times at least, but this I doubt." Coward also remarked wryly, "She can't know, poor girl, being young and in love, that love dies soon and that a future with two strapping stepsons and a man years older than herself would not be very rosy. . . ."

Years later, Townsend himself admitted that the marriage wouldn't have worked, because he could not have compensated for what the princess would have sacrificed to wed him.

Following Margaret's formal renunciation of their relationship, Townsend embarked on a trip around the world, while Her Royal Highness threw herself headlong into London's social whirl. John Moynihan, a reporter whose beat encompassed the local boîtes, recalled the princess's "zest for whisky at various nightclubs . . . her eyes became hard as coins as she dragged on her long cigarette holder. But no assistance was needed as she rose imperiously for the drive back to Buck House, escorted by a number of doting male friends. . . ."

Perhaps to assuage her broken heart, Margaret accepted

a marriage proposal from one of these chinless wonders, Billy Wallace. Right after she said yes, Wallace set off for the Bahamas, where he proved to be the upper-class twit everyone thought he was. He enjoyed a romantic fling while on holiday and when he returned home he told his royal fiancée all about it. Margaret promptly kicked Wallace to the curb.

As the 1950s flew by, rumors began to circulate about the princess's little attitude problem. Lord Mountbatten asserted that Margaret had inherited her mother's "sardonic and really quite bitchy" personality, but not the queen mum's "common touch, her genuine interest in and enjoyment of people." The princess had become a roving international ambassador for the monarchy, but many people noticed her rudeness; instead of gritting her teeth and thinking of England, she had a way of behaving imperiously or churlishly whenever she found an event tedious or not focused enough on *her*.

An unnamed courtier's wife summed up Her Royal Highness's unpredictable moods, observing that Margaret was "nice one day and nasty the next. She was the only one who would come up to you at a party and really talk to you—but the next day she'd cut you. She antagonized her friends with her tricks, being horrid to their wives. She'd come up to a man and get him to dance with her, cutting out his wife. . . ." Others commented on her way of encouraging a person to call her "Margaret," but the next time they'd encounter her and use her Christian name, she'd freeze them out with one of her legendary regal stares.

Margaret's reputation for creating scandals had by then reached global proportions. The caption of a cartoon published in a German magazine depicted an angry Queen

Elizabeth confronting her younger sister and exclaiming, "Say, Margaret, couldn't you do something to distract the horrid world press from our Suez débâcle?"

Margaret's selfishness garnered media attention after she made only the briefest and most begrudging of appearances at her sister's tenth wedding anniversary on November 20, 1957. A royal watcher, who must have been a stranger to sibling rivalry, particularly among the high and mighty, found her rudeness "inexplicable." Perhaps Margaret could not stomach yielding the spotlight to anyone, least of all her sister. Or perhaps she blamed the queen for her (nonetheless unavoidable) lack of support regarding the Townsend affair.

Peter Townsend stepped back into Margaret's life in the spring of 1958, and romantic Britons hoped the match would be rekindled, although Buckingham Palace denied all rumors of a formal reunion. Dogged by the press and pressured by the palace, the star-crossed couple met at Clarence House, but it was clear that dreams of a second chance were hopeless. Townsend would write in his memoirs, "Public curiosity killed our long and faithful attachment. That evening, Princess Margaret and I, warmly, affectionately, said adieu."

A chapter in Margaret's life had closed for good. She would not see Townsend again for another thirty years.

In October 1959, while she was at Balmoral, the princess received a letter from her forty-five-year-old former beau: He was getting married to a nineteen-year-old Belgian heiress, Marie-Luce (nicknamed "Mosquito") Jamagne. Margaret's reaction was swift. As if she had flipped a switch, she suddenly agreed to wed her man-of-the-moment, the society photographer Antony Armstrong-Jones. Years later, she confided to Conservative MP Jonathan Aitken, "I received a letter from Peter in the morning and that evening I decided to marry Tony. It was no coincidence." Margaret took Townsend's news very hard. Evidently, after they had been compelled to end their relationship, the pair had made an unrealistic pact never to wed anyone else. After receiving Peter's letter informing her of his engagement, the princess sent him a scathing reply, rebuking him for breaking their agreement.

That December, as Townsend quietly wed his teenage bride, Margaret and Armstrong-Jones became formally engaged. Tony, as she called her fiancé, gave the princess a ring in the shape of a flower: a ruby surrounded by diamonds. The pair had met in February 1958 at a dinner party hosted by a mutual friend, and their relationship did not become serious until that spring. The same age as Margaret, Armstrong-Jones was five-foot-seven, sandy haired, slender, and handsome. He was the son of a barrister and the nephew of a famous theatrical set designer, Oliver Messel.

Tony belonged to London's bohemian set. Most of his friends were in the fields of theater, fashion, and advertising; several of them were gay (including his uncle Oliver). Perennial royal watcher Nigel Dempster wrote in his column that according to Margaret she was able to keep her affair with Armstrong-Jones a secret for so many months "because no one believed he was interested in women."

But Margaret loved to deliberately shock people. One of her main reasons for choosing to wed Armstrong-Jones was because, as she told the film director Jean Cocteau, "Disobedience is my joy!"

Looking back on her relationship with Tony in the late 1950s, Margaret mused, "He was such a nice person in those days. He understood my job and pushed me to do things. In a way, he introduced me to a new world." They shared common artistic interests and she felt "daring" in his company. And although Tony's background was rather posh (he'd attended Eton and Cambridge), he could hardly be described as an "upper-class twit."

The royal romance was kept discreetly under wraps. Margaret visited Tony's Chelsea flat in Pimlico Road only when there was a group of people present, and the press wasn't even primed for the scent of a princess dating a photographer—a man so many rungs beneath her on the social ladder. The lovers enjoyed private trysts at Tony's "white room," his studio in Rotherhite Street, where the windows faced the Thames and, at high tide, the swans would swim right up to the glass.

According to one of Tony's friends, what the couple had most in common was "sex, sex, sex. Theirs was a terribly physical relationship, they couldn't keep their hands off each other, even with other people present. . . ."

Armstrong-Jones obtained the queen's formal consent to wed her sister in January 1960. Interestingly, it was *his* friends and family who saw the royal match as a mésalliance. Tony's father expressed his apprehensions, and the photographer's pal Jocelyn Stevens thought the princess was too imperious and indulged and Tony too independent and assertive for their union to ever be a success.

Of course, it could have been sour grapes, but Cecil Beaton, the foremost society photographer of the day (who may have surmised that Armstrong-Jones would have a lock on all the royal commissions after his marriage), was rather ungenerous to his professional rival. Beaton tartly characterized Tony as "extremely nondescript, biscuit-complexioned, ratty and untidy . . . the young man is not worthy of this strange fluke [of] fortune, or misfortune, and because he is likeable and may become unhappy makes one all the sorrier."

Right.

The celebrated writer Kingsley Amis had his own tuppence to insert regarding the match:

> Such a symbol of the age we live in, when a royal princess, famed for her devotion to all that is most vapid and mindless in the world of entertainment, her habit of reminding people of her status whenever they venture to disagree with her in conversation, and her appalling taste in clothes, is united with a dog-faced tight-jeaned fotog of fruitarian tastes such as can be found in dozens in any pseudo-arty drinking cellar in fashionable-unfashionable London. They're made for each other.

Tony's wedding attendants had to be vetted by the palace. His first choice for best man had been convicted for a homosexual offense eight years earlier and therefore had to be eliminated from consideration. His fallback was also gay. Tony finally ended up with a best man he barely knew, but whose sexual proclivities passed muster with Buckingham Palace—a wildly hypocritical move, as the royals routinely hobnobbed with Noël Coward, the queen's couturier Norman Hartnell, Tony's uncle Oliver Messel—and Cecil Beaton.

Armstrong-Jones's rarefied status went to his head immediately. The princess was appalled when she caught him ordering her staff about imperiously, prefacing his demands with such flip phrases as, "Do be a darling, and . . ."

The royal wedding took place on May 6, 1960, yet the event was a bit of an embarrassment, as one by one the RSVPs from foreign royals had arrived in the negative from all but Queen Ingrid of Denmark, whose mother had been a British princess. The bride's gown was designed by Armstrong-Jones and created by Norman Hartnell. One of the loveliest wedding dresses to be worn by a twentieth-century luminary, it was deceptively simple: long-sleeved, with a V-neck and a full skirt, constructed from thirty yards of white silk organza. The only sparkle came from the famous Poltimore tiara; its original owner was the daughter of the eighteenth-century playwright, tavern wit, and MP Richard Brinsley Sheridan.

The wedding cost £25,000 (upward of $715,000 today), £16,000 (over $458,000) of which was spent on decorations to line the route from Buckingham Palace to Westminster Abbey. The six-week honeymoon would cost another £40,000 (more than $1.1 million in today's economy).

The couple honeymooned on the royal yacht *Britannia*. Halfway through the voyage they anchored off the Caribbean island of Mustique, which Margaret's friend Colin Tennant was developing into a pleasure paradise for the titled, entitled, and famous. He offered Margaret a parcel of land as a wedding present. Worth £15,000, it was far more than Tony could ever have spent on his wife, and Tennant's largesse made the photographer distinctly uncomfortable. Perhaps it was the reason Armstrong-Jones had no desire to revisit Mustique no matter how much his wife adored it.

It was a good thing for the extravagant Margaret that her Civil List income increased substantially upon her marriage. She would now receive £15,000 annually (over

$429,000 in today's economy). Upon their return to London the newlyweds moved into one of the state apartments in Kensington Palace; but the princess didn't find it grand or comfortable enough; so £6,000 (nearly $172,000 today) was spent on renovations, spearheaded by Armstrong-Jones.

The huge redecorating expenses sent shock waves through Buckingham Palace; and Tony's casual behavior—in his own home—scandalized the Kensington Palace staff. The photographer ate breakfast in his shirtsleeves or popped into the kitchen and ordered the servants about. Of course, they were determined to pretend that Tony didn't exist, bringing a breakfast tray to the couple set with a single teacup, or complaining that he had made off with the car or raided the pantry, as though he were a delinquent teen. His own staff believed that he went out of his way to be difficult and rude to them. Perhaps the root of the problem, as one unnamed insider commented, was that "Tony may have been the head of the house, but he was not the head of the household."

As a measure of the Windsors' continued disapproval of the marriage (even though the queen had given the couple her permission to wed), none of the royal family ever visited. Their dissatisfaction increased when Margaret decided that after spending £6,000 on renovating apartment 10 in Kensington Palace, the residence remained unsatisfactory, necessitating the move to a significantly larger flat, which they redecorated to the tune of another £85,000 (nearly $2.5 million today).

Margaret had to have been footing the bill, which was exponentially larger than her income. Armstrong-Jones had found himself out of a job when he married her, a situation that would soon become intolerable for his ambitious and aggressive personality. He was now more or less a kept man, emasculated by his role as the princess's permanent escort. But when he was finally permitted to garner some design assignments, even if they were in an advisory capacity, he was publicly mocked for receiving them solely because of his lofty marital status. The ridicule hurt all the more because he was a genuine talent who had enjoyed a fairly lucrative and prestigious career prior to his nuptials.

Tony was elevated to the peerage during the spring of 1961 while Margaret was pregnant with their first child. Queen Elizabeth created him Earl of Snowdon, and Viscount Linley of Nymans. The first title was an invented one, a nod to Armstrong-Jones's Welsh ancestry, as Snowdon is the highest peak in Wales. Nymans had been a Messel family estate in Sussex. The viscountcy was a courtesy title that the earl would eventually pass to his son. Margaret would thereafter be styled Her Royal Highness The Princess Margaret, Countess of Snowdon.

She gave birth to a son, David Albert Charles, on November 3, 1961, and the boy inherited his father's courtesy title at birth. The Snowdons' daughter, Lady Sarah Armstrong-Jones, was born on May 1, 1964. Both of Margaret's children were delivered by caesarean section, derided by the princess's biographer Tim Heald as the "too posh to push" system of childbirth.

Just a few months after their son was born, the Snowdons became snowbirds, leaving the infant with a nanny and departing dreary London for the Caribbean sun. Margaret received hate mail calling her "callous, selfish, and perverse" for leaving her little one so soon. The princess's commandeering of the entire first-class cabin of a BOAC jet just for herself, her husband, and pair of domestics did not sit well with the public, either. Lady Jebb, the wife of the British ambassador in Paris, did not mince words when it came to Margaret's behavior abroad and her sense of entitlement:

> Princess Margaret seems to fall between two stools. She wishes to convey that she is very much the Princess, but at the same time she is not prepared to stick to the rules if they bore or annoy her, such as being polite to people. She is quick, bright in repartee, wanting to be amused, all the more so if it is at someone else's expense. This is the most disagreeable side to her character. . . .

As the swinging sixties swept through Britain, Margaret became mod, sporting heavy eye makeup and miniskirts. The Snowdons were the kingdom's hot young glamour couple, frequenting nightclubs, theaters, and the ballet, and jet-setting to exotic locales. But with her regal hauteur, icy stare, tidy coiffure, and Windsor "cut-glass" accent, Margaret never let anyone forget that she was a princess. She was not quite as progressive as people thought; for example, when someone dared to curse in her presence, she looked as if she had smelled something unpleasant.

By the summer of 1965, although the Snowdons were off on an Italian holiday, the royal marriage was headed for the rocks. Margaret's biographer Theo Aronson surmises that the relationship had begun to sour as early as 1964, before their daughter, Sarah, was born. Never happy walking a few paces behind his wife despite the perquisites of their lifestyle, the earl griped, "I am not a member of the royal family, I am married to a member of the royal family." He was not cut out for the rigidity of a lifestyle steeped in centuries of unbreakable tradition. And the spouses had entirely different views on child rearing; just like Charles and Diana, the royal wanted a very old-school upbringing for their offspring, while the commoner wanted the kids to experience a more casual and informal childhood.

An element of commonality that had brought Margaret and Tony together—a mutual self-centered arrogance—was what contributed to tearing them asunder. Neither partner was accustomed to capitulation or compromise. Snowdon would snap at Margaret if she entered one of his rooms without knocking first. She didn't understand his sulks or his need to return to his artistic milieu, viewing his desires for self-expression and self-worth as a personal rejection of her. As her husband accepted increasingly frequent photography assignments that took him to far-flung parts of the globe, the princess, known for her positively Hanoverian amorous appetites, inherited from her libidinous forebears, found herself oversexed and under-appreciated.

In Snowdon's absence, the princess began to indulge in extramarital affairs. Did anyone dare to mention the inconsistencies between Margaret's formal renunciation of Group Captain Peter Townsend based on her rock-solid faith and the Anglican Church's views on the indissolubility of marriage, and her own adulterous flings?

Her first lover, Anthony Barton, was their daughter's godfather and a former school chum of her husband's. The paramours' discretion was commendable until Margaret phoned Barton's wife to confess everything. According to a family friend of the Bartons', the princess "obviously enjoyed the role of *femme fatale*. She is a typical Leo—devious, destructive, and jealous." When Snowdon found out about the affair he was quick to forgive his old friend, but Mrs. Barton was far less cheerful about the matter.

By the final months of 1966 the thirty-six-year-old princess was miserable, guzzling Famous Grouse and drunk-dialing her friends for a pity party. Margaret entered the King Edward VII Hospital for Officers for a "checkup" early in 1967, but according to Theo Aronson it was reported that she had deliberately overdone the liquor and pills and had checked herself into the hospital to dry out.

While Snowdon was on a photographic assignment in Japan, Margaret embarked on a torrid affair with thirty-five-year-old Robin Douglas-Home. Robin was the son of Margaret Spencer, wife of the 6th Earl Spencer—the future Princess Diana's grandmother. Divorced, a heavy drinker, and an equally avid gambler, he was a pianist in popular nightclubs and an advertising executive in the London office of J. Walter Thompson, where a colleague described him as ". . . a nice enough chap, but a lazy bastard."

Robin wrote effusive love letters to his royal mistress, and Margaret responded, though with less ardor than her swain. Only a month after their romance began, the press reported the demise of the Snowdons' marriage.

On February 27, 1967, the earl categorically denied that there was a rift. The couple made a concerted effort to appear cozy. Believing it was in their children's best interests to be raised in a two-parent home, neither of them wanted a divorce or a formal separation. Although the concept of fidelity was rather fluid in their household,

Margaret nevertheless decided to end her affair with Douglas-Home.

On March 25, 1967, the princess sent a maudlin "Dear John" letter to her paramour:

> Trust me as I trust you and love me as I love you. Our love has the passionate scent of new-mown grass and lilies about it. Not many people are lucky enough to have known any love like this. I feel so happy that it has happened to me.

She did, however, express the wish that the two of them could one day rekindle their romance. But after the breakup Douglas-Home became suicidal; and on October 15, 1968, the thirty-six-year-old amateur pianist took his own life by overdosing on pills. Princess Margaret did not attend his funeral.

Meanwhile, Snowdon was enjoying a liaison with the daughter of the Marquess of Reading, Lady Jacqueline Rufus Isaacs, who turned twenty-three in November 1969. But the affair ended and the earl patched up his relationship with Margaret. The royal couple made another attempt at damage control by having themselves photographed looking affectionate as they romped in the Caribbean.

However, the marriage continued to flounder. In the early 1970s, the princess's name was linked with various men who visited Les Jolies Eaux, her home on Mustique, one of whom, according to biographer Theo Aronson, was Mick Jagger. The Rolling Stones front man eventually built his own home on the island. Actor Peter Sellers, known for his portrayal of Inspector Clouseau in the Pink Panther classics, declared himself in love with the princess in the late 1960s, although at the time he was married to the blond bombshell Britt Ekland. The Sellerses were divorced in 1968. Aronson asserts that Sellers sent Margaret love letters expressing his fantasy about marrying her, confessing to a friend, the actor Laurence Harvey, that the princess had "the same cup size, exactly" as one of Sellers's previous infatuations, Sophia Loren.

Unfortunately for Sellers, Margaret considered him "the most difficult man I know." Regardless of the actor's flights of fancy, the princess was aware that he was a womanizer and never viewed him as a prospective spouse.

By this time the Snowdons' marriage had deteriorated to such an extent that although they remained loving parents to their children, they had taken to dealing with each other primarily by writing notes. The communiqués were hardly cordial. One day the earl left a missive on his wife's dressing table titled "20 reasons why I hate you."

Verbal exchanges were even less civil. "Oh, God, you bore me," Snowdon once told the princess when they were out in public. At the end of his tether one day, the earl unleashed an exceedingly bizarre insult intended to wound his wife on multiple levels: "You look like a Jewish manicurist and I hate you!"

Snowdon even had the gall to make out with a shopgirl under a table after the local Red Cross Ball in Barbados. Although he was caught in the act by the event's host (with Margaret's bodyguard in tow as well), the earl expressed no shame about his little episode of flagrante, telling the bodyguard to "Fuck off, arselicker."

Still, divorce remained unthinkable because of the scandal it would cause the royal family—the Duchess of Windsor, Wallis Simpson, looming large in the memories of

Margaret, Queen Elizabeth, and their mother. Additionally, the queen mum was rather fond of Snowdon and tended to view the couple's marital woes as more attributable to Margaret's behavior than to the earl's.

In 1973, the year the queen's daughter, Princess Anne, wed Captain Mark Phillips, Cecil Beaton characterized Margaret as "a little pocket monster" while referring to Snowdon, his archrival in the world of fashion and society photography, as "the horrid husband."

"Poor brute, I do feel sorry for her," Beaton opined, his pen dripping with inky crocodile tears. "She was not very nice in the days when she was so pretty and attractive. She snubbed and ignored friends. But my God, has she been paid out! Her eyes seem to have lost their vigour, her complexion is now a dirty negligee pink satin. The sort of thing one sees in a disbanded dyer's shop window."

Margaret was still viewed as not pulling her weight when it came to public appearances; and as Parliament debated whether to abolish her Civil List annuity, particularly as she had a successful husband who could support her, the princess embarked on another love affair.

A couple of weeks after her forty-third birthday, in August 1973, Margaret met twenty-five-year-old Roddy (Roderic) Llewellyn at the Café Royal in Edinburgh. Llewellyn was her physical "type"—slender, sandy-haired, and slightly fey-looking—and they soon fell in love. The princess's children were said to have quickly accepted the presence of their mother's new boy toy in their lives.

While the princess trysted with Llewellyn on Mustique, Snowdon was carrying on an affair with Lucy Lindsay-Hogg, the ex-wife of renowned director Michael Lindsay-Hogg. By then the Snowdons were estranged, although the earl was still living at Kensington Palace and the royal couple maintained the pretense of civility at public engagements.

Unlike his wife's affair, Snowdon's extramarital relationship was not a social mismatch. Although Llewellyn's father had been an Olympic equestrian, Roddy fit the mold of aimless upper-class twit. What little employment he'd had, he'd secured primarily through nepotism. Like Robin Douglas-Home, Llewellyn was a manic-depressive who was often suicidal. He was also bisexual. Margaret's relationship with Roddy was fraught with tension on a number of counts: Not only was there a significant difference in their ages, but Llewellyn was Margaret's social inferior. His lack of experience in the workplace left him with scant understanding of a paramour who had a highly demanding and very public role. Margaret was also one of the most overbearing and imperious women in the kingdom, and her sexual appetite frightened her young lover, who had never before enjoyed a long-term relationship with a woman.

Toward the end of 1974, Llewellyn panicked and bolted, spending three weeks in Turkey finding himself. He returned to London, and Margaret, but his friends realized he was psychologically unstable. Margaret, too, had become horribly depressed after Llewellyn's disappearance. One evening, a male friend hosting a house party was interrupted by a frantic phone call from the princess, who was threatening to commit suicide by throwing herself from her bedroom window. Panicked, the gentleman rang up the queen, who remained unfazed by her sister's dramatics. With characteristic sangfroid Her Majesty informed the caller to "carry on with your house party. Her bedroom is on the ground floor." According to Theo Aronson, Queen Elizabeth referred to

Margaret's affair with Roddy Llewellyn as "my sister's guttersnipe life."

In November 1975, the forty-five-year-old princess earned a private rebuke from Roy Strong, a self-proclaimed "devoted monarchist," and director of the Victoria and Albert Museum. In one of his diary entries, Strong recorded, "She is, as we all know, tiresome, spoilt, idle and irritating. She has no direction, no overriding interest. All she now likes is la jeunesse dorée and young men."

Margaret seemed uninterested in doing anything that would contradict Strong's observation. Quite the contrary, in fact. In February 1976, Margaret and Llewellyn were photographed romping in the surf on Mustique by Ross Waby, an employee of News International, a conglomerate owned by Rupert Murdoch. Although the princess and her lover had not been the only ones in the original shot, the photo was cleverly cropped to make it appear that the bikini-clad princess was frolicking with her bare-chested twenty-eight-year-old gigolo. Even more damning was the *Private Eye* spoof of the image, which placed the heads of Roddy and Margaret on the bodies of a loinclothed Tarzan and a completely nude Jane, captioning their lampoon, "Margaret & Roddy: The Picture They Tried To Ban: 'Eye' Exclusive."

After the provocative photograph was published in the *News of the World*, there could be no more denials from Kensington Palace; the Snowdons' marriage was over. However, it was Margaret who moved first, citing her husband's affair with Lucy Lindsay-Hogg and thereby casting herself as the wronged party in a potential divorce proceeding. On March 19, 1976, Kensington Palace issued a formal statement announcing the Snowdons' official separation. It was an immense embarrassment for the crown and for the entire royal family.

But Margaret's sybaritic lifestyle showed no signs of abating. She continued to pal around Mustique with pop stars and ex-cons, getting herself snapped skinny-dipping with a number of male friends, and fueling the fires of critics who lambasted her dereliction of duty. Tabloid photo scandals inevitably followed.

She supported Llewellyn's interest in becoming a lounge singer and his fascination with horticulture. And when he suffered an upper gastrointestinal hemorrhage, she stationed herself at his bedside. However, these activities were not exactly in keeping with her obligations as a member of the royal family, and once again Margaret's Civil List income became the subject of debate. Liberal MP Douglas Hoyle referred to the princess as a "parasite" and demanded that Margaret decide whether she wanted to continue "swanning around the West Indies or get on with her job."

On Sunday April 5, 1978, the *Sun* printed an article falsely alleging that the queen had presented her sister with an ultimatum: "Give Up Roddy Or Quit."

The Church then weighed in on the issue. Margaret was scolded by the Bishop of Truro, the Right Reverend Graham Leonard, who reminded her that "if you accept the public life, you must accept a severe restriction on your personal conduct." The bishop then suggested to the princess that she absent herself from society for a while in order to straighten out her private life.

But according to Theo Aronson, it was Llewellyn who received a message from the highest circles requesting that he to skip town for three months. He departed for Africa, and on May 3, 1978, Margaret was hospitalized for hepatitis and advised to abstain from alcohol for a full year.

On May 10, Kensington Palace announced that Princess Margaret was suing the Earl of Snowdon for divorce. Six weeks later the princess had her decree absolute. And on December 15, Snowdon wed Lucy Lindsay-Hogg.

Nineteen seventy-eight was also the year that Group Captain Peter Townsend's memoir *Time and Chance* was published, providing the public with some of the more intimate (if sanitized) details of their star-crossed romance.

Margaret called it the worst year of her life. But her woes were far from over. Colin Tennant's oldest son sold photographs of the princess impersonating Sophie Tucker, the singer nicknamed "the Last of the Red-Hot Mamas." And, for the third time, Roddy Llewellyn's older brother made a few bob on his brother's royal affair, selling a serialized article to the *News of the World*.

Worst of all, early in 1979 Roddy himself was nabbed driving while intoxicated with another woman in his car— Naima Kelly. Kelly's husband sued his wife for divorce, citing Llewellyn as corespondent. Yet Margaret refused to hand Llewellyn his walking papers. People who knew them as a couple observed a genuine and mutual affection between them. Whatever his faults, Llewellyn was not a gold digger.

That same year, Margaret landed in hot water during a formal visit to Chicago, where dinner guests at a charity reception heard her insult the Irish, referring to them as "pigs"—rather bad form in the presence of the windy city's Irish-American mayor, Jane Byrne.

The princess's press got worse when she ostentatiously turned her back on California governor Jerry Brown at a Hollywood function after he inadvertently omitted the word "royal" in addressing her, and then informed Her Royal Highness that he could stay for only the first course because he had to attend another event that evening. When Brown's girlfriend, the pop star Linda Ronstadt, casually touched the princess's shoulder, Margaret "shrugged like a punch from a boxer," observed another guest, the British-born actor Michael Caine.

The forty-nine-year-old princess underwent plastic surgery to smooth out her jawline in January 1980. That year she logged several international visits, including one to Canada, where she was feted at a Wild West frontier-style event, but the populace was unimpressed by her presence. A *Toronto Sun* editorial asserted, "She is out West being given the top hat and curtsy treatment as if she were something special, rather than a Royal Baggage who has, by her lifestyle, forfeited all right to respect and homage."

Perhaps to avoid further bad press, Margaret did not attend Roddy Llewellyn's thirty-third birthday party, hosted by disco owner Peter Stringfellow on October 9, 1980. However, a connection was made there that would sound the death knell for the royal affair. Llewellyn realized that he was falling in love with an old friend, Tatiana ("Tania") Soskin. On Mustique the following February he confessed his passion for Tania to the princess and Margaret let him go, with her blessing. The couple was married in July 1981.

But there was a far more significant wedding that month. After Prince Charles and Lady Diana Spencer exchanged vows on July 29, 1981, Margaret found herself characterized as "the Princess Diana of her day." For many years the queen's sister felt a kinship with Diana that she never had for any of her blood relations. And while the two women shared several interests, such as shopping, the arts, and palling around with pop icons, Margaret was quick to dismiss their reputation as mere glamour girls, remarking, "The Princess of Wales said all the things I was saying twenty-five years ago. Clothes aren't her prime concern. They weren't mine, as if we were just unreal figures straight from *Dynasty*," Margaret insisted.

Her own antics were yesterday's news. Media focus was shifting to the foibles of the next generation of royals and their own soon-to-be-failed marriages and scandalous love affairs.

Margaret and Snowdon's children fared well, though. David, Viscount Linley became a highly respected cabinetmaker and restaurateur, wedding the Honorable Serena Stanhope in 1993. His younger sister, Sarah, now a professional painter, was married to Daniel Chatto the following year.

During the 1980s, the princess's name was perpetually linked with a string of men, and she also continued to enjoy her two biggest vices, "cigarettes and drink," insisting "and I don't see myself giving those up." Misplacing her pack of fags one day, Margaret asked a nearby footman, "Where are my fucking Winstons?" But after a nonmalignant tumor was removed from her lung in 1985, she was asked to kick the habit for a while. The best she could manage were filter-tips.

In the summer of 1992, a very nervous Margaret saw Group Captain Peter Townsend for the first time in thirty-four years. Now seventy-seven years old, he was visiting London from Paris, where he had been enjoying a happy marriage to Marie-Luce Jamagne. During the 1990s two different men stepped forward, each claiming to be the secret love child of Margaret and Peter, but their assertions were quickly and easily dismissed as fabrication and fraud. On June 9, 1995, Townsend died from stomach cancer at the age of eighty. Margaret was "saddened by the news," according to the formal statement issued by Buckingham Palace.

That year, Margaret's Civil List income was terminated, although she was not the only royal to see her annuity dry up. By then the princess was receiving £220,000 annually, on which she was obligated to pay taxes; however she received one hundred percent tax relief on expenses related to her formal duties. The queen personally assumed the tab for the members of the royal family who had been dumped from the Civil List.

In the spring of 1994 some of Margaret's passionate correspondence with her former lover Robin Douglas-Home had been published in a book penned by royal watcher Noel Botham. The princess was mortified by the letters' reappearance but declined to publicly discuss it, on the assumption that if she didn't call attention to the issue it would quietly go away. The palace issued a statement that it was merely "an old story." By then, the press had become sympathetic to the princess, recasting her once-wild behavior as that of a lonely woman searching for love and happiness.

Snowdon had been searching, too, and with similar luck, stepping out on his second wife as well. His lover of more than twenty years, the fifty-five-year-old journalist Ann Hills, committed suicide in 1997 by overdosing on pills and champagne. By then the earl needed a cane to ambulate, thanks to the effects of aging and his childhood bout with polio. Yet his physical impediments didn't diminish his libido. After Ann Hill's death, as his marriage to Lucy Lindsay-Hogg hit the skids, Snowdon took another lover, a magazine editor who bore him a son.

The sixty-seven-year-old Margaret had a stroke while she was on Mustique in February 1998. Although she suffered no paralysis, she became forgetful on occasion and it took a long time for her to recuperate. And in early March 1999, as the result of a faulty thermostat, the princess badly scalded her feet when she turned on the bath tap instead of the shower. For health reasons, Margaret soon gave up her Caribbean retreat, Les Jolies Eaux. The burns she had sustained healed very slowly; the fact that she'd been a heavy smoker since the age of fifteen retarded the process as well. Margaret's biographer Tim Heald claims that for several years she suffered from Raynaud's disease, which affects the body's circulation, an ailment that may also have been caused by her inveterate chain-smoking.

With the help of painkillers, the princess soldiered on, maintaining her royal obligations. On January 3, 2001, Buckingham Palace revealed that she might have had another, milder stroke over the Christmas holidays. And on March 27, the seventy-year-old Margaret suffered a third stroke, losing the sight in one eye and nearly all movement on her left side. From then on, still as vain as ever, she couldn't bear to be seen by men.

The princess gamely attended her mother's hundred-and-first birthday celebration in August 2001. Wheelchair-bound and sporting dark glasses, she looked far worse than the queen mother.

Margaret died on February 9, 2002, at King Edward VII Hospital. She was cremated and her remains were interred in St. George's Chapel beside those of her father, and her mother, who died on March 30, 2002.

The public viewed Margaret as a frivolous hedonist, a drain on the taxpayers, and a royal freeloader because she had no sense of purpose. In their collective opinion, if she had appeared to devote herself to philanthropic causes instead of spending the majority of her time in the company of celebrities and enjoying theater, film, and jazz concerts (or had found a smart balance, as Princess Diana did), she could have redeemed her reputation. Clearly, Margaret's selfishness and sexual escapades overshadowed her accomplishments—because she *did* visit AIDS patients, and was patron of the Migraine Trust and other charitable and philanthropic organizations to which she was genuinely dedicated, including the Royal Ballet and the Girl Guide association. But the princess stubbornly refused to behave graciously when an assignment was more of a task than a pleasure, and that was what people remembered. Those who found themselves on the wrong end of Margaret's attitude had no qualms about expressing their disappointment. One member of a woman's organization that received an official visit from Her Royal Highness admitted, "I'm afraid we weren't very impressed. We had all worked so hard and looked forward to her visit so much. But she just didn't seem to be interested. You felt that she was just getting through the whole business as quickly as she could. . . ." And a prominent Briton privately confided to Margaret's biographer Theo Aronson, "When I meet a princess, I expect her to behave like a princess. It's the least she can do."

Although her revelations of Elizabeth's and Margaret's early lives was always viewed as a betrayal, Margaret's former governess Marion Crawford saw the softer side of the girl, characterizing her as "a plaything. She was warm and demonstrative, made to be cuddled and played with." Although Crawfie had little respect for Margaret's spoiled temperament, when all is said and done it's not such a bad thing to be "made to be cuddled and played with."

Except perhaps if you're a royal, as there's always the pitfall of becoming a royal pain. *Times* journalist and editor Philip Howard observed of Margaret, "She is short of the exquisite discretion and majestic humility we demand from our monarchs. When attacked, her instinct is to bite back." He prefaced these remarks with the assessment that "It was psychologically natural for the lively younger sister to become the royal equivalent of the *enfant terrible.*"

Acknowledgments

Perennial thanks to my agent, Irene Goodman, and my editor, Claire Zion, as well as to my husband, Scott, for his incomparable patience, support, and good humor. Bouquets to the following folks: Christine Trent for enthusiastically cheering me through every stage of the birthing process of *Royal Pains*; for snippets of Russian history, Jennifer Shikes Haines, Cara Elliott, and Simon Boughey; for additional Lettice Knollys background, Elizabeth Johnson; for the correct pronunciation of "Cjesthe," Bob and Joseph Korda; for a quick lesson on Arab linguistics, Ambassador Mark Hambley. A shout-out to Nancy Meyer, for her wealth of knowledge on eighteenth-century law, and to the ladies of the Beaumonde for a lively discussion on the definition of a "wine cock." A tremendous group hug to the community of historical fiction bloggers, including the "Round Table" ladies, who have supported my nonfiction writing with ebullience and enthusiasm. And finally to Dan Nastu, my "computer guru," without whom this book (and many others) could not have been written—literally.

Selected Bibiliography

Books

Aronson, Theo. *Prince Eddy and the Homosexual Underworld.* New York: Barnes & Noble Books, 1994.

———. *Princess Margaret: A Biography.* London: Michael O'Mara Books Limited, 2001.

Baldwin, David. *Elizabeth Woodville: Mother of the Princes in the Tower.* Thrupp, Stroud, Gloucestershire: Sutton Publishing, Ltd., 2002.

Barkeley, Richard. *The Road to Mayerling: Life and Death of Crown Prince Rudolph of Austria.* New York: St. Martin's Press, 1958.

Borman, Tracy. *Elizabeth's Women: The Hidden Story of the Virgin Queen.* London: Jonathan Cape, 2009.

Church, S. D., ed. *King John: New Interpretations.* Woodbridge, Suffolk: The Boydell Press, 1999.

Cook, Andrew. *Prince Eddy: The King Britain Never Had.* Stroud, Gloucestershire: The History Press, 2008.

Florescu, Radu, and Raymond T. McNally. *Dracula: A Biography of Vlad the Impaler, 1431–1476.* New York: Hawthorn Books, Inc., 1973.

Fraser, Antonia, ed. *The Lives of the Kings & Queens of England.* Berkeley, Los Angeles, London: University of California Press, 1999.

Fraser, Flora. *Pauline Bonaparte: Venus of Empire.* New York: Alfred A. Knopf, 2009.

Goldberg, Enid A., and Norman Itzkowitz. *Vlad the Impaler: The Real Count Dracula.* New York: Franklin Watts, 2008.

Hamann, Brigitte (trans. Ruth Hein). *The Reluctant Empress: A Biography of Empress Elisabeth of Austria.* Berlin: Ullstein, 1998.

Haslip, Joan. *The Lonely Empress: Elizabeth of Austria*. London: Phoenix Press, 1965.

Heald, Tim. *Princess Margaret: A Life Unravelled*. London: Phoenix, 2008.

Hibbert, Christopher. *Napoleon: His Wives and Women*. New York and London: W. W. Norton & Company, 2002.

———. *The Royal Victorians: King Edward VII, His Family and Friends*. Philadelphia and New York: J. P. Lippincott Company, 1976.

Judtmann, Fritz (trans. Ewald Osers). *Mayerling: The Facts Behind the Legend*. London, Toronto, Wellington, Sydney: George G. Harrap & Co., Ltd., 1971.

Kendall, Paul Murray. *Richard the Third*. New York/London: W. W. Norton & Company, 2002.

Lewis, Brenda Ralph. *A Dark History: The Kings and Queens of Europe from Medieval Tyrants to Mad Monarchs*. New York: Metro Books, 2008.

Lloyd, Alan. *The Maligned Monarch: A Life of King John of England*. Garden City, New York: Doubleday & Company, Inc., 1972.

McNally, Raymond T., and Radu Florescu. *In Search of Dracula*. New York: Mariner Books, 1994.

Nicholas, Margaret. *The World's Wickedest Women*. London: The Hamlyn Publishing Group, 1994.

Payne, Robert, and Nikita Romanoff. *Ivan the Terrible*. New York: Thomas Y. Crowell Company, 1975.

Penrose, Valentine (trans. Alexander Trocchi). *The Bloody Countess: Atrocities of Erzsebet Bathory*. Solar Books, 2006.

Ronay, Gabriel. *The Truth about Dracula*. Briarcliff Manor, New York: First Day Books, 1979.

Ross, Charles. *Richard III*. Berkeley/Los Angeles: University of California Press, 1981.

Tibballs, Geoff. *Royalty's Strangest Characters: Extraordinary But True Stories from Two Thousand Years of Mad Monarchs and Raving Rulers*. London: Robson Books, 2005.

Tillyard, Stella. *A Royal Affair: George III and His Scandalous Siblings*. New York: Random House, 2006.

Troyat, Henri (trans. Joan Pinkham). *Ivan the Terrible*. New York: E. P. Dutton, Inc., 1984.

Turner, Ralph V. *King John: England's Evil King?* Stroud, Gloucestershire: Tempus Publishing, Limited, 2005.

Vlad the Impaler: The Real Dracula. Filiquarian Publishing, LLC, 2008.

Warren, W. L. *King John.* Berkeley and Los Angeles: University of California Press, 1961, 1978.

ARTICLES

Adams, Simon. "Dudley, Lettice, Countess of Essex and Countess of Leicester (1543–1634)." In *Oxford Dictionary of National Biography*, edited by H. C. G. Matthew and Brian Harrison. Oxford: OUP, 2004. Online ed., edited by Lawrence Goldman, January 2008. http://www.oxforddnb.com/view/article/8159.

———. "Sheffield, Douglas, Lady Sheffield (1542/3–1608)." In *Oxford Dictionary of National Biography*, edited by H. C. G. Matthew and Brian Harrison. Oxford: OUP, 2004. Online ed., edited by Lawrence Goldman, January 2008.

Bradford, Sarah. "Margaret Rose, Princess, Countess of Snowdon (1930–2002)." In *Oxford Dictionary of National Biography*, online ed., edited by Lawrence Goldman. Oxford: OUP, January 2006. Online ed., edited by Lawrence Goldman, January 2009. http://www.oxforddnb.com/view/article/76713.

De-la-Noy, Michael. "Townsend, Peter Woolridge (1914–1995)." In *Oxford Dictionary of National Biography*, edited by H. C. G. Matthew and Brian Harrison. Oxford: OUP, 2004. Online ed., edited by Lawrence Goldman, May 2008. http://www.oxforddnb.com/view/article/59143.

Farrell, S. M. "Grosvenor, Richard, First Earl Grosvenor (1731–1802)." In *Oxford Dictionary of National Biography*, edited by H. C. G. Matthew and Brian Harrison. Oxford: OUP, 2004. Online ed., edited by Lawrence Goldman, January 2008. http://www.oxforddnb.com/view/article/11669.

Gillingham, John. "John (1167–1216)." In *Oxford Dictionary of National Biography*, edited by H. C. G. Matthew and Brian Harrison. Oxford: OUP, 2004. http://www.oxforddnb.com/view/article/14841.

Hicks, Michael. "Anne (1456–1485)." In *Oxford Dictionary of National Biography*, edited by H. C. G. Matthew and Brian Harrison.

Oxford: OUP, 2004. Online ed., edited by Lawrence Goldman, October 2006. http://www.oxforddnb.com/view/article/556.

―――. "Elizabeth (*c*.1437–1492)." In *Oxford Dictionary of National Biography*, edited by H. C. G. Matthew and Brian Harrison. Oxford: OUP, 2004. Online ed., edited by Lawrence Goldman, May 2008. http://www.oxforddnb.com/view/article/8634.

―――. "George, Duke of Clarence (1449–1478)." In *Oxford Dictionary of National Biography*, edited by H. C. G. Matthew and Brian Harrison. Oxford: OUP, 2004. http://www.oxforddnb.com/view/article/10542.

Horrox, Rosemary. "Richard III (1452–1485)." In *Oxford Dictionary of National Biography*, edited by H. C. G. Matthew and Brian Harrison. Oxford: OUP, 2004. http://www.oxforddnb.com/view/article/23500.

Kilburn, Matthew. "Henry Frederick, Prince, Duke of Cumberland and Strathearn (1745–1790)." In *Oxford Dictionary of National Biography*, edited by H. C. G. Matthew and Brian Harrison. Oxford: OUP, 2004. Online ed., edited by Lawrence Goldman, January 2008. http://www.oxforddnb.com/view/article/12963.

―――. "William Henry, Prince, First Duke of Gloucester and Edinburgh (1743–1805)." In *Oxford Dictionary of National Biography*, edited by H. C. G. Matthew and Brian Harrison. Oxford: OUP, 2004. Online ed., edited by Lawrence Goldman, January 2008. http://www.oxforddnb.com/view/article/29456.

Kiste, John Van der. "Albert Victor, Prince, Duke of Clarence and Avondale (1864–1892)." In *Oxford Dictionary of National Biography*, edited by H. C. G. Matthew and Brian Harrison. Oxford: OUP, 2004. Online ed., edited by Lawrence Goldman, January 2008. http://www.oxforddnb.com/view/article/275.

WEB SITES:

http://www.historytoday.com
http://www.nndb.com
http://www.measuringworth.com
http://www.gocurrency.com
http://www.battlefieldstrust.com

N.B.: regarding relative monetary values: During the writing of this book the American dollar fluctuated widely against the British pound, with an average conversion rate of £1 to $1.65. Financial calculations from British pounds in a given year to American dollars as of 2008 (which is as far as the Web site goes as of this writing) were obtained from www.measuringworth.com. The sums I provided "in today's economy" and similar wording are rounded numbers, not intended to be an exact calculation but to give readers a general sense of the monetary values then and now.

Photo by Ron Rinaldi

LESLIE CARROLL is the author of several works of women's fiction and, under the pen name Amanda Elyot, is a multipublished historical fiction writer. She and her husband, Scott, divide their time between New York City and southern Vermont. *Royal Pains* is her third foray into the field of historical nonfiction. Meet the author at www.lesliecarroll.com.

Let's Dish the Dirt on Royal Pains!

For *Royal Affairs*, my maiden voyage into nonfiction, I set up a blog at www.royalaffairs.blogspot.com, and over the years it's become a lively discussion hub for my royal nonfiction titles.

Please visit the blog to chat with me about the fascinating lives and tempestuous personalities profiled in my books, as well as juicy tidbits about other notorious royals. I welcome reading group leaders to set up a "tryst," choosing a blog day all to yourselves, where I'll discuss the book interactively with your members. Alternatively, we can set up an interactive speakerphone chat during your book club meeting. To do so, please contact me through my Web site.